DISHING UP® NEW JERSEY

DISHING UP®
NEW JERSEY

150 RECIPES FROM THE GARDEN STATE

JOHN HOLL

Photography by Amy Roth • Foreword by Augie Carton

Storey Publishing

Heritage

Where water folds across the stones
A kid glove over knuckle bones

And idles into pools, the trout
Lifts his speckled body out

Once, twice, and thrice he hurls
A whip of steel against the swirls,

Then leaps the rapids, and in air
Curves a note of music there

And with a swift contrary will
Climbs the staircase of the hill

A. M. Sullivan

DEDICATION

To the staff of the New Jersey Network News, especially John Williams, Judy Goetz, William Jobes, Dave Frick, and Jim Hooker. When I was 16, NJN gave me the opportunity to travel the state in search of news and the training to tell it properly. And to all the editors at *The New York Times* and *The Star-Ledger* who allowed me to cover the state I love, seeking out stories and eating well along the way. I'm here today, professionally, because of them.

*The mission of Storey Publishing is to serve our customers by
publishing practical information that encourages
personal independence in harmony with the environment.*

Edited by Margaret Sutherland and Sarah Guare
Art direction and book design by Jeff Stiefel
Text production by Liseann Karandisecky
Indexed by Christine R. Lindemer, Boston Road Communications

Cover and interior photography by © Amy Roth, except: front cover (top center),
   vii, 88, and 267 by Jeff Stiefel; back cover (author) by Jaime Lawson
Map of New Jersey by © Anne Smith

Storey Publishing
210 MASS MoCA Way
North Adams, MA 01247
www.storey.com

Printed in the United States by Versa Press
10 9 8 7 6 5 4 3 2 1

Library of Congress Cataloging-in-Publication Data on file

CONTENTS

viii   **ACKNOWLEDGMENTS**

ix   **FOREWORD** by Augie Carton

1   **INTRODUCTION**

2   **IN SEASON**

5   Chapter 1: **RISE AND SHINE**

29   Chapter 2: **APPS AND SNACKS**

49   Chapter 3: **PUTTING THE GARDEN IN GARDEN STATE**

89   Chapter 4: **DOWN THE SHORE**

117   Chapter 5: **THE MAIN EVENT**

155   Chapter 6: **SANDWICHES, SAUCES, AND SPREADS**

177   Chapter 7: **THE MELTING POT**

213   Chapter 8: **SWEET TREATS**

247   Chapter 9: **COCKTAILS**

260   **FESTIVALS**

261   **RESTAURANT WEEKS OF NOTE**

262   **RESTAURANTS, FARMS, AND FAMILIES BY COUNTY**

268   **INDIVIDUAL RECIPE CONTRIBUTORS**

269   **INDEX**

ACKNOWLEDGMENTS

There's a recording of "Tenth Avenue Freeze-Out," performed live at Madison Square Garden, where Bruce Springsteen introduces the E Street Band. He tells a tale about standing at the edge of a forest, knowing that on the other side success awaits him. He encounters a gypsy woman who tells him that what he needs is a band; he needs some help to get to where he wants to go. Writing a book is a lot like that — to get to the end, you need some help. And that's why I'm so glad to introduce you all to the following people.

My wife, April Darcy, of Edison, is the true writer and explorer in the family, and she is the most encouraging, supportive, and loving partner anyone could ask for. My parents, John and Carolyn, and my mother-in-law, Teresa, are the kind of role models everyone should be blessed with in life. The same is true for my siblings, Tom, Amanda and Todd, Bill and Valerie, and Dan.

My Aunt Dellsie has long been a source of encouragement and love, and has again and again generously donated her time and resources to my various writing projects. We used her house along the Musconetcong River to prep and photograph many of the recipes contained within.

Although no longer with us, my grandmothers — Adel Holl and Helen Gibbons — helped shape my relationship, appreciation, creativity, and experience with food. Their kitchens were very different, but both produced meals that I remember and cherish to this day.

Since I started working with Storey Publishing in 2011, I've been pushing to write this book, and along the way there has been no greater cheerleader than Margaret Sutherland. Not only is she a very talented (and patient) editor, but she is a calming force and a great lover of food. Sarah Guare took over the editing reins from Margaret, with great care and skill. Nancy Ringer gave every line in this book the careful and wise eye of an experienced copy editor. Together, they made this book better. My thanks also to Deborah Balmuth, Dan Reynolds, Sarah Armour, Alee Moncy, Jeff Stiefel, and everyone else at Storey for their commitment to quality books, their talents, and their kindness toward writers.

I was privileged to work with Amy Roth, a true artist and food enthusiast. We traveled around the state together while she took many of the beautiful photographs contained in the following pages. Her stellar work brings these recipes to life throughout the book.

For the last several years I've served as editor of *All about Beer Magazine*, and it's just the best job I've ever had. This is thanks to my colleagues Daniel Bradford, Chris Rice, Ken Weaver, Peter Johnstone, Jeff Quinn, Daniel Hartis, and Jon Page, a North Carolinian with a sometimes-acerbic and dry wit that often makes me believe he was born here in Jersey.

Thanks to Jenny Stephens and everyone at Sterling Lord Literalistic for wonderful guidance, support, and representation.

My thanks also to Allyson O'Brien, Rob Hurff, Scott Miller, Vince Baglivo, Warren Bobrow, John Kelly, Chris Oney and the Cape May County Chamber of Commerce, Jennifer Guhl and the Princeton Regional Chamber of Commerce, Mark Allen, Kathy Simon, Jennifer Lea Cohan, Vicki Jakubovic, Daria and Theodore Romankow, Susan Belfer, Wolf Sterling, Paul Kermizian, Jackie Pappas and the Asbury Park Chamber of Commerce, John Cifelli, Jeremy Lees, Rich Eldert, Augie Carton, and Jeff Cioletti.

This book is largely a collection of recipes gathered from talented chefs, cooks, and restaurateurs from every county in the state. I am indebted to their kindness, generosity, and creativity. Their names are attached to their recipes, and I encourage you to visit them in person.

Finally, I've become the clichéd writer who takes the time to thank the dog. Long days at the computer and in the kitchen were helped by Pepper, our mutt rescued from a shelter in Sussex County seven years ago, who has become my shadow, my sounding board, and a great excuse to get outside and work off the extra pounds associated with writing a cookbook. She's a good girl.

FOREWORD

If America is a melting pot, New Jersey is its heat source. The "barrel tapped at both ends" has everything and every type flowing through it at a zooming pace.

Within five blocks of my brewery, in a small town that is both the best in the world and your regular ordinary Jersey berg with a shore vibe, you can choose between three local pizza places, each with a deli making better sandwiches than are available at most places in the known universe. You can also have exceptional Thai, a world-class bagel, two proper diner breakfasts, a respectable cheesesteak, and the best Southwestern cuisine I've ever had. You can choose Memphis ribs or a Tuscan trattoria dinner, either aspirational or traditional pub fare. And the best croissant I have had on any continent can be found in this town any morning between 6:30 and whenever the bakery runs out. All of these representations are as good as any others to be had anywhere, as long as you know what you want and how to filter the options.

Sure, you can figure out New Jersey's culinary jumble for yourself, and doing so is well worth it. There is as much pleasure in a life that knows where the perfect "Pork Roll (don't entertain the misguided notion that Taylor Ham is or ever was a thing; you want to end up on the right side of history, don't you?), Egg, and Cheese on a hard roll with SPK" is to be found as there is in discovering which of an area's roadside farm stands has this August's best Beefsteak tomato.

It's a rewarding endeavor, to be sure, but it will require a thick skin and the acceptance of some shenanigans along the way. Locals know best, and to locals Jersey is like our mom: we're the only ones allowed to pick on her. New Jersey isn't a small-talk kind of place; we are brash, candid, and proudly opinionated, which adds a wrinkle to finding your own way. The things we pick on the most are the most loved. It's a safe bet that the best place for you to eat in a Jersey town is the one the locals tell the most jokes about. Short of a willingness and determination to wade in these waters solo,

the camaraderie of a fluent and fluid tour guide will be your best way.

There are thousands of Jerseyans with whom I would happily spend hours debating the merits of one shop's sub roll over another's, but few who I will blindly follow into their chosen deli, let alone a linen tablecloth restaurant. John Holl has spent his life, from adolescence, as one of the last true newsmen, wandering each corner of New Jersey getting to know our home state. Typically proud and atypically egalitarian, John will candidly discuss the merits of ingenious local fare in the most pragmatic way, looking for a truth to it regardless of whether it is a Sloppy Joe, Oysters Braten, or the best stop on the route from Jersey City to LBI on a summer Saturday. Here, John has assembled a spread of Jersey samples only a man with his pedestrian knowledge of how we live could do; enjoy it.

Augie Carton
Carton Brewing
Atlantic Highlands, NJ

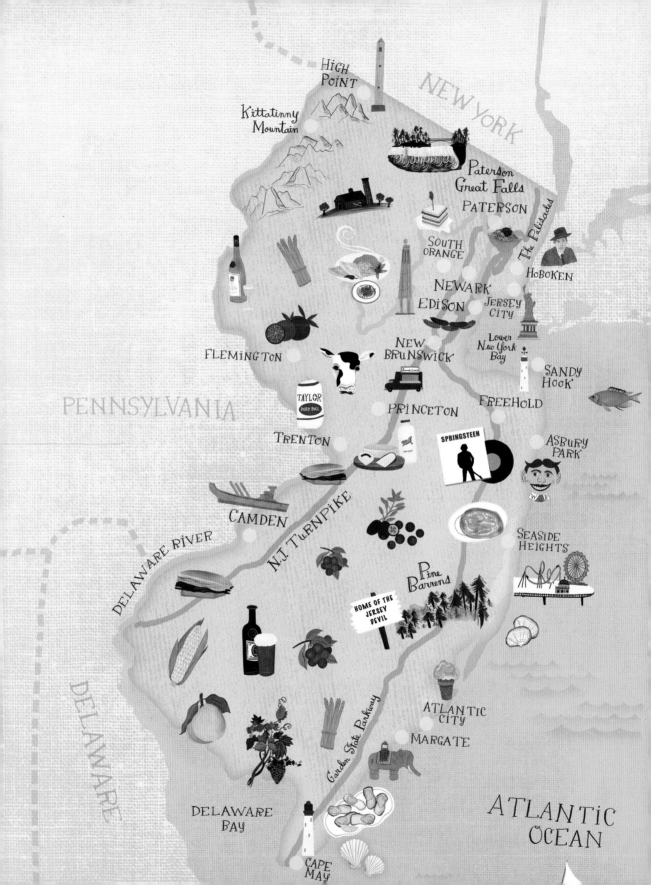

INTRODUCTION

Pride. If you're from Jersey, it's what you have. If you're not from here, it's that attitude you pick up on within minutes from Garden State natives.

Long the butt of national jokes, the insufferable "What exit?" questions, the "armpit of America" references, teasing about the smells, the mob, the traffic, the cities, party kids down the shore, and our endless stream of indicted politicians — we've heard it all, and worse. But we endure, because we know better.

We know that there is more to the state than the view from the airport, the parkway tolls, the turnpike traffic, and the occasional patches of blight. We know that our shoreline is unrivaled, that our farms produce some of the most flavorful fruits and vegetables anywhere on the planet. Throughout the state, we hunt and fish. We can hike a tough stretch of the Appalachian Trail or visit historic sites like the spot where Washington crossed the Delaware. We do this while snapping along to Sinatra and rocking out to Springsteen.

We're a complicated state, split into sections that are often tough to unify culturally, geographically, and socially. When it comes to sports, the northern part roots for the Giants and Jets, which, though they play, practice, and keep offices here in New Jersey, identify with New York. The southern half bleeds green for the Eagles of Philadelphia, a city that rarely shows its eastern neighbor any love. In the spring and summer, we may root for the Yankees or Mets or Phillies, but we also catch minor-league games at the dozen or so parks spread across the state. Our last proud-to-be-in-Jersey team is the Devils. We love them for bringing home the Stanley Cup and for their mascot, the legendary creature of New Jersey history.

Because New Jersey is all about the lore. We're about the mysterious. Hell, there is a magazine that celebrates our weird (it's *Weird NJ*, in case you didn't know).

It's the food, however, that truly unites us. A quality meal is never hard to find. Whether you're on the highways, winding through cities and past factories and infrastructure and swamplands, or on the back roads, passing through bucolic towns, shore communities, forests, or farmlands, you're guaranteed to find a great restaurant serving up recipes that represent the very best of the Garden State.

This includes everything from cultural dishes with roots in Italy, Poland, Portugal, Ireland, China, India, and Japan to fresh-caught fish from the shore. More than anything, New Jersey lives up to its Garden State reputation as a leader in tomato, corn, cranberry, blueberry, and apple crops. There are bison farms, bee farms, wineries, breweries, distilleries, and artisan producers of all manner of food. From fine dining to food trucks, we have it all.

And while we love fresh, we also don't mind indulging in fried foods and sweet treats now and again. What else are you going to eat on the boardwalk?

For us, quick is not a bad thing either. Corner bodegas and delis are good for a snack or sandwich in a pinch. A diner, resplendent in chrome, mirrors, and Formica, can serve up awesome food at a lightning-fast pace. Breakfast is served all day long.

This book is a celebration of all that. It's about the people, the towns, and the food that make Jersey what it is: a place to be proud of.

I started working as a reporter when I was 16, and over the next two decades I was able to travel through all 21 counties covering the news of the day, the trends, and the residents. I never missed an opportunity to try the local specialty.

What follows is a collection of recipes that come from restaurants and home kitchens all across Jersey. There are familiar diner dishes and shore specialties, fine-dining options and deep-fried goodies, and farm bounty and melting-pot traditions.

I hope you will visit these places in person. Get in the car, explore, and eat like a local; you might be surprised at what you find.

Most of all, stand tall. Be a good steward for our beloved state. There's more for visitors than the view from Newark Liberty International Airport and no need to cross the Hudson or Delaware to visit those major cities. New Jersey will win over your heart through your stomach. And we'll do it with pride.

By the way, my exit is 14C. Stop by and say hello.

John Holl
Jersey City

IN SEASON

Jersey is the Garden State for a reason. Get beyond the cities and congested roadways and it's easy to find a garden or farm. How easy? Well, the state currently boasts more than 9,000 farms on more than 720,000 acres. Agriculture in the state is a multibillion-dollar business that encompasses not only produce but an equine industry, dairy farms, and nursery plants.

New Jersey is among the top national producers of several major crops. The state might not be number one in numbers, but anyone who has had Jersey corn (ninth in the nation with 68.4 million pounds produced), tomatoes (seventh in the nation with 56.7 million pounds produced), blueberries (fifth in the nation with 51.5 million pounds produced), and cranberries (third in the nation with 550,000 barrels produced) knows that our produce has the most flavor.

The state is also a national leader in bell pepper, spinach, peach, cucumber, squash, apple, and snap bean production, according to the state department of agriculture. Farming is the state's third largest industry, and Jersey farmers produce more than 100 different kinds of vegetables and fruit.

The chart on the facing page, from the Jersey Fresh program, a division of the state department of agriculture, represents key harvest dates for the fruit, vegetables, and herbs that grow in gardens and farms from the north to the south. Fresh produce tastes best when it's in season, so mark your calendar, and when it's time, head out to your local farmers' market or roadside stand and celebrate the best of the spring, summer, and fall. (And to find out more, look up the Jersey Fresh program at jerseyfresh.nj.gov.)

KEY HARVEST DATES FOR JERSEY PRODUCE

Fruits & Berries	Early	Most Active	Late
Apples	July 15	Sept. 1–Oct. 25	Oct. 31
Blackberries	July 10	July 15–July 30	Aug. 10
Blueberries	June 20	July 5–Aug. 10	Aug. 15
Cherries	June 10	June 10–June 25	June 25
Cranberries	Sept. 20	Oct. 1–Nov. 1	Nov. 10
Grapes	Aug. 25	Sept. 10–Sept. 20	Sept. 30
Peaches and nectarines	July 5	July 20–Sept. 1	Sept. 15
Pears	Aug. 1	Aug. 10–Aug. 31	Sept. 10
Plums	July 1	July 15–Aug. 15	Sept. 1
Red raspberries (traditional)	July 1	July 5–July 21	Aug. 1
Red raspberries (fall bearing)*	Aug. 15	Sept. 1–Sept. 20	Oct. 15
Strawberries	May 20	June 1–June 10	June 25
Vegetables	**Early**	**Most Active**	**Late**
Asparagus	April 23	May 1–May 30	June 25
Beets	June 1	July 1–Oct. 31	Nov. 30
Broccoli	June 20	July 1–Oct. 31	Nov. 1
Cabbage	June 1	June 10–Oct. 31	Nov. 15
Cauliflower	Sept. 1	Oct. 5–Nov. 20	Dec. 5
Collards	May 15	Aug. 20–Oct. 31	Nov. 20
Cucumbers	June 25	July 5–Aug. 15	Sept. 15
Eggplant*	July 10	July 20–Sept. 30	Oct. 15
Lettuce (late spring)	May 15	May 20–July 15	Aug. 31
Lettuce (early fall)	Sept. 1	Sept. 15–Nov. 15	Nov. 30
Lima beans	July 10	July 15–Aug. 31	Oct. 31
Okra*	July 15	Aug. 15–Sept. 15	Oct. 15
Onions	June 25	June 25–July 31	Sept. 30
Peas	May 20	June 15–June 25	July 5
Peppers	July 5	July 15–Oct. 31	Nov. 5
Potatoes	July 10	July 20–Sept. 30	Oct. 15
Pumpkins	Sept. 15	Oct. 1–Oct. 15	Oct. 31
Snap beans	June 10	June 20–July 20	Aug. 31
Spinach	April 15	May 5–June 25	June 30
Squash	June 15	June 25–Sept. 1	Sept. 30
Sweet corn	July 1	July 5–Aug. 31	Sept. 25
Tomatoes*	July 5	July 10–Sept. 15	Oct. 15
Other	**Early**	**Most Active**	**Late**
Everlastings, flowers, herbs	July 1	July 15–Sept. 15	Oct. 1

*Late date is Oct. 15 or killing frost.

1 Rise and Shine

We know that breakfast is the most important meal of the day, and there's no shortage of options no matter where in New Jersey you travel: A cup of coffee to go from the deli, bodega, or drive-through — just something to sip on while you're commuting (and likely stuck in traffic) or taking that road trip down the shore. Eggs the way you want them at the diner, with your choice of toast. You want a side of bacon, sausage, or Taylor ham with that? On a sandwich with salt, pepper, and ketchup? What about a bagel with cream cheese? A hard roll wrapped in waxed paper? Seize the day.

Here are some favorites from popular Jersey kitchens, cut down to size so you can make them in your own kitchen, the way you like.

Buttered Roll

Let's be honest: this is a ridiculous recipe to include in a cookbook. It's a roll with butter. Two ingredients. One spread on the other. Easy. Brainless. Plus, why do it at home when every deli in the state has these ready-made, sitting on the counter next to the coffee pots, ready for you to take on the road? Then again, how can we talk about Jersey food without talking about this classic breakfast-to-go? Yeah. That's what I thought.

Kaiser roll
2 tablespoons butter, softened

Makes 1 roll

Cut the roll in half lengthwise. Spread 1 tablespoon butter on each half, place the roll back together, and slice down the middle. Wrap in waxed paper and secure with a strip of masking tape.

Or forgo that process and head to your local deli, grab one at the counter, and pair with a cup of coffee.

Pork Roll Surprise

Cheese *inside* pork roll? Genius! This was the winning recipe, created by Anthony McDonald and Rob Rossetti, at the first annual Pork Roll Recipe Contest held at the 2014 Pork Roll Festival in Trenton. Serve the sliced pork roll log on a roll with eggs, or on a plate with your other favorite breakfast foods.

1 pound bacon

1 (3-pound) pork roll log

1 cup shredded Asiago cheese

1 cup shredded cheddar cheese

1 cup shredded Monterey Jack cheese

4 cherry peppers, diced

Salt and freshly ground black pepper

Garlic powder

1 cup Frank's RedHot hot sauce, or a hot sauce of your choice

1 cup Worcestershire sauce

½ stick butter, melted

Makes 8–12 servings

1. Preheat the oven to 300°F.

2. Create a bacon weave: Place about two-thirds of the strips side by side lengthwise, and then interweave the other strips sideways, like you're making a basket, to form a rectangular weaving. Set aside.

3. Cut the pork roll log in half lengthwise and dig out the middle of both sides (like a canoe), keeping the edges intact. Combine the Asiago, cheddar, and jack with the cherry peppers in a mixing bowl, and mix well. Pack the mixture into the pork roll cavities. Fit the two halves back together to form a log. Season the outside of the log with salt, black pepper, and garlic powder to taste. Starting on a corner, roll the pork roll log in the bacon weave, tucking in the sides as you roll.

4. Combine the hot sauce, Worcestershire, and melted butter in a mixing bowl and stir to combine.

5. Place the bacon-wrapped pork roll on a baking sheet and brush with the hot sauce mixture. Bake for 1 hour, reapplying coats of sauce every 20 minutes.

6. Remove the pork roll from the oven and allow to rest for 10 minutes. Slice into ½-inch pieces and serve.

Classic Pork Roll, Egg, and Cheese Sandwich

It seems simple enough, right? Three ingredients stacked inside a hard roll — what's so complicated? For a sandwich with slippery contents, construction is key, as is the ingredients ratio. I remember once being at a South Jersey diner that served this breakfast staple with a dozen slices of Taylor ham. It was a glorious sight — until my first bite sent slices of ham sliding out the back end to plop down onto the plate below. A sandwich should stick together — that's what makes a sandwich a sandwich, rather than something you have to eat with knife and fork.

¼ tablespoon butter

3 slices Taylor ham or pork roll

2 eggs

Salt and freshly ground black pepper

3 slices yellow American cheese

1 kaiser or round crusty roll, cut in half, lightly toasted

Coleslaw, pickle, ketchup (optional, but really mandatory)

Makes 1 sandwich

1. Melt the butter in a skillet over medium heat. Cut four evenly spaced slits around the edges of the ham (to prevent curling), add to the skillet, and cook until the edges are beginning to brown, about 5 minutes. Set aside on a plate lined with a paper towel to absorb any excess grease.

2. Crack the eggs into the skillet and season with salt and pepper. Cook gently over medium heat until you reach your desired level of doneness. Turn off the heat. Cover the eggs with one slice of cheese and let stand until softened, 30 seconds.

3. Meanwhile, put the bottom half of the toasted roll on a plate. Top with one slice of cheese, then the meat, then the remaining slice of cheese. Add the egg and cheese from the pan, followed by the top half of the roll. Serve immediately, with a side of coleslaw, a pickle spear, and ketchup.

PORK ROLL: WHAT IS IT?

The state's official breakfast meat is pork roll, but many folks — especially in the northern part of the state — will call it Taylor ham. It is a mildly spicy pork-based meat product that is sold in cylindrical solid rolls wrapped in a cotton sack of varying weights, from 1 pound up to 5. Best cooked in a pan or griddle, it's important to notch the edges on each side after you slice it to prevent curling while cooking.

Several companies manufacture the salty, slightly tangy meat, which originated in Trenton by the Taylor Pork Roll company. It is also packaged presliced, but most purists will tell you to buy the roll and cut slices to your desired level of thickness. It's most commonly served on a roll or bagel accompanied by a fried egg and American cheese.

Recipe from RUNNING DEER GOLF CLUB, PITTSGROVE

Stuffed French Toast

This is a great Sunday-morning breakfast recipe from Stephen Pennese, the executive chef at Running Deer Golf Club, for those weekends when brunch is enjoyed at home. Better than any toaster variety, the fresh ingredients in this French toast make all the difference here. Crunchy, creamy, and vibrant with fresh fruit, all you need to round out this meal is a side of bacon and a strong pot of coffee.

1 French baguette

6 eggs

½ cup light cream

2 tablespoons Myers's dark rum (optional)

2 tablespoons vanilla extract

3 tablespoons sugar

1 tablespoon ground cinnamon

1 tablespoon ground nutmeg

12 ounces mascarpone cheese, softened

6 strawberries, sliced

½ cup fresh blueberries

2 tablespoons clarified butter

Pure maple syrup

Makes 6 servings

1. Cut the French bread into 1-inch slices on a heavy bias. To make a pocket, cut a slit in the middle of each piece, three-fourths of the way down but not all the way through, at the same angle.

2. To make the batter, combine the eggs, cream, rum, vanilla, sugar, cinnamon, and nutmeg in a medium mixing bowl and whisk vigorously until well combined.

3. Carefully open the pocket of the bread with your hands and place about 1 tablespoon of cheese on each inner side of the bread. Place 1 sliced strawberry and 6 blueberries, or the amount desired, inside the pocket with the cheese.

4. Working in batches, place the stuffed bread slices in the batter, pressing lightly with your hands to make sure the batter is absorbed.

5. Add the butter to a nonstick skillet over medium heat. When hot, add the battered stuffed bread and cook until the egg is cooked through and the toast is golden brown, about 3 minutes per side.

6. Serve immediately with maple syrup and any leftover or additional fruit.

Hash Browns

Good hash browns are a staple of diner breakfasts, but I've never understood why more people don't make these at home. Four ingredients are all you need. Have a hot cast-iron skillet ready, and you'll have a crispy breakfast potato pancake in minutes.

1 pound russet potatoes, peeled

3 tablespoons butter

Salt and freshly ground black pepper

Makes 4 servings

1. Shred the potatoes into long strips with a box grater. If you have a potato ricer, pass the shredded potato through the ricer to squeeze out extra moisture. Otherwise, gather up the shreds in a piece of cheesecloth and wring well.

2. Place a cast-iron skillet over medium-high heat and let warm for 5 minutes. Melt the butter in the hot skillet, tipping the pan to distribute it evenly. Immediately add the potato shreds, evenly covering the surface of the skillet. Press down with a spatula to form the potato into a pancake. Cook until the underside turns golden brown, taking care not to burn the potato (turn down the heat if necessary); this takes about 5 minutes.

3. Flip the pancake and cook until the other side is also golden brown, 3 to 5 minutes. Tip the pancake out onto a cutting board, slice, and serve.

Recipe from CONFECTIONS OF A ROCK$TAR, ASBURY PARK

Fresh Doughnuts with Beer Glaze and Chocolate-Covered Potato Chip Crumbles

Salty and sweet. This is the kind of snack where you can't have just one. You'll want to use a chocolate that, once melted, hardens quickly and evenly. You can buy specialty melting chocolate for this, but in general, most high-quality chocolate will do the job. These doughnuts use beer as their liquid; if you want to go a more traditional route, simply substitute ¾ cup buttermilk plus 2 tablespoons water for the beer. *Read about Confections of a Rock$tar on page 15.*

THE CRUMBLE

1½ cups Valrhona or other premium milk chocolate

4¼ ounces kettle chips (about half of a big bag)

THE DOUGHNUTS

¾ cup plus 2 tablespoons India pale ale

2 teaspoons active dry yeast

⅓ cup granulated sugar

1 large egg

2½ tablespoons butter

2¾ cups all-purpose flour

1 teaspoon salt

Vegetable oil, for frying

THE GLAZE

¼ cup India pale ale

2 cups confectioners' sugar

Makes 10–12 doughnuts

1. The crumble begins with melted chocolate: Place the chocolate in a microwave-safe bowl and microwave on high for 20 seconds. Stir. If there is still unmelted chocolate in the bowl, heat in 10-second bursts until fully melted.

2. Carefully coat the potato chips by dipping into the chocolate, and place on a parchment-lined baking sheet. Allow to cool completely.

3. Once the chips are completely cool, crush them into crumbles. Transfer to a bowl and set aside.

4. Time to make the doughnuts: Heat the beer in a saucepan over medium-high heat until it reaches 105°F. Pour the warm beer into the bowl of a stand mixer and sprinkle the yeast and half of the granulated sugar (2 tablespoons + 2½ teaspoons) over the surface; let stand for 5 to 10 minutes, until foamy. Add the remaining granulated sugar (2 tablespoons + 2½ teaspoons), the egg, and the butter, and whisk to combine well.

5. In a separate bowl, whisk the flour and salt together, and then add to the wet ingredients. Use a dough hook attachment to mix until the batter forms a ball, 2 to 3 minutes. Place the dough in a greased bowl, cover, and let rise in a warm place for 1 hour.

RECIPE CONTINUES ON PAGE 14

6. Remove the dough to a floured surface and roll it out to ¼-inch thickness. Use a doughnut cutter to make 10 to 12 doughnuts. You can reroll and cut extra dough, but those doughnuts will be denser. Place the cut doughnuts on a tray and let sit, uncovered, in a warm place for 30 minutes.

7. Pour about 3 inches of oil into a large heavy pot and heat to 265°F. Set up a rack with paper towels underneath for draining the fried doughnuts. Fry the doughnuts in batches until golden brown, 2 to 3 minutes on each side. Set on the prepared rack to cool.

8. To make the glaze, pour the beer into a mixing bowl and whisk gently to release some of the bubbles. Slowly add the confectioners' sugar and whisk until smooth. If the glaze is too thick, add a bit of water to thin it out.

9. When the doughnuts are room temperature, you're ready to glaze them. (If they're still warm, the chocolate will melt off the potato chip topping.) Dip each doughnut in the glaze, then set back on the rack. Once the glaze sets (just a few minutes), sprinkle the chocolate-covered potato chips over the top.

CONFECTIONS OF A ROCK$TAR

Bright pink walls. Musical instruments. Sweet treats. "These are the three things that I love the most," says Kimmee Masi, owner of Confections of a Rock$tar. So it makes sense that the bakery she opened in 2013 — as seen in *3 Days to Open with Bobby Flay* on the Food Network — has all three prominently placed. While it's not hard to find familiar baked goods, Masi and her staff also offer some offbeat selections like cupcakes topped with candied bacon. A former musician who played drums for a number of bands throughout Jersey, Masi has been working with musical acts on special bakery collaborations. It's the perfect fit for a town like Asbury Park.

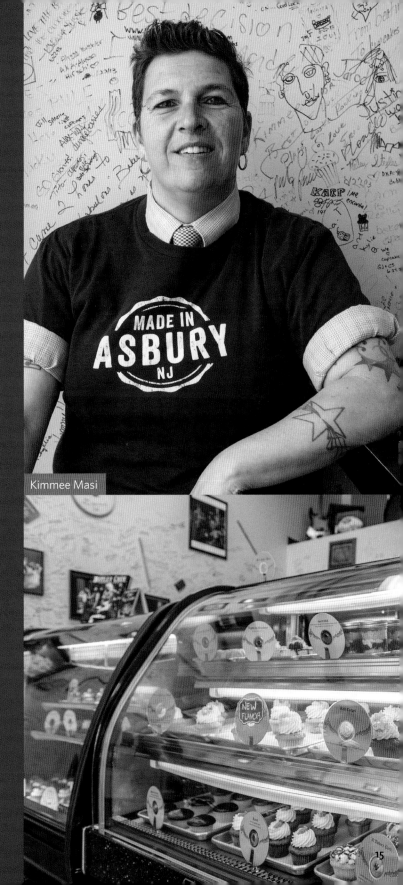

Kimmee Masi

Recipe from BUSY BEE ORGANICS

Almond-Cherry Pancakes
with Coconut Flakes

Pancakes are one of breakfast's great indulgences. Chef Michelle Berckes takes some of the guilt out of this dish with a collection of healthy, organic ingredients. A satisfying option for anyone with a breakfast sweet tooth, these dynamite pancakes might just become a weekend tradition in your house. *Read about Busy Bee Organics on page 18.*

1 cup almond flour/meal

1 teaspoon baking powder

1 teaspoon ground Saigon or Ceylon cinnamon

⅛ teaspoon sea salt

½ cup milk (the chef suggests almond milk or any other seed/nut-based milk)

2 egg whites

1 whole egg

1 teaspoon vanilla extract

2 tablespoons honey, preferably raw

½ cup pitted frozen cherries

Coconut oil or butter, for cooking

¼ cup shredded unsweetened coconut

Makes 4 servings

1. Mix the almond flour, baking powder, cinnamon, and salt in a medium bowl. Create a well in the center of the dry mix, add the milk, egg whites, whole egg, vanilla, and honey, and stir until the mixture is smooth and pourable.

2. Place the cherries in small saucepan and cook over medium heat, covered, until soft, 5 to 7 minutes. Remove the cover and continue cooking until the liquid in the pan has reduced slightly. Remove the pan from the heat and allow to cool slightly.

3. Heat a skillet over medium heat and add a bit of coconut oil or butter, swirling it around the pan as it melts. (Berckes suggests grass-fed butter, ghee, or unrefined coconut oil for this application, to keep with the theme.) Dollop the batter in small portions (about ⅛ cup or 2 tablespoons) into the hot skillet; you're aiming here for silver-dollar-size pancakes. Let cook for 1 to 2 minutes, then use a spatula to flip. Cook for 1 to 2 minutes longer.

4. Layer the pancakes and cherries on a plate, sprinkle with coconut, and enjoy!

NOTE: For added flavor, add chocolate or carob chips to the batter. The flavors complement each other very nicely!

CHEF MICHELLE BERCKES, BUSY BEE ORGANICS

When asked about her relationship with food, chef Michelle Berckes is candid. "I developed an eating disorder in my teens that carried into my twenties. I strived for the skinny body by eating fat-free and sugar-free options of every processed food because cookbooks and diet books told me that was the best way to a 'fit' body. I deprived my body of nutrients and struggled with body image and bulimia without an end in sight. I lost hope in myself and thought that I would eventually find my demise in that disease."

She focused her attention on solving the issue, received a degree in dietetic nutrition, and founded Busy Bee Organics, a food company that helps people embrace natural ingredients, promoting health without compromising flavor. Through her website, and in person at farmers' markets and events, she is erasing confusion and intimidation that some people might have about organic ingredients and is promoting the concept that natural eating can help solve many food-related problems.

Chef Michelle Berckes

Recipe from THE CINNAMON SNAIL

Chocolate Cashew Milk

This chocolate milk is a hit with everybody, especially those with chronic chocolate dependency. Chocolate addiction runs deep in my family, and we self-medicate often. For serious chocolate fixes, chef Adam Sobel suggests using pure unroasted cacao powder; it provides the most intense flavor and is the best way to access all of chocolate's antioxidants and alkaloids. For a more subtle, typical-tasting chocolate milk, replace half the cacao powder with roasted or Dutch-process cocoa.

1 cup raw cashew pieces

¼ cup cacao or unsweetened cocoa powder

¼ cup agave nectar

2 tablespoons coconut butter

¼ teaspoon salt

3½ cups water

Makes 1 quart

1. Place the cashews, cacao, agave, coconut butter, salt, and 1 cup of the water in a blender. Let the contents sit for 15 minutes, to start softening the cashews.

2. Blend for 40 seconds at high speed. Add the remaining 2½ cups water and blend until the milk is creamy, smooth, rich, and just a wee bit thicker than regular chocolate milk, 20 seconds.

3. Serve immediately. Store any leftover milk in a sealed container in the refrigerator, where it will keep for up to 3 days.

Recipe from SAM A.M., JERSEY CITY

Chicken and Waffles

A staple in the South, chicken and waffles are treated to a northern spin in this recipe that evokes memories of Thanksgiving dinner. This any-time-of-day meal features roasted chicken instead of the usual down-home fried variety. While you can use prepared ingredients, make it from scratch for a rewarding experience that's worth the effort. *Read about Sam a.m. on page 22.*

THE ROASTED CHICKEN

1 (3- to 4-pound) free-range chicken

3 tablespoons unsalted butter, softened

3 sprigs fresh sage

1 tablespoon kosher salt

2 teaspoons freshly ground black pepper

1 teaspoon smoked paprika

THE GRAVY

Drippings from the roasted chicken

¼ cup sifted all-purpose flour

2 cups hot water

THE CRANBERRY SYRUP

2 cups fresh cranberries

½ cup granulated sugar

½ cup light brown sugar

½ cup freshly squeezed orange juice

½ cup water

THE WAFFLES

2 cups self-rising flour

2 tablespoons granulated sugar

2 cups whole milk

2 eggs

2 tablespoons canola oil

Makes 4–6 servings

1. Preheat the oven to 425°F.

2. Pat the chicken dry with paper towels. Place the chicken breast side up in a cast-iron skillet. Gently pull the skin up from the top of the neck bone and slide two fingers down the back to the bottom of the chicken, loosening the skin from the entire backbone area. Massage 2 tablespoons of the softened butter under the loosened skin, then put the sage sprigs under the skin and pat the loose skin down. Mix the salt, pepper, and paprika with the remaining 1 tablespoon butter to create a paste and gently massage that mixture over the entire bird.

3. Roast for 50 minutes or so, until the wings and legs wiggle loosely and the juices run clear or the chicken reaches 165°F at the thickest point of the thigh. Remove from the oven and let rest for 20 minutes. Then pull off the meat and shred it or cut it into bite-size pieces.

4. To make the gravy, place a skillet over low heat and add the drippings from the chicken pan. Cook until they reach a slow simmer and begin to darken. Gradually whisk the sifted flour into the drippings, and let cook for 2 minutes, whisking constantly. Add the hot water, raise the heat to medium-high, and let simmer, whisking constantly, until the gravy thickens and reaches a creamy consistency. Pour into a separate container or gravy boat and set aside.

5. To make the syrup, combine the cranberries, granulated sugar, brown sugar, orange juice, and water in a medium saucepan over medium-low heat and bring to a simmer. Stir occasionally to prevent sticking. Let simmer until the berries have popped and the syrup has reduced by half, 15 minutes. Pour the contents through a fine-mesh strainer set over a bowl; use a whisk to work the syrup through. Let cool to room temperature.

6. For the waffles, grease and heat a waffle iron.

7. Combine the self-rising flour, granulated sugar, milk, eggs, and oil in a large bowl and mix until well blended. Pour ¼ cup of the batter into the waffle iron and cook until golden brown and crispy. Repeat until all the batter is used up. (If you want to keep waffles warm while you finish cooking, set them on a tray in a just-warm oven.)

8. To serve, place a waffle in the center of a plate. Top with ½ cup of chicken meat, pour ¼ cup of gravy over the chicken, and drizzle with 1 teaspoon of cranberry syrup.

SAM A.M.

Sam a.m. is a neighborhood café on a leafy street full of brownstones, just three blocks from the Hudson River. When you visit, it's like walking into a friend's house — you know, the friend with great design style and an effortless knack for cooking delicious food. Locals and tourists alike flock to Sam a.m. for a quick coffee, full weekend brunch, or casual weekday lunch.

Chef Francis Samu

Corned Beef Hash

With this recipe, you'll never reach for a can of hash again. Cooking low and slow is the key to getting this dish right. Great for lazy Sunday mornings, the recipe demands only a handful of ingredients. Serve with your favorite toast and eggs, the way you like them.

3 tablespoons unsalted butter

1 cup finely chopped green bell pepper

1 cup finely chopped yellow onion

3 cups finely chopped cooked corned beef

3 cups finely chopped raw unpeeled russet potato

Salt and freshly ground black pepper

Fresh parsley, minced, for garnish

Makes 4–6 servings

1. Melt the butter in a cast-iron skillet over medium heat, then add the bell pepper and onion. Cook, stirring occasionally, until fragrant, about 3 minutes. Remove from the heat and let cool slightly.

2. Combine the corned beef and potato in a mixing bowl. Add the onion mixture and stir well.

3. Warm the same skillet you used for cooking the onion over low heat. Spread the corned beef mixture evenly into the skillet. Press the mixture flat with a sturdy spatula; add a cooking weight if possible. Cook for 10 minutes, taking care not to let the hash burn. Flip the hash, again pressing the mixture down into the pan, and cook for another 20 minutes.

4. Remove the hash from the heat and sprinkle with parsley and salt and pepper, to taste. Serve hot with the rest of your breakfast.

Recipe from HOBBY'S DELICATESSEN AND RESTAURANT, NEWARK

Cheese Blintzes

Slightly crispy on the outside, warm and soft on the inside, this breakfast pastry brings the bakery right into your kitchen. This is a large-scale preparation, great for big gatherings, holiday brunches, kids' sleepovers, or any situation where you're likely to have a crowd gathered in the earlier part of the day. *Read about Hobby's on page 26.*

9 eggs (3 separated)

2 cups water

4 tablespoons cooking oil, plus more for sautéing

1 teaspoon salt

1½ cups all-purpose flour

1 quart farmer cheese

4 tablespoons confectioners' sugar

2 tablespoons vanilla extract

Sour cream or fresh fruit (optional)

Makes about 2 dozen blintzes

1. Make the batter: Combine the 6 whole eggs, water, oil, and salt in a bowl and mix well. Add the flour slowly, stirring until it is fully incorporated.

2. Make the filling: Combine the cheese, egg yolks, sugar, and vanilla in a bowl and mix thoroughly.

3. Heat a tablespoon or so of oil in a medium skillet over medium-high heat. Pour about 2 tablespoons (1 ounce) of batter into the center of the pan. Swirl the pan to evenly distribute the batter across the cooking surface. Cook for about 30 seconds, then flip (the batter will have a crepelike appearance and consistency) and cook on the other side for 15 seconds. The key here is to make sure the pancake is cooked through, but still soft and not crispy. Remove from the heat and slide the pancake out onto a cutting board. Repeat until all the batter is used up, stacking the pancakes on the cutting board as you go.

4. To assemble the blintzes, lay out a pancake on a plate. Place 2 tablespoons of the cheese mixture on the lower third of the pancake. Wrap the sides over the cheese, burrito-style, and then roll away from you, keeping the blintz tight.

5. Heat another tablespoon or so of oil in the skillet over medium heat. Add the blintzes in batches and cook until lightly browned, 2 minutes on each side.

6. Serve warm, with sour cream or fresh fruit, if you like.

HOBBY'S

An old-fashioned Jewish delicatessen and Newark dining institution, Hobby's has been run by the Brummer family since 1962. While the city has changed considerably since then, the deli has not — and that's a great thing.

In America today the sandwich shop is ubiquitous but has become bland with uninspired ingredients or menu items chasing a fad. You can taste the authenticity in everything on Hobby's menu. Corned beef is pickled in 50-gallon stainless-steel vats; the potato pancakes fried just right. Brothers Marc and Michael keep the business hopping these days, deftly making their way through the always bustling kitchen and dining room, which displays decades' worth of letters from notable locals and news clippings touting Hobby's many great attributes.

Marc Brummer

The sandwich that made the deli famous — corned beef and pastrami on rye, topped with coleslaw and Russian dressing — remains a fan favorite. But who can ignore the fresh and hearty soups, giant omelets, overstuffed deli sandwiches, and all the other great fare you can get here? It's a dizzyingly big menu that always delivers. And speaking of deliveries, Hobby's is also the proud sponsor of Operation Salami Drop, an effort to send salamis to American soldiers serving overseas. OSD, as it's known, has shipped more than 18 tons of salami to grateful troops.

New Jersey Iced Tea

This recipe is homage to that staple beverage found in coolers across the state, from delis and bodegas to bagel shops and convenience stores. You used to find it in pint-size waxed cardboard containers, but now it's more commonly packaged in plastic bottles. New Jersey iced tea is a less sweet version of its southern counterpart, with more of an emphasis on the black tea and lemon. It's best served with your favorite Jersey sandwich.

5 cups cold water

⅓ cup sugar

3 black tea bags

2 tablespoons freshly squeezed lemon juice

Ice

Makes 5 cups

1. Bring 3 cups of the water to a boil. Pour the boiling water over the sugar, tea bags, and lemon juice. Stir to dissolve the sugar and let steep for 10 minutes. Then remove the tea bags and let the tea cool to room temperature.

2. Fill a large pitcher one-quarter full with ice. Add the remaining 2 cups cold water, then add the tea and stir. Serve over ice, if desired.

2

Apps and Snacks

Do you have the house where everyone gathers? Big family celebrations, Sundays during football season, holidays, or just because it's a Thursday? These dishes are built to serve a crowd. Some are bar favorites, some celebrate the seasons, some highlight a particular ingredient or theme. All will disappear quickly after hitting the table. They are just that good.

Fried Chicken Wings with Sauce Two Ways

Bruno Pascale has a passion for wings. There's no disputing that. Just visit his Marley's Gotham Grill in Hackettstown and take your time (you'll need it) reading through the 130-plus sauces he has available for his plump and crispy wings. Bring your friends and let everyone order a different flavor. You'll still need many return visits to get through them all to find your favorite.

Pascale offers here two of his personal favorites, and they're easy to make at home. So grab your ingredients and call friends over to watch the game. You'll need a moist towelette after you're finished licking your fingers. Pair with a quality beer (like the kind Pascale serves at his place) and you're ready for a bar night at home.

Canola or soybean oil, for frying

2 cups all-purpose flour

1 cup plain breadcrumbs

1 tablespoon cayenne pepper

4 pounds chicken wings

2 cups Bang Bang Sauce (page 32) or Kung Foo Sauce (page 32)

½ cup chopped scallions, for garnish

3 tablespoons sesame seeds, for garnish (optional)

Makes 4–6 servings

1. Fill a deep fryer or large cast-iron pot with 4 inches of oil and heat to 375°F. Line a large plate with paper towels.

2. Combine the flour, breadcrumbs, and cayenne in a mixing bowl and mix well. Working in batches, lightly coat the wings in the flour mixture, shaking off any excess flour, and set on a platter.

3. Fry the wings in batches; don't crowd the pot. When the wings are done, they will turn golden brown and float to the surface; it takes 10 to 12 minutes. Remove from the oil and transfer to the towel-lined plate to drain while you start the next batch.

4. Let the hot wings rest for 1 minute, then toss with the sauce. Serve with a garnish of fresh scallions. Sesame seeds are good with the Kung Foo Sauce, if desired.

RECIPE CONTINUES ON PAGE 32

Bang Bang Sauce

Ka-pow! Just as the heat is smacking your taste buds, the soothing honey and cooling mayo come to the rescue, tamping down the spice, until that next bite, when the sensations repeat themselves. This sauce whips up in a snap. It's great on hot wings, but also try it on fried calamari, roasted tofu, or shrimp.

1 cup mayonnaise
1 cup Thai sweet chili sauce
¼ cup Sriracha hot sauce
2 tablespoons honey

Makes 2 cups

Combine the mayonnaise, chili sauce, hot sauce, and honey in a small bowl. Whisk until well combined. Store any leftover sauce in an airtight container in the refrigerator for up to 5 days.

Kung Foo Sauce, "a Bruce Lee Favorite"

No need for blue cheese with a sauce like this. Spicy and savory, it gives a different kind of kick to the taste buds. Serve with carrots and celery on the side.

1 cup aged balsamic vinegar
1 cup honey
½ cup soy sauce
½ cup sugar
½ teaspoon ground ginger
½ teaspoon cornstarch
1 tablespoon water

Makes 2 cups

1. Combine the vinegar, honey, soy sauce, sugar, and ginger in a medium saucepan and bring to a simmer over low heat. Let simmer for 6 minutes.

2. Whisk together the cornstarch and water in a small bowl. Add the cornstarch mixture to the sauce, stir, and let simmer until the sauce thickens slightly, 1 minute. Let cool slightly before tossing with wings.

Buffalo Chicken Dip

I've come to make a spare, smaller dish of this when hosting parties, because I know that as soon as it hits the table I won't be able to get past the crowd for my own taste. It's also popular at tailgates in the Meadowlands, during Rutgers' games, or anywhere crowds gather to watch sports. This dip incorporates many of the flavors of chicken wings, but with the convenience of a dip (no sticky fingers!).

4 large boneless, skinless chicken breasts

8 ounces blue cheese dressing

8 ounces cream cheese, softened

8 ounces hot sauce, such as Frank's RedHot

4 stalks celery, finely minced

2 large carrots, shredded

Salt and freshly ground black pepper

½ cup shredded cheddar cheese

Corn chips, celery, and carrot sticks, for serving

Makes 6–8 servings

1. Place the chicken in a pot and cover with water. Bring to a gentle boil over medium-high heat and cook until the chicken is cooked through and has an internal temperature of 170°F, 10 to 15 minutes. Remove the chicken from the water, pat dry, and shred the meat using two forks.

2. Preheat the oven to 350°F.

3. Combine the dressing, cream cheese, hot sauce, celery, carrots, and shredded chicken in a mixing bowl. Mix until fully combined. Season with salt and pepper to taste.

4. Transfer the mixture to a large casserole dish and bake for 15 minutes. Top with the cheddar cheese and bake for 15 minutes longer. Serve hot, with chips and vegetables for dipping.

Cantaloupe and Prosciutto

This is a good alternative to a starter salad. Sweet and savory with a simple citrus kick, this is a light start that can lead into a heavy meal. It's best whenever melons are in season — during the summer months — but those brought in from a warmer climate during our colder months work in a pinch. When picking out prosciutto, have the deli counter slice it thin.

2 medium cantaloupes, rinds removed, and sliced into 16 equal slices

16 slices prosciutto

2 limes, quartered

Makes 8 servings

Starting at one end and moving in a circular manner, wrap one slice of prosciutto around one cantaloupe spear. Repeat for each slice of cantaloupe. Place two slices on each plate and serve with a lime wedge for garnish.

Cauliflower Buffalo Wings
with Roasted Garlic Ranch Dip

You can make vegetarian buffalo "wings" out of tofu, tempeh, seitan — heck, just about anything, even vegetables! And it's a handy coincidence that small cauliflower florets naturally have a drumsticklike shape. In this recipe chef Adam Sobel suggests using a gluten-free flour mix, but if that doesn't matter to you, at home you can easily substitute equal parts all-purpose flour for the mix of gluten-free flours.

THE ROASTED GARLIC RANCH DIP

- 8 garlic cloves
- 3 tablespoons olive oil
- ⅔ cup Vegenaise
- 1 tablespoon agave nectar
- 2 teaspoons stone-ground mustard
- Zest and juice of 1 lemon
- 1 tablespoon minced dill pickle
- 1 scallion, minced, green and white parts
- 2 tablespoons minced fresh parsley
- 1 tablespoon minced fresh dill

THE BATTER

- 1½ cups gluten-free flour
- 1 tablespoon paprika
- 1 teaspoon dried thyme
- 1 teaspoon salt
- 2 cups soy milk
- 1 teaspoon apple cider vinegar
- 1 teaspoon stone-ground mustard

Makes 6 servings

1. Preheat the oven to 400°F.

2. To roast the garlic for the dipping sauce, toss the cloves with 1 tablespoon of the olive oil in a small bowl, then spread them on a parchment-lined baking sheet. Roast for 12 to 14 minutes, until golden brown. Remove from the oven and let cool for 10 minutes.

3. Transfer the garlic and the 2 remaining tablespoons oil to a blender along with the Vegenaise. Blend on high speed for 45 seconds, until smooth. Add the agave, mustard, lemon zest and juice, pickle, scallion, parsley, and dill, and pulse a few times to incorporate, just until the dip is speckled with bits of fresh herbs and pickle throughout.

4. To make the batter, whisk together the flour, paprika, thyme, and salt in a medium bowl. Add the soy milk, vinegar, and mustard, and whisk thoroughly until well blended.

5. To make the wings, heat the oil in a large skillet over medium-high heat. Put the cauliflower pieces in a medium bowl, add the rice flour, and toss gently until all sides are well coated.

⅔ cup canola or safflower oil, for frying

1 medium head cauliflower, cut into 18 to 24 drumstick-shaped florets

½ cup rice flour

⅓ cup habanero hot sauce or any thick hot sauce of your choice

2 tablespoons chopped fresh parsley, for garnish (optional)

2 tablespoons finely minced red onion, for garnish (optional)

6. Divide the cauliflower florets into two batches for frying. For each batch, submerge the cauliflower in the batter (this is easiest if you work with just three or four pieces at a time), remove, let excess batter drip back into the bowl, and quickly place the florets in the hot oil. Make sure the florets aren't touching one another in the pan. Fry until the pieces have turned golden brown on the bottom side, 2 to 3 minutes, and then flip and fry until the other side is golden brown, another 1 to 2 minutes. Stir the pieces in the pan, and flip and fry any remaining sides that show uncooked batter. When they're done, remove the cauliflower florets to a plate lined with paper towels.

7. Toss the cauliflower wings with the hot sauce in a medium bowl. Serve warm, with the ranch dip in a ramekin on the side, and if you like, garnish the wings with chopped parsley and minced onion.

Recipe from JERSEY GIRL BREWING COMPANY, HACKETTSTOWN

Grilled Shrimp and Sausage Skewers

This surf and turf is served on a stick, and everyone knows that food always tastes better on a stick. Fire up the grill, assemble some skewers, pair with an American brown ale (like the one made by Jersey Girl Brewing Company), and you're in for an excellent eating experience. Serve these skewers with the Jersey Tomato and Corn Salsa (page 66). This recipe can easily be scaled up if you're cooking for a large crowd.

THE GLAZE

- ½ cup honey
- ⅓ cup spicy brown mustard
- 3 tablespoons apple cider vinegar
- 2 teaspoons garlic powder

THE KABOBS

- ½ pound large shrimp, peeled and deveined
- ½ pound sweet Italian sausage, cut into rounds
- 1 medium green bell pepper, cut into large chunks

Makes 4 appetizer servings

1. Prepare a medium-hot fire in a gas or charcoal grill and oil the grill grates. If you're using wooden skewers, soak them in water for at least 15 minutes.

2. To make the glaze, combine the honey, mustard, vinegar, and garlic powder in a small bowl and mix well.

3. To assemble the kabobs, thread the shrimp, sausage, and bell pepper onto skewers. Brush the kabobs with some of the glaze and reserve the remaining sauce.

4. Place the kabobs on the grill, over medium heat, or 4 to 6 inches from the coals if you're using a charcoal grill. Cook until the shrimp turns pink and the sausage is cooked through, 8 to 10 minutes. Turn frequently and keep brushing with the glaze. Remove to a platter and serve.

JERSEY GIRL BREWING COMPANY. Founded in 2014 and opened a year later, Jersey Girl Brewing Company is part of the new wave of modern microbreweries that took advantage of recent changes to state law that allowed for easier beer production and distribution.

Charles Aaron and Mike Bigger, the cofounders, opened the brewery in Hackettstown with a goal of offering fresh beer packed with flavor.

As the brewers are fond of saying, "Jersey Girl is not what we are, but what we love. Our inspiration comes from the true essence of a Jersey girl — complex, deep, layered, bitter, sweet, subtle, and sophisticated."

Garlic Knot Fries

Like the classic baked knots of Italian bread, these homemade French fries are topped with fresh garlic, cheese, and parsley. It's basically substituting one starch for another, with the same delicious results. The potatoes require advance prep time, so plan ahead.

4 large russet potatoes, skin on

2 tablespoons distilled white vinegar

3 cups vegetable oil

2 teaspoons olive oil

3 garlic cloves, chopped

¼ cup grated Parmesan cheese

2 tablespoons chopped fresh parsley

2 teaspoons sea salt

Makes 6–8 servings as a side dish

1. Cut the potatoes into long strips about ¼ inch thick and wide. Put the cut potatoes in a strainer and rinse under cold water for a few minutes. This removes some starch, which prevents them from sticking together and stops the oxidizing process. Place the potatoes in a large bowl and fill the bowl with enough cold water to completely cover them. Add the vinegar to the water and stir. Cover the bowl and refrigerate for at least 6 hours, but no longer than 24 hours. The vinegar will give the fries a crispy finish.

2. In a pot fitted with a thermometer or a fryer, heat the vegetable oil until it reaches 325°F. Drain the potatoes and pat dry. Working in small batches, fry the potatoes until they go from shiny to matte, 3 to 5 minutes. Remove from the oil and drain well on paper towels.

3. Warm the olive oil in a small skillet, add the garlic, and sauté until barely golden, 2 to 3 minutes.

4. Reheat the oil in the pot or fryer until it reaches 350° to 375°F. Add the potatoes, again in small batches, and fry until they are golden brown and crispy on the outside but soft and chewy on the inside, 3 to 4 minutes. Remove from the oil, drain well, and toss with the sautéed garlic, Parmesan, parsley, and salt. Serve hot and enjoy!

PUDGY'S STREET FOOD

Before she started Pudgy's Street Food, a food truck, in 2010, Mary Voorhees had no professional culinary training. She just knew that she wanted to cook and didn't want to be confined to a building. She started simple, learning as she went, and focused on serving quality hot dogs and French fries.

It didn't take long for people to notice and flock to her truck daily.

After just a few years, the two-fryer setup couldn't handle the demand, so the ride had to be upgraded to one with five deep fryers. That growth led to a change in the menu as well, with the fries becoming the star. "The side has become the entrée," says Voorhees. Focusing on the community aspect of food truck cuisine, the fries now come topped with everything from pulled pork to buffalo chicken, and always several forks for sharing.

Short Rib Poutine

This is one hearty side. It's a rich blend of meat, vegetable, and potato . . . just maybe not the way Grandma used to make. *Read about The Shannon Rose Irish Pub on page 203.*

THE SHORT RIBS

1 tablespoon olive oil

2 pounds boneless short ribs

Salt and freshly ground black pepper

½ cup diced carrot

½ cup diced celery

½ cup diced onion

2 garlic cloves, minced

¼ cup red wine, preferably Chianti

2 tablespoons tomato paste

1 bay leaf

1 sprig fresh rosemary

1 sprig fresh thyme

1 quart beef stock

THE HORSERADISH GRAVY

1 quart beef gravy, preferably homemade

4 tablespoons prepared horseradish

FOR SERVING

1½ pounds frozen French fries, or make your own (see Garlic Knot Fries, page 38)

½ pound mozzarella cheese curds

4 teaspoons chopped chives

Makes 4 servings

1. Preheat the oven to 350°F.

2. To prepare the short ribs, heat the oil in a large pot over medium-high heat. Season the short ribs with plenty of salt and pepper. Set the short ribs in the hot oil and brown all over, about 2½ minutes per side. Remove the ribs and set aside. Add the carrot, celery, onion, and garlic to the pot and sauté until browned, about 10 minutes. Deglaze with the red wine (add the wine, then scrape up the browned bits from the bottom of the pot) and simmer until the liquid is reduced by half, about 10 minutes. Add the tomato paste, bay leaf, rosemary, thyme, and stock, and stir to mix. Return the short ribs to the pot, raise the heat, and bring to a boil. Cover with foil, place in the oven, and let cook for 2½ hours, or until the short ribs are very tender.

3. Remove the short ribs from the liquid and let cool slightly. Shred the beef and set aside. Strain the braising liquid into a large saucepan and set aside.

4. To make the horseradish gravy, combine the beef gravy and horseradish in a saucepan. Bring to a boil, then reduce the heat and let simmer for 5 minutes. Keep warm.

5. Cook the French fries according to the package instructions.

6. Add the shredded short ribs to the reserved braising liquid and bring back to a simmer.

7. Divide the French fries and the shredded beef among four plates. Divide the cheese curds evenly among the plates, scattering them over the fries. Ladle ½ cup or so of the horseradish gravy over each serving. Garnish with the chopped chives.

Recipe from TAPASTRE, SOMERVILLE

Drunken Clams on Fire

If the name doesn't make you smile, the taste sure will. Bursting with heat and spice, this recipe from chef Carlton Greenawalt is one for the adults to enjoy. You won't go wrong with your favorite beer to cut the heat.

1 tablespoon olive oil

1 jalapeño, sliced, and seeded if you want to temper the heat

2 tablespoons minced garlic

2 tablespoons minced shallots

2 tablespoons red pepper flakes

1 (12-ounce) bottle pale ale

½ cup marinara sauce

4 tablespoons unsalted butter

4 dozen littleneck clams, washed well

Crusty bread, for serving

Makes 4–6 servings

1. Heat the oil in a large pot over medium-low heat. Add the jalapeño, garlic, shallots, and pepper flakes. Cook slowly over low heat until softened, 5 to 7 minutes.

2. Add the ale, marinara sauce, butter, and clams. Cover and bring to a simmer over medium-high heat. Cook until all the clams have opened, about 5 minutes. Remove clams as they open and discard any clams that do not open after 10 minutes. Serve immediately, with fresh bread for dipping in the sauce.

Recipe from ABELES & HEYMANN

Sweet and BBQ Salami

Simple and delicious, this will likely become a party staple after you try it once. In fact, it's a good idea to have extra ingredients on hand to whip up a second batch, once that first disappears. The brainchild of kosher food blogger Chani Apfelbaum, this recipe calls for Abeles & Heymann salami, made locally in Hillside, New Jersey, but any good-quality salami will do. If you're cooking for a larger crowd, opt for the 2-pound salami in the deli case, and scale up the sauce recipe.

½ cup duck sauce

½ cup tangy barbecue sauce

1 (14-ounce) Abeles & Heymann salami

Makes 4–6 appetizer servings

1. Preheat the oven to 400°F.

2. Combine the duck sauce and barbecue sauce in a small bowl, whisking well to fully combine.

3. Remove the labeled casing from the salami and place the meat on a cutting board. Make deep cuts in the salami, about ¼ inch apart, taking care not to cut all the way through. The salami should remain intact. Place the whole salami on a baking sheet lined with parchment paper.

4. Using a pastry brush, liberally coat the salami with the prepared sauce. Brush the sauce on both sides and across the top. Be careful not to tear apart the slices, so the salami remains intact.

5. Bake for 45 minutes, basting the salami with the sauce several times during that time. (Watch for burning, as the sauce has a high sugar content.) As it cooks, the salami slices will fan out.

6. Slice apart and serve warm, with toothpicks and extra sauce for dipping.

Cider Fondue

Great for autumn, when sweet cider is abundant across the state. (New Jersey is not the biggest apple producer in the nation, but it's no slouch, either; in 2014 the state produced 35 million pounds of apples.) Cheddar is a classic and tasty pairing with apples, so it makes the most sense in this recipe, but feel free to mix it up with your favorite fromage. Make sure you have plenty of dipping options available, such as grilled bread, fresh crudités, and, of course, sliced apples.

10 ounces fresh apple cider

1 garlic clove, minced

12 ounces extra-sharp yellow cheddar cheese, shredded

8 ounces white cheddar cheese, shredded

1 teaspoon freshly ground black pepper

1½ teaspoons cornstarch

1 tablespoon Dijon mustard

1 tablespoon water

Makes 4–6 servings

1. In a fondue or any small heavy-bottomed pot, combine the cider and garlic and bring to a simmer. Gradually add the yellow and white cheddar, stirring constantly. Bring the mixture to a gentle simmer and let cook, still stirring, until all the cheese is melted and the mixture is smooth. Stir in the pepper.

2. In a small bowl, whisk together the cornstarch, mustard, and water to make a slurry. Stir the slurry into the cheese mixture and let cook at a low simmer, uncovered, for 20 minutes. Season with additional pepper if needed.

3. Transfer to a serving pot (or right to the table if you're using a fondue pot) and serve immediately, with accoutrements.

Deep-Fried Salami Chips

Before you serve these to your guests, put a few aside for yourself. Once these chips hit the table, they'll be gone in a flash. This is a sometimes treat obviously not for the diet conscious, but it's a fun game-day snack and a step above the usual meat tray. Serve these chips with a spicy mustard for dipping.

Vegetable oil, for frying

3 cups all-purpose flour

1 tablespoon onion powder

1 tablespoon paprika

1 tablespoon garlic powder

1 tablespoon freshly ground black pepper

1 tablespoon cayenne pepper

1 tablespoon dried oregano

2 cups buttermilk or beer (a porter or a stout)

1 (16-ounce) salami, sliced into ¼-inch rounds

Makes 4–6 servings

1. Place the oil in a large pot, Dutch oven, or deep fryer, and heat to 350°F.

2. Combine the flour, onion powder, paprika, garlic powder, black pepper, cayenne, and oregano in a large mixing bowl and whisk together. Pour the buttermilk into a separate bowl.

3. Dredge a salami slice with flour, then dip into the buttermilk, and then put it back in the flour mixture. Shake off any excess flour. Repeat with the remaining chips. Tip: Use one hand for dipping the salami in the flour and the other for dipping in the liquid. This prevents the mixture from caking on your fingers.

4. Working in small batches, fry the chips until golden, about 1 minute. Using a slotted spoon, transfer the chips to a plate lined with paper towels and allow to cool while releasing any excess oil. Let rest for 1 minute before serving. Repeat with the remaining chips.

Recipe from ANTHONY DAVID'S GOURMET SPECIALTIES, HOBOKEN

Lamb Tartare

Tartare is back in fashion these days. Eating fresh, raw meat allows us to better experience the natural flavors. In the case of this recipe from chef Anthony Pino, it's the grassy flavor of lamb that we're enjoying. Fresh herbs and a pungent piece of blue cheese add an additional pop of flavor. For a bit of Italian authenticity, after you grill the bread until crisp and drizzle it with the olive oil, call it *fettunta*.

8 ounces best-quality lamb loin, finely chopped

Sea salt and freshly ground black pepper

2 teaspoons finely chopped fresh parsley

1½ teaspoons crushed capers

½ teaspoon chopped fresh thyme

Extra-virgin olive oil

Microgreens, for garnish

4 ounces blue cheese, cut into 4 pieces

4 slices Italian bread, grilled and drizzled with extra-virgin olive oil

4 pickled baby radishes, sliced in half

Makes 4 servings

1. Season the chopped lamb loin with salt and pepper. Mix in the parsley, capers, and thyme. Stir well and finish with a drizzle of olive oil.

2. Using two spoons, form the tartare into four quenelles (small oval shapes).

3. Arrange a small handful of microgreens on each of four plates. For each serving, place a cube of blue cheese, a lamb quenelle, a slice of grilled bread, and two pickled radish slices on or around the greens. Serve immediately.

ANTHONY DAVID'S. Anthony Pino doesn't hide his enthusiasm. "I'm doing what I love. What I do as a chef, owner and operator, husband, father, and beachgoer — I want to make sure I have no regrets," Pino says. Inspired by his mother, who told him to get a trade, and a friend's father, who was a chef, as well as by teachers who encouraged his creative side, he studied cooking and then nearly 20 years ago opened Anthony David's in Hoboken. The restaurant has grown in size, along with its fan base.

Serving breakfast, lunch, and dinner every day of the year (they are closed only on Christmas), it's one of Hoboken's most popular spots, with people lining up early for brunch (the menu includes 10 varieties of eggs Benedict), and through the night (the pork chop has pleased taste buds of more than one generation).

Deviled Eggs

If you think this is an hors d'oeuvre that was left behind in the 1950s, you clearly haven't been to some of the hottest restaurants around these days. Deviled eggs, the slippery two-bite treat packed with protein and a bit of spicy zip, are back in fashion. While a bit time consuming to make, they are guaranteed to disappear quickly once placed on a table for guests. You can fill each egg cavity with a spoonful of the filling, but using a pastry bag with a decorative fitting makes for a much nicer presentation. There are also special serving trays designed for deviled eggs, and if you make this recipe more than once, a tray is a worthy investment.

12 hard-boiled eggs, peeled, halved, and yolks removed and saved

¼ cup mayonnaise

2 tablespoons Dijon mustard

2 tablespoons sweet pickle relish

½ teaspoon cayenne pepper

Paprika, for garnish

Gerkins, for garnish

Makes 10–12 servings

1. Set the eggs on a serving tray, cavity side up.

2. Place the egg yolks in a medium mixing bowl and mash with a fork until completely crumbled and fine. Add the mayonnaise, mustard, relish, and cayenne, and mix together until fully incorporated. If using a pastry bag, transfer the filling to it.

3. Spoon or squeeze about 1 tablespoon of filling into each egg cavity. Store, uncovered, in the refrigerator for 30 minutes before serving.

4. Dust the eggs lightly with paprika just prior to serving and place a bowl of gherkins on the tray as an accompaniment.

3

Putting the Garden
in Garden State

It's called the Garden State for a reason. Jersey hosts more than 9,000 farms, operating on more than 720,000 acres. Let others believe what they want, but we know that the best tomatoes, corn, blueberries, cranberries, and other fruits and vegetables come from our soil. From the west to the south, our harvests are strong, flavorful, great to look at, and even better to eat. Enjoy these dishes that celebrate our farmers' bounty.

Radish Bread

Easy to prepare with a few garden-fresh ingredients, these appetizers offer an intriguing array of flavors, from tart and sharp to earthy and spicy. The instructions call for toasting the bread in the oven, but by all means use the grill if you'd rather.

1 loaf crusty French bread, cut into ½-inch slices (about 30 slices)

1 bunch scallions, minced

3 ounces cream cheese

6–8 radishes, sliced into thin rounds

Celery salt

Makes about 8 servings

1. Preheat the oven to 200°F.

2. Spread the bread slices on a baking sheet and toast until lightly golden, 5 to 7 minutes. Meanwhile, fold the scallions into the cream cheese.

3. Spread each toast with a thin layer of the cream cheese mixture. Top each with one or two radish slices and lightly sprinkle with celery salt.

Recipe from JOHN CIFELLI, GARDEN STATE WINE GROWERS ASSOCIATION

7 Fishes Caesar Salad

Caesar salad has become bland. Too often the dressing comes from a bottle or a packet, poured over generic greens. This recipe from John Cifelli marks a return to the bold, assertive flavors that made the salad famous in the first place. Easy to assemble, the dressing will cure you forever of bottled versions. Add a grilled protein of your choice on top to make it an entrée. To round this out, try pairing with a Jersey-made Pinot Grigio or dry Riesling.

THE DRESSING

- 1½ cups packaged garlic croutons
- ½ cup shaved Parmesan cheese
- 7 anchovies
- 5 garlic cloves, roasted
- ¾ cup extra-virgin olive oil
- ½ cup red wine vinegar
- ¼ cup Worcestershire sauce
- 3 tablespoons Dijon mustard
- 1 tablespoon capers
- Juice of 2 lemons

THE SALAD

- 2 hearts romaine lettuce, sliced lengthwise, then shredded sideways
- ¼ cup lightly toasted pine nuts
- 2 tablespoons diced red onion
- Freshly ground black pepper
- Croutons

Makes 4–6 servings and roughly 2 cups of dressing

1. To make the dressing, combine the croutons, Parmesan, anchovies, garlic, oil, vinegar, Worcestershire, mustard, capers, and lemon juice in a food processor. Process until thoroughly blended, about 25 seconds.

2. To make the salad, toss the lettuce, pine nuts, and onion together in a salad bowl. Refrigerate for 15 minutes.

3. Drizzle one-quarter of the dressing over the salad and toss well. Season with pepper to taste, and add croutons as desired. Serve immediately with the remaining dressing on the side. Any leftover dressing will keep in the refrigerator for up to 3 days.

Recipe from 12 FARMS RESTAURANT, HIGHTSTOWN

Honey-Balsamic Roasted Beet Salad

Roasting helps concentrate much of beets' earthy, sweet flavor. Combined with the tang of the vinegar and the uplifting freshness of goat cheese, this is a simple yet elegant starter salad.

2 teaspoons honey

2 teaspoons balsamic vinegar

3 ounces chèvre

¼ cup heavy cream

3 large beets, peeled and sliced into ⅛-inch-thick rounds

Salt and freshly ground black pepper

Makes 4 servings

1. Preheat the oven to 400°F.

2. Combine the honey and vinegar in a small mixing bowl. In a separate bowl, stir together the chèvre and cream.

3. Spread the beet slices on a parchment-lined baking sheet. Brush half of the honey vinegar on the tops of the slices. Season with salt and pepper to taste. Roast for 10 minutes, then flip the beets, brush the other side with the remaining honey vinegar, and season again with salt and pepper. Roast for 5 to 10 minutes longer, or until the beets begin to caramelize.

4. Remove the beets from the oven and allow to cool slightly. Arrange into four servings on small plates and drizzle the cream mixture on top. Serve immediately.

Farm-Fresh Beet Salad

Vibrant color and earthy flavor combine to make this simple-to-prepare salad a favorite; it won't last long on the table. This is a recipe that is easy to scale up for larger gatherings and tastes best when fresh beets are at their peak, between July and October. *Read about Flaim Farms on page 74.*

10 medium beets

1 bunch leeks (approximately 4 large), white parts only, washed and sliced into thin rounds

½ cup red wine vinegar

¼ cup olive oil

¼ teaspoon salt

⅛ teaspoon freshly ground black pepper

Makes 4–6 servings

1. Place the beets in a large pot and cover completely with water. Bring to a boil, then reduce the heat and let simmer until the beets are tender, 12 to 16 minutes. Drain and allow the beets to cool. Slip off the skins, then chop the beets into bite-size pieces.

2. Combine the leeks, vinegar, oil, salt, and pepper in a large bowl. Add the beets and mix well. Serve immediately, while the beets are still warm, or refrigerate for several hours and serve chilled.

Recipe from COMMUNITY FOODBANK OF NEW JERSEY, HILLSIDE

Acorn and Butternut Squash Soup

Over the past 10 years, chef Paul Kapner has made many different kinds of soup for the Community FoodBank of New Jersey. "I love winter squash," he says. "It is grown in abundance in New Jersey, and we receive a lot of squash varieties throughout the year." This squash soup, created by Kapner, offers an amazing combination of flavors and is a great warming meal in late fall and winter. Kapner suggests freezing it in batches and eating it year-round. One of his favorite variations is to add some diced cooked chicken, creating a more complete meal for very low cost.

This is a central tenet for the Community FoodBank of New Jersey, which was founded in 1975. In 2014, the organization distributed 43 million pounds of food to more than 1,000 nonprofit programs, as well as more than 400 programs served by its partner distribution organizations. A designated 501(c)(3) charitable organization, the FoodBank, through the combined efforts of all its programs, feeds more than 900,000 hungry people in 18 New Jersey counties.

½ cup (1 stick) butter

½ acorn squash, peeled and diced (about 2½ cups)

½ butternut squash, peeled and diced (about 2½ cups)

½ Spanish onion, diced

½ sweet potato, diced

1 carrot, diced

6 cups vegetable stock

½ cup instant mashed potatoes (optional)

2 tablespoons maple syrup

1½ teaspoons granulated garlic

¼ teaspoon ground cloves

⅛ teaspoon ground allspice

⅛ teaspoon ground cinnamon

½ cup heavy cream

Salt and freshly ground black pepper

Makes 8 servings

1. Melt the butter in a soup pot or Dutch oven over medium heat, then add the acorn squash, butternut squash, onion, sweet potato, and carrot. Cook until tender, 5 to 7 minutes.

2. Add 4 cups of the stock. Bring to a boil, then reduce the heat and let simmer until the vegetables are soft, about 10 minutes. Use a stick blender (or a regular blender if that's all you have) to purée the soup.

3. Add the remaining 2 cups stock. Bring to a simmer over medium heat. By now the soup should have a thick consistency, coating the back of a spoon. If the soup seems thin, mix the potato flakes with 1 cup of water or stock. Gradually stir the mixture into the soup until it reaches your desired consistency. Stir in the maple syrup, garlic, cloves, allspice, and cinnamon, and let simmer for a few minutes longer.

4. Stir in the cream and turn off the heat. Season with salt and pepper to taste. Serve hot.

Recipe from MUIRHEAD FOODS, TRENTON

Autumnal Brown Rice Salad

Packed with the rich flavors of the season, this salad from Barbara Simpson of Muirhead Foods has an earthy depth, a sweet acidic bite, and a snap of heat from the ginger. Plan on making this at least 2 hours before serving to allow the flavors to mingle and intensify.

1 cup cooked brown rice, at room temperature

1 cup grated carrots

½ cup dried cranberries

½ cup unsalted roasted pumpkin seeds or walnuts

4 scallions, finely sliced

¼ cup extra-virgin olive oil

2 tablespoons orange juice

1 tablespoon ginger juice

1 teaspoon orange zest

¼ teaspoon sea salt

⅛ teaspoon freshly ground black pepper

Makes 4–6 servings

1. Combine the rice, carrots, cranberries, pumpkin seeds, and scallions in a medium bowl and mix well.

2. Whisk together the oil, orange juice, ginger juice, orange zest, salt, and pepper in a small bowl.

3. Pour the vinaigrette over the rice mixture 30 minutes before serving and stir to blend. Refrigerate until ready to serve.

Tomato and Onion Salad

This salad comes together in minutes, and it's a good bet that you'll have these ingredients on hand, especially during the summer months. Great with grilled meats, this can be made several hours in advance and stored covered in the refrigerator before serving.

4 medium tomatoes, each cut into 8 wedges

1 medium onion, halved and thinly sliced

1½ tablespoons fresh oregano

2 tablespoons extra-virgin olive oil

1 tablespoon balsamic vinegar

½ teaspoon sea salt

Makes 4–6 servings

Combine the tomatoes, onion, and oregano in a large mixing bowl and toss together. Add the oil and vinegar and toss again. Top with the salt and toss a third time. Transfer to a serving bowl and serve.

MUIRHEAD. Barbara Simpson is carrying on the work started by her parents back in 1974. From the moment Muirhead opened it was known to locals and customers from beyond as the fine-dining establishment in the celery green painted farmhouse. Inside, Ed and Doris Simpson served guests in a quiet, unrushed fashion and focused on fresh, seasonal foods. Ed was the host and Doris ran the kitchen, preparing five-course gourmet meals every weekend.

Soon customers wanted to leave with more than just full, satisfied stomachs and happy memories. They wanted to leave with jars of the restaurant's butters, dressings, and mustards. So over time Muirhead morphed into a specialty food company and now operates a full production facility in Trenton, not far from the family's original restaurant in Ringoes. Barbara brings the same care and attention to detail to the products — including sauces, chutneys, and mincemeats — as her parents brought to the restaurant.

Recipe from OLDE MILL INN AND GRAIN HOUSE RESTAURANT, BASKING RIDGE

Stuffed Zucchini Blossoms
with Heirloom Cherry Tomato Salad

If you're used to picking up zucchini from the farmers' market or store, there's a chance you've never encountered a zucchini blossom — you have to get them fresh from the garden. As the name suggests, it's the flower that grows on the tip of the green squash, a big bulbous twisty affair that flames into a vibrant yellow and orange at its top. There's not much to it in the flavor department — subtle, a bit sweet, evoking the flavor of the zucchini itself. But because of their size, squash blossoms are great for stuffing. The stems are often considered the best part thanks to the crunch, so look for blossoms that still have stems attached.

Olive oil, for frying

1 cup grated Pecorino Romano cheese

1 pound ricotta cheese, such as Calabro

2 tablespoons chopped chives

2 tablespoons chopped flat-leaf parsley

Sea salt and freshly ground black pepper

8 zucchini blossoms, preferably with stems attached

2 cups all-purpose flour

12 ounces cold sparkling water, such as Pellegrino

1 pint heirloom cherry tomatoes, halved

3 tablespoons crushed tomatoes

2 tablespoons extra-virgin olive oil

10 fresh basil leaves

⅛ teaspoon dried Mediterranean oregano

Makes 4 servings

1. Pour about 3 inches of the frying oil into a large heavy pot and heat to 350°F.

2. In the meantime, combine the Pecorino, ricotta, chives, and parsley in a mixing bowl. Season with salt and pepper to taste and mix well.

3. Transfer the cheese mixture to a pastry bag fitted with a large tip. Carefully open the blossoms and fill with the cheese mixture until they just start to overflow. (Don't worry if the mixture spills a little from the sides.)

4. Combine the flour and sparkling water in another mixing bowl and whisk well to combine. Coat the stuffed blossoms in this batter, and then gently place the blossoms into the hot oil. Fry until golden brown, 2 to 3 minutes, or approximately 1 minute on each side. Remove from the oil, transfer to a plate lined with paper towels, and season with salt.

5. Toss together the cherry tomatoes, crushed tomatoes, olive oil, basil, and oregano in another mixing bowl. Serve the warm fried blossoms on top of the tomato salad.

NOTE: You can make a simple pastry bag by filling a ziplock bag and snipping the tiniest bit from one of the bottom corners. Then grab the bag at the top, twist to tighten, and push the filling from the cut corner.

Recipe from DIANE HENDERIKS

Arugula and Papaya Salad
with Pomegranate-Lime Vinaigrette

A fresh vinaigrette makes all the difference in a salad. This dressing is full of sweet, tart, and spicy flavors that add an intriguing element to a light and refreshing salad. *Read about Diane Henderiks on page 109.*

THE DRESSING

¼ cup pomegranate juice

2 tablespoons rice wine vinegar

1 tablespoon honey or ¼ teaspoon powdered stevia

1 teaspoon Dijon mustard

Juice of half a lime

1 garlic clove, minced

¼ teaspoon smoked paprika

¼ cup olive oil

Salt and freshly ground black pepper

THE SALAD

5 cups baby arugula

½ papaya, seeded, peeled, and cubed

½ red onion, thinly sliced

½ cup pomegranate seeds

Makes 4–6 servings

1. Make the dressing: Combine the pomegranate juice, vinegar, honey, mustard, lime juice, garlic, and paprika in a small bowl and whisk until incorporated. Whisk in the oil and season to taste with salt and pepper.

2. Make the salad: Toss the arugula, papaya, onion, and pomegranate seeds in a large bowl. Add half the dressing and toss thoroughly. Add additional dressing as needed or serve a little extra on the side. Serve immediately.

Recipe from JENKINSON'S BOARDWALK BAR & GRILL, POINT PLEASANT BEACH

Summer Strawberry-Avocado Salad
with Broiled Scallops

Sweet, creamy, and salty come together in this inventive salad. When all of the ingredients are ripe and fresh, you can practically hear it singing in harmony on the plate. A double portion makes this a meal, and no one will fault you if you go back for seconds.

12 large scallops

  Salt and freshly ground black pepper, or your favorite seafood seasoning

8 ounces spring lettuce mix

1 cup strawberries, halved

½ cup pecans

1 avocado, thinly sliced

2 ounces goat cheese, crumbled

2 tablespoons raspberry vinaigrette of your choice

Makes 4 servings

1. Preheat the broiler to high.

2. Pat the scallops dry and season with salt and pepper to taste. Place the scallops in an oven-safe dish and cook under the broiler for 6 to 8 minutes, until the scallops are lightly golden brown on top.

3. Combine the lettuce, strawberries, pecans, avocado, cheese, and dressing in a mixing bowl. Toss well to combine.

4. Divide the salad among four serving plates. Top each plate with three scallops. Serve immediately.

JENKINSON'S BOARDWALK BAR & GRILL. From the second-story balcony overlooking the boardwalk, a new visual world is opened. There's the mighty Atlantic battering the shore, and the throngs of people happily splashing in the waves or soaking up the sun. There's the endless parade of families, couples, or teenagers walking the planks, and the sounds of games, laughter, and the boisterous nature that envelops Point Pleasant Beach on summer days. All of this is available for your sensory pleasure while enjoying a casual dinner and stiff drink from this Jersey Shore institution. With a typical beach bar on the ground level, those in the know head upstairs to get the full experience.

Recipe from CARTON BREWING CO., ATLANTIC HIGHLANDS

The Heal-Your-Liver Paleo Salad

Augie Carton of Carton Brewing Co. created this salad for brewers, who tend to have high carbohydrate intakes. Bitter greens and omega-3 fatty acids are believed to be good for the liver; Augie ties them up together in a very tasty salad on the bitter end of the spectrum. The garlicky dressing takes a while to make but will keep for a month in the refrigerator.

THE DRESSING

20 garlic cloves

1 cup extra-virgin olive oil

6 ounces oil-cured anchovies, drained

THE SALAD

8 ounces dandelion greens (any bitter/chicory green will do but dandelion is best)

2 tablespoons extra-virgin olive oil

Juice of one-quarter of a lemon

Kosher salt

Makes 2–4 servings

1. To make the dressing, place the garlic in a small saucepan with ½ cup of the oil and cook over very low heat for 3 hours. If the oil starts to bubble, turn the heat off for 10 minutes or so and then back on. What you want is very light brown (pecan-colored or lighter) softened garlic. Take the pan off the heat and let the oil cool.

2. Put the garlic, the oil from the saucepan, and the remaining ½ cup oil in a blender and whiz them about. With the blender running, add the anchovies, a couple at a time, and purée to as smooth a mixture as possible. Transfer to a small airtight container and store in the refrigerator until salad time.

3. To make the salad, chop the greens into 1-inch pieces. Place in a large bowl and add the oil, lemon juice, and salt to taste. Toss to combine. Cover and set aside for at least 1 hour to allow the greens to soften a bit. If the garlic dressing is in the refrigerator, remove it now and let it warm to room temperature.

4. When you're ready to serve, divide the salad among serving plates. Top each plate with dressing to taste.

Escarole and Sun-Dried Tomato Salad

The pleasing bitter taste of escarole and the savory depth of the sun-ripened tomatoes make for ideal bedfellows. This simple salad has a lot of flavor, thanks to the tang of the cheese, acidity of the balsamic vinegar, and earthiness of the nuts. It is quick to prepare and great any time of year.

5 cups escarole, washed, dried, and chopped

¼ cup dry sun-dried tomatoes, roughly chopped

2 tablespoons balsamic vinegar

3 tablespoons extra-virgin olive oil

Kosher salt and freshly ground black pepper

¼ cup feta cheese, crumbled

¼ cup toasted pecans, crushed

Makes 4–6 servings

1. Combine the escarole and tomatoes in a large salad bowl. Add the vinegar, oil, and salt and pepper to taste, and toss well to combine.

2. Add the cheese and the pecans, and toss together. Serve immediately.

Recipe from WILDFLOUR BAKERY/CAFÉ, LAWRENCEVILLE

Fresh Jersey Corn Cakes
with Avocado Crème and Tomato Salsa

Here's a great use for all the corn piled high during the peak of the season: a crumbly, spicy, baked treat. Think corn bread, Jersey-style. From the acclaimed bakery in Mercer County, Marilyn Besner offers up this gluten-free recipe that is great alongside your favorite salad, chili, or barbecue. Besner says that any gluten-free baking blend will work. WildFlour uses a custom blend of sweet white rice, millet, sorghum, and potato starch.

THE CAKES

- 4 ears fresh corn or 2 cups corn kernels
- ½ cup finely diced red bell pepper
- ½ cup chopped scallions
- ¼ cup chopped fresh cilantro
- ½ jalapeño, minced
- 4 tablespoons vegetable oil
- 4 eggs, separated
- ¼ cup cornmeal
- ¼ cup gluten-free flour
- 1 teaspoon salt
- ½ teaspoon freshly ground black pepper

THE AVOCADO CRÈME

- 1 avocado, mashed
- 1 tablespoon sour cream or yogurt
- 2 teaspoons freshly squeezed lemon juice
- Salt and freshly ground black pepper

THE TOMATO SALSA

- 3 plum tomatoes, cored and diced
- ¼ cup chopped fresh cilantro
- 1 small red onion, finely diced
- ½ jalapeño, minced (optional)
- Freshly squeezed lime juice
- Salt and freshly ground black pepper

Makes 6 servings

1. If you're working with fresh corn, cut the kernels from the cobs. Mix the corn, red bell pepper, scallions, cilantro, and jalapeño together in a large bowl. Add the oil and egg yolks; whisk to combine. Mix the cornmeal, flour, salt, and pepper in a separate bowl, then combine this flour mixture with the corn mixture.

2. Beat the egg whites to soft peaks; fold into the batter, which will end up being quite thick.

3. Heat a griddle over medium heat. Pour the batter onto the griddle in cakes about 3½ inches across. You should be able to cook the cakes without adding oil to the griddle, but feel free to add a thin film of oil if you like. Cook until lightly browned, about 3 minutes, then flip and cook for 1 minute longer.

4. To make the avocado crème, combine the avocado, sour cream, lemon juice, and salt and pepper to taste in a bowl; mix well.

5. To make the tomato salsa, combine the tomatoes, cilantro, onion, jalapeño, lime juice, and salt and pepper to taste in a bowl. Mix well.

6. Serve the corn cakes topped with the salsa and crème.

Recipe from JERSEY GIRL BREWING COMPANY, HACKETTSTOWN

Jersey Tomato and Corn Salsa

When Jersey's best produce is in season, homemade salsa is just plain terrific. This recipe from Charles Aaron and Mike Bigger is great with chips, on burgers, or with burritos, but it really shines when paired with the Grilled Shrimp and Sausage Skewers on page 36. *Read about the Jersey Girl Brewing Company on page 36.*

1 small red onion, finely diced

2 cups fresh corn kernels

2 large Jersey tomatoes, diced

2 tablespoons minced fresh flat-leaf parsley

1 tablespoon freshly squeezed lemon juice

1 teaspoon minced fresh thyme

1 garlic clove, finely minced

¾ teaspoon salt

¾ teaspoon freshly ground black pepper

Makes 3 cups

1. Put the onion into a strainer, and the strainer in a bowl of ice water. Let the onion soak for 10 minutes; this dulls some of its bite. Remove, drain, and dry the onion, then transfer to a mixing bowl.

2. Add the corn, tomatoes, parsley, lemon juice, thyme, garlic, salt, and pepper to the onion and stir to combine.

3. Let the mixture sit for at least 30 minutes, then drain and discard any excess liquid before serving. The salsa will keep in the refrigerator for up to 3 days.

Recipe from RUNNING DEER GOLF CLUB, PITTSGROVE

Cracked Black Pepper–Salmon Pinwheel Salad

Fresh salmon combined with a variety of garden delights makes for a great appetizer that will show off your kitchen creativity. This multistep recipe takes a bit of advance planning. Stephen Pennese, the executive chef at Running Deer Golf Club, says this can also be used as an appetizer and portioned into individual servings.

8 ounces Atlantic salmon, cut into a ¾-inch-thick strip lengthwise

2 strips bacon

2 teaspoons cracked black pepper

4 tablespoons extra-virgin olive oil

1 small shallot, finely diced

4 ounces local mushrooms, quartered

2 ounces Chablis wine (preferably local)

8 ounces heavy whipping cream

2 tablespoons Dijon mustard

Kosher salt

White pepper

2 cups fresh baby spinach, washed and dried

1 sprig fresh dill, finely chopped

Makes 4 servings

1. Preheat the oven to 375°F.

2. Place the salmon on a cutting board. Place the bacon on top of the salmon and roll up the salmon and bacon into a pinwheel, so you can see the edge of the bacon in between the salmon.

3. Place the cracked black pepper on a small plate and press one side of the salmon and bacon pinwheel into the pepper to coat.

4. Place 2 tablespoons of the oil in a skillet over medium heat. Place the salmon, pepper side down, into the pan and cook until you have a nice peppercorn crust, about 4 minutes. Flip with a fresh spatula and cook on the other side until golden brown, about 2 minutes.

5. Place the salmon on a roasting pan and finish in the oven for 8 to 12 minutes, or until the fish feels firm.

6. While the skillet is still hot, add the shallot and cook over medium heat until translucent, about 2 minutes. Add the mushrooms and toss.

7. Turn off the heat and add the wine. Return the pan to medium heat and cook until the wine is reduced slightly and the drippings have come away from the pan, about 5 minutes.

8. Add the heavy cream and cook until the liquid is reduced by half, about 2 minutes. Add the mustard, then salt and white pepper to taste. Continue to cook until the sauce is reduced to creamy, about 2 minutes. Turn off the heat.

9. To make the spinach, warm the remaining 2 tablespoons of oil in a large pan over medium heat. Add the spinach and cook until it becomes wilted, about 4 minutes. Remove from the heat and roll in paper towels to remove excess oil and moisture.

10. Place the spinach on a serving plate. Place the salmon on top of the spinach leaves and spoon the sauce over half the salmon to show off the beautiful pinwheel. Top with fresh dill.

Crunchy Broccoli Salad

After seeing this salad pop up at supermarket deli counters over the last few years, and then seeing how quickly bowls of it emptied at parties, I took the best features of a few variations and combined them into this recipe. Colorful and cool, it's a great cookout complement to more traditional side salads. Crunchy broccoli salads are also open to personal interpretation. I've seen recipes with almonds or raisins; you can substitute apple cider vinegar for the white vinegar, or sugar for the honey. Start with this, and then build on it to make it your own.

¾ cup mayonnaise

2 tablespoons honey

2 tablespoons white wine vinegar

½ teaspoon garlic powder

5 strips bacon, cooked, cooled, and crumbled

4 large heads broccoli, cut into bite-size florets

4 stalks celery, finely diced

1 large red onion, finely diced

1 large carrot, finely diced

1 large red bell pepper, finely diced

1 large yellow bell pepper, finely diced

½ cup dried cranberries

¼ cup sunflower seeds (optional)

Salt and freshly ground black pepper

Makes 12–14 servings

1. Combine the mayonnaise, honey, vinegar, and garlic powder in a small mixing bowl and whisk to thoroughly combine.

2. Combine the bacon, broccoli, celery, onion, carrot, bell peppers, cranberries, and sunflower seeds, if using, in a large salad bowl. Toss to combine. Pour the dressing over the salad and toss until fully incorporated. Season with salt and black pepper to taste. Can be served immediately, or refrigerated for 30 minutes to allow flavors to mingle.

NOTE: Add some extra crunch to this salad by using the broccoli stems alongside the florets. Trim off the rough end, peel the exterior layer, like you would a carrot, and then finely dice.

Cucumber Dill Salad

A summertime salad that never goes out of style, this cool salad is a staple in our family, often made from the cucumbers grown in the backyard garden. It's great alongside grilled chicken or lamb. Make it ahead and refrigerate for at least an hour and up to overnight. Before serving, be sure to drain any excess liquid that has accumulated in the bowl.

4 large cucumbers, peeled, seeded, and diced

½ cup mayonnaise

½ cup plain yogurt

2 tablespoons chopped dill

1½ garlic cloves, mashed

1 tablespoon freshly squeezed lemon juice

Kosher salt

Makes 6–8 servings

1. Combine the cucumbers, mayonnaise, yogurt, dill, garlic, and lemon juice in a mixing bowl. Combine thoroughly. Season with salt to taste.

2. Cover and refrigerate for at least 1 hour before serving.

Recipe from FLAIM FARMS, VINELAND

Baked Cauliflower Casserole

Cauliflower is enjoying a renaissance these days. High in vitamin C and other nutrients, the vegetable is also a bit of a chameleon, able to absorb the flavors of other ingredients it's cooked with, boosting the overall taste.

1 large head cauliflower, chopped into florets

2 tablespoons butter

2 bunches leeks, sliced

10 mushrooms, sliced

1 tablespoon garlic powder

Salt and freshly ground black pepper

1 (10¾-ounce) can cream of mushroom soup

¼ cup white wine or sherry

Makes 4–6 servings

1. Preheat the oven to 350°F.

2. Place the cauliflower in a steamer basket over a pot with water. Bring the water to a boil and steam the cauliflower until the florets begin to soften, about 10 minutes. Drain and transfer to a baking dish.

3. Melt the butter in a large skillet over medium heat. Add the leeks, mushrooms, garlic powder, and salt and pepper to taste; sauté until the leeks are softened, about 10 minutes. Add the soup and wine to the skillet, mix well, and bring to a simmer for 5 minutes.

4. Pour the leek mixture over the cauliflower in the baking dish, mix well, and bake for 20 minutes, or until the cauliflower is fork-tender. Serve immediately.

FLAIM FARMS. From the beginning, Flaim Farms has been a family affair. Founded on a large patch of land in Cumberland County in 1934 by Anthony and Catherine Flaim, the farm quickly became known for its peaches and vegetables. As the family grew, new generations came into the business, and eventually they decided to remove the peach trees and focus solely on vegetables.

Today two grandsons of the founders — Robert Flaim Jr. and Kevin Flaim — keep the family business thriving with a combination of old farming traditions and new farming innovations. Flaim Farms produces the well-known Panther Brand romaine lettuce, along with leeks, spinach, collard greens, Swiss chard, kale, turnips, napa cabbage, squash, eggplants, peppers, escarole, endive, and scallions.

Recipe from MANISCHEWITZ COMPANY, NEWARK

Apple, Fennel, and Tarragon Slaw

Both tarragon and fennel have an aniselike flavor, which means they are perfect partners in a fresh salad. Developed for Manischewitz by chef Shifra Klein, this slaw is crunchy and sweet and utterly delicious. *Read about the Manischewitz Company on page 124.*

2 medium crunchy apples, such as Fuji or Gala, thinly sliced

1 fennel bulb, thinly sliced

¼ cup tarragon leaves, chopped

¼ cup extra-virgin olive oil

2 tablespoons red wine vinegar

1 tablespoon Dijon mustard

1 tablespoon honey, preferably Manischewitz

¼ teaspoon freshly ground black pepper

¼ teaspoon salt

Makes 4 servings

1. Place the apples and fennel in a serving bowl.

2. Combine 2 tablespoons of the tarragon with the oil, vinegar, mustard, honey, pepper, and salt in a jar with a tight-fitting lid. Shake to mix.

3. Pour the dressing over the apple mixture and toss well. Garnish with the remaining 2 tablespoons tarragon. The slaw can be made up to 12 hours in advance; keep refrigerated.

Recipe from DIANE HENDERIKS

Asian Slaw

Packed with those wonderful umami flavors, this slaw is a great complement to grilled salmon or tuna steak and breaks up the routine of more traditional slaws. Don't just save it for summer; this recipe is great any time of year. *Read about Diane Henderiks on page 109.*

¼ cup rice vinegar

2 tablespoons grated fresh ginger

2 tablespoons sesame oil

1 tablespoon light soy sauce

1 teaspoon freshly squeezed lime juice

1 teaspoon honey

1 teaspoon natural peanut butter

1 teaspoon chili powder

1 teaspoon dry mustard

¼ teaspoon freshly ground black pepper

2 cups thinly sliced green cabbage

2 cups thinly sliced red cabbage

2 cups grated carrots

1 cup chopped kale leaves

¾ cup toasted slivered almonds

Makes 6–8 servings

1. Whisk together the vinegar, ginger, oil, soy sauce, lime juice, honey, peanut butter, chili powder, mustard, and pepper in a small bowl.

2. Combine the green and red cabbage, carrots, and kale in a large serving bowl. Add half the dressing and toss together. Add ½ cup of the almonds and toss again. Serve immediately, with extra almonds and dressing on the side.

Tomato and Mozzarella Salad

When Jersey tomatoes hit their peak in the summer, this is my family's go-to salad. Not only is it bursting with the fresh flavors and colors of the season, but it's also a beautiful presentation. It's easy to prepare, but be sure to use a good-quality olive oil as the drizzle. It's the deep, rich, nutty flavor that ties this all together.

1½ pounds fresh mozzarella, sliced into ½-inch rounds

3 large heirloom tomatoes, sliced into ½-inch pieces

½ cup finely sliced fresh basil

2 tablespoons olive oil

Sea salt

Crusty bread, for dipping

Makes 6 servings

1. Lay out the mozzarella slices on a large platter. Alternate with the tomato slices. Sprinkle with the basil, drizzle with the oil, and finally sprinkle the salt over everything.

2. Put out a spatula or large fork with the platter, for serving. The platter will collect juices from the tomato, cheese, and oil, so have some bread on hand to sop up the mixture.

Recipe from TALULA'S PIZZA, ASBURY PARK

Swiss Chard and Poached Egg Toast

By the time this is assembled, it's almost too pretty to eat. Still, poke the egg and let the yolk mix with the leafy vegetables and the tangy bread. Don't wait to dive in. Great for brunch, this will impress your guests with its presentation and flavor. They'll be so busy eating, you'll have to wait for the plate to clear before getting the compliments. *Read about Talula's on page 83.*

2 tablespoons extra-virgin olive oil, plus more for drizzling

4 garlic cloves, thinly sliced

½ teaspoon Aleppo pepper or your favorite red pepper flakes, plus more to finish

1 small bunch chard, stems removed and leaves torn into 2-inch pieces

2 tablespoons freshly squeezed lemon juice

½ teaspoon sea salt, plus more to finish

Freshly ground black pepper

2 slices thick-cut sourdough bread

2 garlic cloves, peeled but left whole

2 tablespoons distilled white vinegar

2 eggs, preferably organic

Easter egg radishes, sliced thin with a mandoline

Makes 2 servings

1. Fill a small saucepan with water and set over medium heat.

2. Warm the oil in a large skillet over medium heat. Add the sliced garlic and cook, stirring occasionally, until golden brown, about 2 minutes. Add the Aleppo and half the chard and cook until wilted, about 4 minutes. Add the lemon juice and the remaining chard and cook about 1 minute longer, until all the chard is wilted. Season with the salt and pepper to taste.

3. Toast the sourdough slices, then rub the surface of each slice with one clove of garlic. Set each slice on a serving plate. Divide the cooked chard between the slices, placing it on top. Set aside.

4. Raise the heat under the pan of water and bring it to a gentle boil. Stir the vinegar into the water. Crack the eggs into two small bowls, then tip them gently into the bubbling water. Cook until firm, 4 to 5 minutes. Remove with a slotted spoon and nestle into the cooked chard. Finish with a pinch of salt and Aleppo pepper. Dot with radish medallions for added crunch.

TALULA'S PIZZA

Even between mealtimes, the pizzeria and bar are crowded. But Talula's is not your average pizza place and bar. No slices, no ice-cold mugs of generic suds. The bar menu is local and inventive, and what comes out of the kitchen is oven-baked wonderful. It's the wood-burning oven, really, that is the heart of the restaurant. It was the inspiration for partners Steve Mignogna, Shanti Church, and Josh Stewart to get together to open a restaurant, focusing on breads, pizza, and more that celebrate local ingredients, from brunch to dinner.

Steve Mignogna and Shanti Church

Recipe from BUSY BEE ORGANICS

Cucumber Gazpacho with Crabmeat

This cool, refreshing soup uses the best of the garden. It's ready in a flash, and the recipe is easily tailored to vegan diets by simply removing the crabmeat. *Read about Busy Bee Organics on page 18.*

3 cucumbers, peeled, roughly chopped

1 medium red bell pepper, roughly chopped

1 medium green bell pepper, roughly chopped

1 medium heirloom tomato, cored

½ small red onion, roughly chopped

¼ cup packed fresh cilantro leaves

Juice of 1 lime

¼ teaspoon sea salt

4 ounces cooked lump crabmeat (optional)

¼ teaspoon Old Bay seasoning (if using crabmeat)

Makes 2 servings

1. Measure out ¼ cup of the chopped cucumber and ¼ cup of the chopped red bell pepper and dice that portion. Set aside.

2. Combine the remaining cucumber and red bell pepper with the green bell pepper, tomato, onion, cilantro, lime juice, and salt in a food processor and purée until smooth. Thin the soup with water, if desired.

3. Toss the crabmeat with Old Bay seasoning in a small bowl.

4. Divide the soup between two bowls. Top with the crabmeat, if using, and garnish with the reserved diced cucumber and red bell pepper. Serve immediately.

Caramelized Shallots

Slow and low is the name of this game. Cooking shallots (or onions) for several hours releases an earthy sweetness, and in the case of this recipe, the added sugar and spice give it a bit more punch. Cook on your lowest stovetop setting and keep an eye on the onions, making sure they don't burn but take on a deep, rich brown color. This is a great addition to a large meal, like Thanksgiving or a family Sunday dinner.

¾ cup (1½ sticks) butter

24 shallots or small onions, peeled, with any roots snipped but the bottoms intact

1½ cups sugar

½ teaspoon red pepper flakes

Makes 10–12 servings

1. Melt the butter in a Dutch oven over low heat. When completely melted, arrange the shallots, root end down, in the pot. Cover with the sugar and pepper flakes. Cover and cook for 1 hour.

2. Roll the shallots carefully to one side with tongs or a spatula when the base is brown and gooey. Continue cooking until that side is also fully caramelized. Repeat to brown on all sides, about 3 hours total.

3. Carefully transfer the shallots to a deep serving dish using tongs or a plastic spatula. Drizzle the sauce from the pan on top. Serve immediately.

Rosemary-Citrus Soda Syrup

Making your own soda syrup is relatively easy, and the flavor it delivers is rewarding. In the summer, when your garden rosemary is growing like crazy, this is one more good use for the fragrant and potent herb. Make a delicious sparkling drink by combining 2 ounces of the syrup with 16 ounces of soda water, plus plenty of ice.

1 cup sugar

½ cup plus 3 tablespoons freshly squeezed lemon juice

½ cup plus 3 tablespoons freshly squeezed orange juice

¼ cup wildflower honey

2 sprigs fresh rosemary

Zest of 1 lemon

Makes 16 ounces

1. Combine the sugar, lemon juice, orange juice, honey, rosemary, and lemon zest in a large saucepan and bring to a boil over medium-high heat. Boil for 1 minute. The mixture will bubble up when it's boiling, which is why you should use a large saucepan.

2. Turn off the heat and let the syrup sit for 10 minutes. Then strain the syrup through a fine sieve or cheesecloth-lined strainer into a jar or bottle. Chill before using.

SMALL WORLD COFFEE. Just half a block from Princeton University, Small World Coffee opened its doors on December 22, 1993. It was an almost immediate success, with lines of customers waiting to order drinks. Owners Jessica Durrie and Brant Cosaboom have created a comfortable spot for locals and visitors alike, where cups of locally roasted coffee and other flavorful drinks are served with a friendly neighborhood smile.

4

Down the Shore

Starting at Sandy Hook, with its views of lower Manhattan, and extending 124 miles south to its end at the tip of Cape May, the shore is our treasured space. From quiet beaches swept with dune grass to carnival-like boardwalks with rides and attractions to hulking 24/7 casinos, Jersey's full diversity displays itself along the pounding surf of the Atlantic. The food runs the gamut as well. From fresh-caught seafood to deep-fried everything, there's a reason that down here it's all right.

Recipe from ASBURY FESTHALLE & BIERGARTEN, ASBURY PARK

Oysters Braten

These oysters have become a house favorite at the Asbury Festhalle. In this preparation, chef James Avery takes a classic seafood dish, Oysters Rockefeller, and mashes it up with classic *biergarten* flavors of pretzel and sauerkraut. At the restaurant, the kitchen uses day-old house-made pretzels for the crumbs, but a package of store-bought sourdough pretzels will do just fine at home. The recipe may make more filling than you need, but it will hold up in the refrigerator for about 5 days, or you can freeze it for another batch of oysters. Prost! *Read about Asbury Festhalle & Biergarten on page 92.*

THE MORNAY SAUCE

2 tablespoons butter

3 tablespoons all-purpose flour

2½ cups milk

1 cup Parmesan cheese

2 egg yolks

2 dashes hot sauce

⅛ teaspoon salt

THE OYSTERS

1 cup minced leeks

1 cup sauerkraut, drained

½ cup (1 stick) butter

12 East Coast oysters, such as Wellfleets or Blue Points

Salt

2 tablespoons minced chives

2 tablespoons coarse sourdough pretzel crumbs

Makes 4–6 servings

1. To make the Mornay sauce, melt the butter in a saucepan over low heat. Add the flour and cook, while whisking, for 2 minutes. Raise the heat to medium-high, add the milk, and bring to a boil. Immediately reduce the heat and add the Parmesan, egg yolks, hot sauce, and salt, stirring to fully combine. Remove from the heat and set aside to cool completely.

2. In the meantime, combine the leeks, sauerkraut, and butter in a saucepan over medium heat. Cover, and cook until the leeks are soft, 7 to 10 minutes.

3. Scrub the oysters under cold running water to remove sharp edges and sand. Shuck the oysters over a bowl, being sure to save all the liquid. Discard the flat shell and save the "cup" or deep shell.

4. Strain the reserved oyster liquid through a fine-mesh sieve into the sauerkraut mixture. Cook until almost dry, but not browning or taking on color. Season with salt to taste and allow to cool.

5. Set the oven to broil. Lay out the reserved oyster shells on a baking sheet. Place 1 tablespoon of the sauerkraut filling in each shell, then nest a shucked oyster into the filling. Top with 1 teaspoon of Mornay sauce. Place on a rack in the middle of the oven and broil for 8 to 10 minutes, until browned and bubbly.

6. Arrange the oyster shells on a platter and garnish each oyster with chives and pretzel crumbs.

ASBURY FESTHALLE & BIERGARTEN

The Germans call it *gemütlichkeit*. It's friendliness, the kind that comes with a good time, often accompanied with beer. While *biergartens* are thought of during Oktoberfest in Germany, the good feeling and hospitality is now available year-round in Asbury Park.

Chef James Avery has taken much of the German food traditions associated with beer and given them a modern slant, a Jersey twist, and above all, the seafood treatment. It works, and since its opening in the spring of 2015, the festhalle — with a 9,000-square-foot outdoor rooftop *biergarten* and 6,000-square-foot indoor hall — is often comfortably packed with revelers sitting at communal tables. Add in the 25 beers on draft and another 50 in bottles, and you have no need to get to Munich.

James Avery

Bier vom Faß!

- FESTHALLE ORIGINAL (GER) 4.8%
- RADEBERGER PILSNER (GER) 4.8%
- HOFBRÄU MÜNCHEN ORIGINAL (GER) 5.1%
- HOFBRÄU DUNKEL (GER) 5.5%
- KÖSTRITZER (GER) 5.6%
- STIEGL (AUSTRIA) 4.9%
- PALM (BEL) 5.4%
- PILSNER URQUELL (CZECH REP) 4.4%
- SCHOFFERHOFER (GER) 2.5%
- BLANCHE DE BRUXELLES (BEL) 4.5%
- DAB (GER) 4.8%
- ERDINGER WEISBIER DUNKEL (GER) 5.3%
- REISSDORF KÖLSCH (GER) 4.8%
- BRAUFACTUM PROGSTA IPA (GER) 6.8%
- SPATEN OKTOBERFEST (GER) 5.9%
- SPATEN LAGAR (GER) 5.2%
- FRANZISKANER HEFE-WEISSBIER (GER)
- WEIHENSTEPHANER HEFE-WEISSBIER (GER) 5
- WÜRZBURER PILSNER (GER) 4.9%
- SCHNEIDER AVENTINUS (GER) 8.2%
- HACKER PSCHORR DARK (GER) 5%

Recipe from BLUE ROSE INN & RESTAURANT, CAPE MAY

Cape May Salt Oyster and IPA Chowder

For centuries cooks have known that beer can impart new depths of flavor to soups and stews. Think of it as a spice cabinet in a bottle. In this recipe, a citrus-forward India pale ale gives zesty flavor to oyster chowder, an age-old shore favorite. The folks at the Blue Rose Inn won first place with this chowder at a local competition in 2014. Give it a try and you'll soon understand why.

4 tablespoons butter

3 garlic cloves, thinly sliced

1 (2-inch) piece fresh ginger, chopped

1 stalk lemongrass, thinly sliced

1 shallot, thinly sliced

4 cups shellfish stock

1 (12-ounce) bottle Cape May Brewery IPA or similar India pale ale

1 cup diced cherrywood-smoked (or similar) bacon

1½ cups diced celery

1½ cups diced onion

2 cups heavy cream

1 cup milk

2 pounds Yukon Gold potatoes, peeled and diced

3 sprigs fresh thyme

2 teaspoons fine sea salt

1 teaspoon freshly ground black pepper

8 Cape May salt oysters, shucked, liquor reserved

Lemon oil, for garnish

Chives, finely chopped, for garnish

Makes 6–8 servings

1. Melt 2 tablespoons of the butter in a large soup pot over medium heat. Add the garlic, ginger, lemongrass, and shallot, and sauté until tender, about 8 minutes.

2. Stir in the shellfish stock and ale. Bring to a boil, then reduce the heat and let simmer for 20 minutes, stirring frequently. Strain the soup through a fine-mesh strainer and reserve the broth.

3. Return the empty soup pot to the stove and melt the remaining 2 tablespoons butter over medium heat. Add the bacon and cook until the fat is rendered. Add the celery and onion and sauté until tender, about 8 minutes. Pour the reserved shellfish broth into the pot.

4. Combine 1 cup of the cream with the milk, potatoes, and thyme in a separate saucepan and bring to a simmer over medium heat; cook until the potatoes are tender, 10 to 15 minutes. Remove and discard the thyme sprigs. Add half of the potato mixture to the shellfish stock. Transfer the rest of the potato mixture to a blender with the remaining 1 cup cream and purée until smooth. Add this mixture to the chowder. Stir in the salt and pepper.

5. Bring the chowder to a simmer. Just before serving, add the oysters and reserved liquor. Garnish with lemon oil and chives as desired.

Jersey Green Clam Chowder

Clams, really fresh good ones, taste of the ocean. In this dish, chef James Avery embraces the traditional chowder mixture of clams, potatoes, and pork but adds his own spin by incorporating parsnips, poblano peppers, and fennel sausage instead of bacon. The chowder gets its bright color from a parsley purée, which is added at the last minute.

25 chowder clams, cleaned
2 cups water
2 cups dry white wine
2 ounces Pernod liqueur
¼ cup cooking oil
1 cup peeled and diced
   fennel sausage
1 cup diced celery
1 cup diced onion
1 cup diced parsnip
1 cup diced poblano pepper
1 cup diced red potato, skin on
3 bay leaves
3 sprigs fresh thyme
2 teaspoons green Tabasco sauce
1½ teaspoons Worcestershire sauce
   Salt and freshly ground
      black pepper
1 cup parsley leaves
1 cup spinach leaves
¼ cup olive oil
   Crackers or toast, for serving

Makes 6–8 servings

1. Place the clams in a large pot and cover with the water, wine, and Pernod. Cover and bring to a boil. When the clams have opened — after 6 to 10 minutes — turn off the heat. Strain out the clams, reserving the liquid. Remove the clams from their shells and chop. Discard the shells. Discard any clams that do not open.

2. Heat the cooking oil in a large pot over medium-low heat. Add the sausage and cook until the fat has rendered and the sausage has a nice golden brown color. Add the celery, onion, parsnip, poblano, potato, bay leaves, and thyme, and cook until soft (do not allow to color). Add the clams and the reserved liquid. Stir in the Tabasco and Worcestershire and season with salt and pepper to taste — remember that the clams can be very salty, so taste before adding salt.

3. Have ready a bowl with ice water and a strainer small enough to sit in it. Bring a pot of salted water to a boil, add the parsley and spinach, and blanch until bright green, about 30 seconds. Remove from the pot with a slotted spoon and place in the strainer in the ice water to stop the cooking. Wring out the greens in a clean kitchen towel, then place in a blender along with the olive oil and purée until smooth. Add a little more oil if the blades aren't moving smoothly.

4. Stir the purée into the chowder just before serving. Serve with crackers or toasted bread.

Recipe from SALTWATER CAFÉ, CAPE MAY

Crab and Corn Chowder

This chunky and flavorful chowder combines the best of shore and farm. Don't skimp on the extra time it takes to roast the corn; the sweet flavors intensify with roasting and complement the savory nature of the other ingredients. This is a dish designed for a large party; it yields about a gallon of soup. But it's worth it, and there are unlikely to be leftovers.

4 ears fresh white corn, unshucked
¾ cup (1½ sticks) butter, melted
¾ cup all-purpose flour
1 teaspoon olive oil
3 stalks celery, diced
½ Spanish onion, diced
3½ quarts chicken stock
1½ quarts seafood stock
1 tablespoon seafood seasoning
2 teaspoons Sriracha hot sauce
1 teaspoon dried thyme
3 large potatoes, peeled and diced
½ green bell pepper, diced
½ red bell pepper, diced
2 cups heavy cream
16 ounces cooked crabmeat

Makes 16 servings

1. Adjust an oven rack to the middle of the oven and preheat to 225°F. Place the whole, unshucked cobs on the middle rack and roast for 40 minutes. Cool and then shuck the corn. Slice off the kernels; you should have about 3 cups. Reserve the kernels and the cobs.

2. Mix the melted butter and flour in a medium bowl. Stir until smooth and set aside.

3. Heat the oil in a large pot over medium heat and add the celery and onion. Cook until tender and translucent, stirring often, about 5 minutes.

4. Add the chicken stock, seafood stock, and reserved corn-cobs to the pot and bring to a boil. Boil until reduced by one-third, about 15 minutes. Remove the corncobs and discard. Reduce the heat to bring the stock down to a simmer.

5. Stir in the seafood seasoning, hot sauce, and thyme. Gradually whisk in the butter mixture until the stock has thickened; stir frequently.

6. Add the potatoes, bell peppers, and corn kernels, and bring back to a boil. Reduce the heat and let simmer until the potatoes are tender, about 15 minutes. Turn off the heat and stir in the heavy cream.

7. Portion into bowls and garnish each with 1 ounce of crabmeat and an additional shake of seafood seasoning (as desired) before serving.

SALTWATER CAFÉ

With a calming, often inspiring marina view, the Saltwater Café is a very popular place; don't be surprised if you show up and see a line of people waiting to eat. But don't worry: it always moves quickly, as this restaurant has the efficiency of a Jersey diner and the menu of a specialty café.

Serving breakfast and lunch, it's the place to stop to get fortified before heading out onto the water (or just after, if you had an early start). There's no doubt where the seafood on the menu comes from, and the café also serves plenty of delicious options for the carnivores and vegetarians. It's like having a meal on a welcoming friend's patio. Return visits are encouraged.

Grilled Octopus with Romesco Sauce, Frisée, and Marcona Almonds

Octopus is a seafood dish that, in my opinion, is often overlooked. When well prepared — especially grilled — it's a marvel on the plate. Complemented with a savory sauce, there's a good chance that this will become your new go-to octopus recipe. It's okay to replace the frisée with endive.

THE OCTOPUS

- 1 (4- to 6-pound) Spanish octopus
- ½ cup dry white wine
- 2 tablespoons distilled white vinegar
- 2 tablespoons red wine vinegar
- 1 large Spanish onion, diced
- 2 large carrots, thickly sliced
- 2 stalks celery, chopped
- ¼ cup kosher salt
- 2 tablespoons whole black peppercorns
- 1 tablespoon red pepper flakes
- 2 bay leaves

THE ROMESCO SAUCE

- 4 whole nora chiles (see note)
- 1 Spanish onion, roughly chopped
- 6 medium (8 ounces) plum tomatoes
- ¼ cup hazelnuts
- ¼ cup smoked almonds
- 6 garlic cloves
- 1½ teaspoons sweet paprika
- ½ teaspoon kosher salt
- ½ teaspoon freshly ground black pepper
- ⅛ cup red wine vinegar
- ⅓ cup extra-virgin olive oil

Makes 4–6 servings

1. Place the octopus in a large stockpot and add enough cold water to cover it completely. Set over high heat. Add the wine, white vinegar, and red wine vinegar, followed by the onion, carrots, celery, salt, peppercorns, pepper flakes, and bay leaves. Bring to a boil, then reduce the heat to medium-low and simmer until the tentacles easily pull away from the body and the thickest part of the tentacles is tender, 2½ hours. Be careful not to overcook. Remove from the heat, strain, and remove the octopus from the strainer. Discard the other ingredients. When cool enough to handle, remove the tentacles from the body.

2. Preheat the oven to 350°F.

3. For the romesco sauce, place the chiles in a pot with enough water to cover them by a couple of inches. Bring to a boil and cook until tender, about 10 minutes. Turn off the heat and let the chiles steep for 30 minutes. Remove the chiles from the water, remove their stems and seeds, and set aside; reserve the water.

4. While the chiles are soaking, place the onion and tomatoes in a roasting pan and roast for about 30 minutes, until the onions are golden brown.

5. Grind the hazelnuts, almonds, and garlic together in a food processor. Slowly add the boiled chiles, roasted onion and tomatoes, paprika, salt, and pepper. Purée to form a smooth paste. Add the vinegar. With the motor running, add the ⅓ cup oil and process until fully incorporated. If the sauce seems too thick, add some of the chile-soaking water as needed.

1 cup diced potato, in ½-inch cubes

2 tablespoons olive oil

½ cup red wine vinaigrette

2 heads frisée, trimmed and chopped

½ cup Marcona almonds

NOTE: The Spanish nora (or nyora) pepper originated in the Guardamar region of Valencia. This chile variety is used in making paprika and is sometimes referred to as the paprika pepper. Look for it in specialty or gourmet stores. In a pinch, substitute with Ancho chile.

6. For the final dish, bring a pot of water to a boil. Add the diced potato and let cook for 3 minutes. Drain and let cool.

7. Heat a grill pan over medium-high heat. Place the octopus tentacles in the pan and cook until warm and charred, about 10 minutes. Remove from the grill and cut into 1-inch pieces.

8. Warm the 2 tablespoons oil in a skillet over medium-high heat. Add the blanched potatoes and fry until golden brown, about 4 minutes. Add the octopus and ¼ cup of the vinaigrette. Toss until warm and very tender, about 1 minute. Transfer to a mixing bowl and toss the octopus and potatoes with the frisée and Marcona almonds.

9. Place a large spoonful of romesco sauce on each serving plate. Spoon the octopus mixture on top of the sauce.

RAT'S. The name Rat's might not evoke thoughts of culinary elegance, but as anyone who has visited will tell you, this restaurant is a wonderful French country cuisine experience. Rat's is named for character Ratty from Kenneth Grahame's storybook The Wind in the Willows. That book was a favorite of J. Seward Johnson, a sculptor and philanthropist who founded the Grounds for Sculpture, the serene garden setting in which the restaurant is sited. With that background as a starting point, the restaurant is designed to make guests feel like they have stepped back in time to Claude Monet's beloved town of Giverny. The restaurant grounds feature Johnson's own Impressionist-inspired sculptures, and often the man himself. Johnson tries to emulate Ratty — being everything a host should be. As such, he tries to throw the best parties with the best wine, and everyone who comes to the restaurant is a welcomed guest.

Recipe from TRE PIANI, PRINCETON

Pignolia-Crusted Sea Scallops
with Honey-Lemon Beurre Blanc

Chef Jim Weaver started making this dish in 1987, and it's been a go-to favorite for customers ever since. The combination of textures and flavors, from the crunchy crust to the sweet scallops, wins over diners every time. Local scallops are, of course, the preferred way to go.

THE SCALLOPS

- ½ cup pignolia (pine nuts), finely chopped
- ¼ cup unseasoned breadcrumbs
- ½ cup all-purpose flour
- 3 eggs
- 10 large sea scallops
- Salt and freshly ground black pepper
- ¼ cup olive oil

THE SAUCE

- 1 cup dry white wine
- 2 tablespoons honey
- Juice of 1 lemon
- 1 teaspoon chopped fresh parsley
- 4 tablespoons butter, cut into small pieces and chilled

Makes 2 entrée servings or 5 appetizer servings

1. Combine the nuts and breadcrumbs in a small bowl. Put the flour in a separate bowl and beat the eggs in a third bowl. Season the scallops on all sides with salt and pepper. Lightly coat with flour, then dip in the eggs, and then coat with the nut mixture.

2. Preheat the oven to 350°F. Lightly oil a rimmed baking sheet.

3. For the sauce, combine the wine, honey, and lemon juice in a small saucepan and cook over medium heat, stirring often, until the liquid is reduced to about ½ cup, about 20 minutes. Remove from the heat, add the parsley, and whisk in the butter, one piece at a time, until fully melted and incorporated. Set aside and keep warm.

4. Heat the oil in a skillet over medium heat, add the scallops, and brown for 1 to 2 minutes per side. Transfer the scallops to the prepared baking sheet and bake for about 10 minutes, until cooked through.

5. Place a generous spoonful of the sauce on each plate, top with hot scallops, and serve immediately.

TRE PIANI. With a refined ambience and a menu that brings regulars back for the familiar as well as the new and inventive, Tre Piani, headed by chef Jim Weaver, has been a Mercer Country culinary institution for nearly 20 years. With a mix of Mediterranean and Italian dishes, and an extensive wine list, Tre Piani is one of those rare restaurants that serve many needs well. From a quick drink and a snack at the bar, to a dinner to celebrate a special occasion, or the simple Saturday date night, it's the food and hospitality that keep everyone coming back again and again.

Recipe from THE BERNARDS INN, BERNARDSVILLE

Barnegat Inlet Scallops
with Charred Corn, Jalapeño, Cherry Tomatoes, Cilantro, and Lime

This is a great appetizer when you want to showcase the summer bounty of New Jersey. Barnegat Inlet scallops are considered to be some of the best in the world, and corn and tomatoes, obviously, are a given for New Jersey. Here, they are fire-roasted to caramelize their sugars and give them a smoky quality that goes so well with the sweetness of the scallops. This is a convenient recipe for entertaining; executive chef Corey Heyer says everything but the scallops can be prepared the day before. Sear the scallops right before eating.

2 ears fresh corn, husked

4 tablespoons extra-virgin olive oil

Kosher salt

12 cherry tomatoes, halved

½ cup rice wine vinegar

½ cup water

¼ cup sugar

Zest and juice of 2 limes

1 garlic clove, finely chopped

1 jalapeño, seeds removed, finely chopped

1 small red onion, finely chopped

1 tablespoon canola oil

8 large sea scallops, preferably from the Barnegat Inlet

1 tablespoon unsalted butter

2 tablespoons roughly chopped fresh cilantro

Makes 4 servings

1. Coat the corn with 1 tablespoon of the olive oil and a sprinkle of salt. Heat a cast-iron pan over medium-high heat, add the corn, and roast until charred, rolling the ears to get even color; not all of the kernels need color. Remove from the heat and let cool.

2. Toss the tomatoes with another tablespoon of the olive oil and a sprinkle of salt. Add to the cast-iron pan and cook over high heat until softened, 3 to 5 minutes. Do not overcook the tomatoes; they should retain their shape.

3. Heat the vinegar, water, and sugar in a small pot over medium-high heat until the sugar is dissolved. Remove from the heat and let cool, then stir in the lime juice.

4. Remove the corn kernels from the cobs. Combine the corn with the garlic, jalapeño, red onion, and lime zest. Pour the vinegar mixture over the corn mixture and season with salt to taste. Stir in the remaining 2 tablespoons olive oil. At this point you can pause your preparations, if you like, and put the corn salad and the roasted tomatoes in the refrigerator overnight; just be sure to let them sit at room temperature for 1 hour before serving.

5. To prepare the scallops, heat a cast-iron pan over high heat. Add the canola oil to the pan. Carefully place the scallops in the pan, making sure that they do not not touch one another. Cook until the bottom sides are evenly caramelized, 2 to 3 minutes, gently moving them around with a spatula or tongs. Then add the butter to the pan and turn the heat down to medium-high. Season the scallops with salt. Continue to cook, still moving the scallops around, until they are deeply and evenly caramelized, about 2 minutes. Turn off the heat and flip the scallops. Allow them to cook for 1 or 2 minutes longer in the butter.

6. Divide the corn mixture among four plates and add one-quarter of the tomatoes. Place two scallops on each plate. Sprinkle the chopped cilantro over the scallops and serve.

Recipe from THE OHANA GRILL, LAVALLETTE

Pan-Seared Lobster Tail
over Corn and Asparagus Risotto

There's a common misconception that risotto is difficult to make at home. Following this recipe from chef James Costello, you'll see that's simply not the case. Even better, the risotto can be made a few hours before dinner and held until you're ready to eat. Farm-fresh asparagus and fresh-caught lobster are both musts; the quality of the ingredients is one of the reasons that Costello medaled with this recipe during the 2014 Jersey Seafood Challenge.

8 shallots, minced

¾ cup olive oil

10 cups shrimp or seafood stock

1 teaspoon freshly ground white pepper

1 cup cooking sherry

2 cups Arborio rice

3 bunches New Jersey asparagus

8 lobster tails, removed from shells

Sea salt and freshly ground black pepper

3 cups cooked corn kernels

4 ounces Pecorino Romano cheese, grated

Makes 8 servings

1. To make the risotto, combine the shallots and ¼ cup of the oil in a small dish. Pour the stock into a saucepan and bring to a gentle simmer over medium heat. Heat a large, deep skillet over high heat for 2 minutes. Add the shallots in oil and the white pepper; sauté, stirring often, for 2 minutes, then add the sherry. Cook for a few minutes to burn off the alcohol.

2. Add the rice and stir well to coat with the oil and sherry. Reduce the heat to a low simmer. Add 2 cups of the hot stock and simmer, stirring every few minutes, until the stock is fully absorbed. Repeat this process three times. The rice will start to look creamy. Don't rush this process; working slow and steady is the key here.

3. Taste the risotto to be sure it is cooked through but not mushy. If it's still too firm, add a little more stock and keep cooking. When it's ready, spread the risotto on a rimmed baking sheet and let cool to room temperature. At this point, if you want, you can cover the rice and store it in the refrigerator until you're ready to finish the dish.

4. To prepare the asparagus, bring about 4 cups of water to a boil and prepare an ice water bath large enough to hold the asparagus. Add the asparagus to the boiling water and blanch for 3 minutes. Do not overcook or the asparagus will become mushy after it's added to the risotto. Cool in the ice bath to stop the cooking process. Then cut the asparagus into bite-size pieces.

5. Preheat the oven to 400°F.

6. Season the lobster with salt and pepper. Heat a large skillet over high heat and add the remaining ½ cup oil. Heat until shimmering. Add the lobster and sear on both sides, about 2 minutes per side. Transfer the lobster to a baking sheet and bake for 10 minutes, or until the lobster meat is firm.

7. Meanwhile, return the skillet to the stovetop, add 1½ cups of the remaining stock, the asparagus, the corn, half of the Pecorino, and the cooked risotto. Toss together and cook over medium-low heat until all the ingredients are warmed, about 5 minutes.

8. Portion the risotto into shallow bowls or plates and sprinkle with the remaining Pecorino. Top each bowl with a lobster tail.

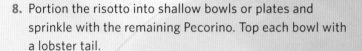

Grilled Swordfish Panzanella with Cherry Tomatoes, Cucumbers, and Baby Kale

Maybe it's just the threatening name, but some people are intimidated by cooking swordfish. Don't be: the meaty fish is filling and satisfying, and it's quick and easy to grill. Once you try it, you'll come back to swordfish again and again. This recipe from chef Evan Victor requires some marinating and planning ahead for the panzanella salad. The cut bread really benefits from drying out in a warm area for up to 3 days.

THE PICKLED ONIONS

- 1 red onion, thinly sliced
- 2 tablespoons red wine vinegar
- 2 tablespoons sherry vinegar
- 1 tablespoon olive oil

THE SWORDFISH

- 4 (6-ounce) fresh swordfish steaks, bloodline removed
- 3 garlic cloves, crushed
- 4 tablespoons olive oil
- 3 tablespoons caper brine
- 1 tablespoon freshly squeezed lemon juice
- Salt and freshly ground black pepper

THE DIJON AIOLI

- 2 tablespoons sherry vinegar
- 2 garlic cloves
- 2 teaspoons fresh tarragon
- ¼ cup Dijon mustard
- 2 tablespoons mayonnaise
- 2 tablespoons freshly ground black pepper
- 1 tablespoon freshly squeezed lemon juice
- 3 tablespoons extra-virgin olive oil

Ingredients continue on page 108

Makes 4 servings

1. To pickle the onion, combine it with the red wine vinegar, sherry vinegar, and oil in a nonreactive container. Cover and refrigerate for at least 2 hours and up to 36 hours.

2. Put the swordfish steaks and garlic in a shallow nonreactive dish. Whisk together the oil, caper brine, and lemon juice in a small bowl. Pour this mixture over the swordfish, cover, and let marinate in the refrigerator for 2 to 8 hours, turning occasionally.

3. To make the aioli, combine the vinegar, garlic, and tarragon in a food processor and pulse until smooth. Add the mustard, mayonnaise, pepper, and lemon juice, and purée until the sauce is smooth. Add the oil and pulse until fully blended. Store in a covered container in the refrigerator until needed.

4. To make the tapenade, combine the mustard, vinegar, and garlic in a food processor and pulse until smooth. Add the olives, bell peppers, capers, and mint, and pulse for 10 seconds. Add the black pepper and oil and pulse for 5 seconds. Store in a covered container in the refrigerator until needed.

5. To prepare the salad, put the stale bread cubes in a large salad bowl. Drain the pickled onions and toss the onions in with the bread. Add the tomatoes, cucumber, and capers and brine, and mix well. Add the kale, feta, and oil, and mix again. Set aside; the salad should sit for at least 15 minutes before serving.

RECIPE CONTINUES ON PAGE 108

THE TAPENADE

- 2 tablespoons Dijon mustard
- 1 tablespoon sherry vinegar
- 3 cloves garlic
- ½ pound assorted pitted Spanish olives
- 2 red bell peppers, grilled, skin removed, seeded, and chopped
- 4 tablespoons capers
- ¼ cup fresh mint
- 2 tablespoons freshly cracked black pepper
- 2 tablespoons extra-virgin olive oil

THE SALAD

- 1 loaf stale crusty bread, crust removed, cut into ½-inch cubes
- 1 pint grape tomatoes, halved
- 1 English cucumber, diced in ⅛-inch cubes
- 6 tablespoons capers plus 1 tablespoon brine
- 1 pound baby kale
- 2 ounces feta cheese, crumbled
- 2 teaspoons olive oil

6. In the meantime, prepare a medium-hot fire in a gas or charcoal grill and brush the grates lightly with cooking spray or vegetable oil. Remove the swordfish from the marinade and blot off any excess marinade to avoid flare-ups. Season the fish with salt and pepper. Grill the swordfish for 4 minutes per side, moving the fish once at a 45-degree increment to achieve proper grill marks. Allow to rest for 3 minutes before serving.

7. Set out four serving plates. On each plate, smear Dijon aioli in a teardrop shape and dollop on 1 tablespoon of olive tapenade. Divide the salad among the plates, setting it on top of the tapenade, and add a swordfish steak atop.

Recipe from DIANE HENDERIKS

Backyard Clambake

A summer staple and an experience that everyone should have at least once (but preferably more than once), the clambake is a delight. While the classic clambake is done on the beach, in a pit with coals, this recipe is suited for the backyard grill. Grab your ingredients and some bottles of your favorite beverage, and call some friends over for a warm-weather feast.

2 dozen steamer clams (more if you'd like)

2 dozen fresh mussels

4 medium red potatoes

1 large bunch seaweed or rockweed, soaked in water

4 ears corn, shucked and cut in half

4 live lobsters

8 extra-large shrimp (11/15 count), peeled and deveined, tails on

Banana leaves (optional)

4 links turkey sausage, grilled or baked until done (optional)

4 tablespoons butter, melted

3 lemons, cut into wedges

Makes 4 servings

1. Prepare a hot fire in a gas or charcoal grill. Wash the clams, mussels, and potatoes thoroughly.

2. Spread a layer of seaweed across the grill and top with the potatoes and corn. Place the lobsters on top of the corn and potatoes, then make another layer with the clams, mussels, and shrimp. Cover the entire clambake with banana leaves or another layer of seaweed. Close the lid and roast for 30 minutes.

3. If you're using the sausage, add it to the top of the pile and continue to cook for another 15 minutes.

4. Check the bake: Search for and discard any unopened clams or mussels. Lobster is done when it turns red and you can twist the small legs and antennae. Remove everything from the grill and transfer to a large serving bowl. Serve immediately with drawn (melted) butter and lemon wedges.

DIANE HENDERIKS. Diane Henderiks has long held a passion for healthy cooking, realizing early in her career that food that is good for the body does not need to taste bland. A Monmouth University graduate, she would later complete the Dietetic Internship Program at the University of Medicine and Dentistry in New Jersey.

From there her career took off. She first started a nutritional consulting firm, and then she self-published a cookbook and started Diane's Daily Dish, her personal chef and catering business, as well as a video series. She now regularly lectures at food festivals, teaches cooking classes, and brings her own Jersey can-do attitude with the goal of encouraging people to eat healthy.

Black Pepper Tuna Tataki
with Edamame Succotash, Marinated Cabbage, and Grapefruit Ponzu

A joyous combination of summer flavors and textures, this dinner is a treat for the senses, colorful and bursting with aromas of the sea and garden. There is a bit of advance preparation time in the kitchen, but the tuna cooks quickly. Eat this dinner in August at a house down the shore, or enjoy it during the winter as a reminder of summer's heat.

THE CABBAGE

1 small head green cabbage, thinly sliced

1 carrot, coarsely grated

1 red bell pepper, seeded and julienned

1 bunch fresh cilantro, stemmed

1 bunch scallions, sliced on a 1-inch bias

¼ cup rice wine vinegar

3 tablespoons olive oil

1 tablespoon sesame oil (optional)

THE GRAPEFRUIT PONZU

½ cup freshly squeezed grapefruit juice

¼ cup soy sauce

2 tablespoons clover honey

1 tablespoon freshly squeezed orange juice

1 tablespoon rice wine vinegar

1 teaspoon freshly ground black pepper

3 scallions, finely sliced

1 (½-inch) piece fresh ginger, grated on a Microplane or finely chopped

Makes 4 servings

1. To marinate the cabbage, combine it with the carrot, bell pepper, cilantro, scallions, vinegar, olive oil, and sesame oil, if using, in a large nonreactive bowl and mix until fully blended. Cover and store in the refrigerator until needed (it will keep there for up to 36 hours).

2. To make the ponzu, combine the grapefruit juice, soy sauce, honey, orange juice, vinegar, black pepper, scallions, and ginger in a jar with a tight-fitting lid. Shake well to combine. Store in the refrigerator until needed (it will keep there for up to 2 weeks).

3. Preheat the oven to 325°F.

4. For the succotash, season each ear of corn with salt and pepper. Wrap each in foil and roast for 20 minutes. Let cool, and then slice off the kernels and transfer to a bowl. Add the onion, bell peppers, cilantro, scallions, jalapeño, vinegar, and 2 tablespoons of the olive oil, and mix until well combined.

5. Warm the remaining 2 tablespoons olive oil in a medium skillet over medium heat. Add the edamame and cook for 1 minute, then stir in the corn mixture and sauté until warm. Do not overcook or the vegetables will be mushy. Season to taste with salt and black pepper.

6. To prepare the tuna, pat the steaks dry with paper towels. Mix the pepper and salt on a small plate and coat the tuna by pressing each steak into the mixture.

2 ears fresh corn, husked

Salt and freshly ground black pepper

1 small red onion, finely diced

½ green bell pepper, finely diced

½ red bell pepper, finely diced

Leaves from 3 sprigs fresh cilantro

3 scallions, sliced on a 1-inch bias

1 jalapeño, seeded and finely diced (optional)

3 tablespoons sherry vinegar

4 tablespoons extra-virgin olive oil

¼ cup frozen edamame, defrosted

THE TUNA

4 ahi tuna steaks

5 tablespoons freshly ground black pepper

1 tablespoon kosher salt

2 tablespoons vegetable oil

7. Warm the vegetable oil in a heavy skillet over medium heat. Gently add the tuna to the pan. Sear each side of the steaks for 1 minute, or until a crust forms. Remove from the heat and let rest for 3 minutes. Then slice the steaks into ⅛-inch pieces, or whatever thickness you desire.

8. Spread the marinated cabbage on a serving platter, and arrange the sliced tuna over the top. Spoon the warm corn succotash on top of the tuna and serve with the ponzu dipping sauce on the side.

Crab Cakes

Often, crab cakes are a dish reserved for restaurants. But with just a few ingredients — many that are likely in your pantry — and fresh crabmeat, these can come together quickly. Served over pasta, or with a side of potatoes and vegetables, it's a great weeknight meal. If you're unfamiliar with Poultry Magic seasoning, it comes from chef Paul Prudhomme's line (and should be a staple of your spice cabinet). However, Old Bay seasoning is an acceptable substitute. *Read about Jenkinson's Boardwalk Bar & Grill on page 60.*

1 pound lump crabmeat

½ cup Italian breadcrumbs

2½ tablespoons mayonnaise

1½ teaspoons brown mustard

1 teaspoon Poultry Magic
seasoning blend

1 teaspoon Worcestershire sauce

2 tablespoons olive oil

Salt and freshly ground
black pepper

Makes 4 servings

1. Combine the crabmeat, breadcrumbs, mayonnaise, mustard, poultry seasoning, and Worcestershire in a large bowl and mix well. Mold into 3-ounce cakes, or eight total (two per person).

2. Preheat the oven to 350°F.

3. Heat the oil in a skillet over medium-high heat and, working in batches if necessary, sear the crab cakes until lightly golden, about 2 minutes per side.

4. Transfer the crab cakes to a baking dish and bake for 10 minutes, or until hot throughout. Season with salt and pepper as desired.

Raspberry Tartar Sauce

Ubiquitous at seafood restaurants and grocery-store seafood counters, tartar sauce is a condiment that most people don't think about making at home. And that's too bad, because not only is the sauce more flavorful when fresh, but it's also very easy to make. A few years back, I started experimenting with fruited tartar sauce and eventually settled on raspberry as my berry of choice. A little goes a long way, but the tart-sweet fruit offsets some of the salt and oil and adds color to flaky whitefish, the kind most associated with fried fish dishes and fish sticks.

1 pint fresh raspberries

¼ cup sugar

2 tablespoons freshly squeezed lemon juice

1 cup mayonnaise

¼ cup finely chopped dill pickle

1 tablespoon minced fresh parsley

Makes about 2 cups

1. Combine the raspberries, sugar, and 1 tablespoon of the lemon juice in a saucepan and cook over medium heat, stirring occasionally, until the berries have released their juice, 15 minutes.

2. Increase the heat and bring the mixture to a boil. Cook until the liquid has reduced but is not fully thickened, 5 minutes. Strain through a fine-mesh strainer to remove any seeds and skin, then set aside to cool.

3. Combine the mayonnaise, pickle, parsley, and remaining lemon juice in a small bowl and mix until fully blended. Add the raspberry sauce and mix again. Store in an airtight container in the refrigerator until ready to serve. It will keep for up to 1 week.

The "Health Be Damned Tonight" Jersey Disco Fries

Sometimes you just need to throw nutrition out the window. This is usually helped along after a few drinks, so it should come as no surprise that this recipe comes from Augie Carton, the namesake of Carton Brewing Co. Of course, using hot oil is not something that should be done under the influence. So plan ahead, or have a responsible adult handle the cooking duties.

Peanut oil, for frying

4 medium russet potatoes, skin on, julienned

Kosher salt

1 (¼-pound) segment pork roll, diced

2 tablespoons all-purpose flour

1 cup milk

½ cup half-and-half

1 teaspoon freshly ground white pepper

1 cup grated sharp cheddar cheese

½ cup sliced scallions

Sea salt

Makes 6–8 servings

1. Fill a deep fryer or a large pot with 3 inches of oil and heat to 315°F.

2. Cut the potatoes into French fries no bigger than ¼ inch thick. Deep-fry for 4 minutes. Remove with a wire spider or small mesh strainer and lay out on paper towels or a wire rack to drain.

3. Heat the oil to 350°F. Return the fries to the oil and cook until crispy and golden, about 3 minutes. Remove from the oil, drain, and toss with Kosher salt to taste.

4. Lower the oil temperature to 305°F. Add the pork roll and fry until crispy, 2 to 3 minutes. Remove, drain, and toss with the French fries.

5. Ladle 2 tablespoons of the oil from the fryer into a medium saucepan over medium heat. Add the flour, stirring with a whisk until well combined. A little browning here is good. Add the milk and half-and-half and white pepper, stir to combine, and increase the heat to medium-high. When the sauce just reaches a boil, reduce the heat to low and let simmer until the sauce is thick enough to coat the back of a spoon, 10 minutes. Whisk in the cheese ¼ cup at a time, until fully incorporated.

6. Arrange the fries and pork roll on a plate and top with cheese sauce and sliced scallions. Add a sprinkling of sea salt as desired. Serve hot.

NOTE: A package of cream cheese combined with a jar of nacho cheese sauce and heated in a microwave is a quick and tasty substitute for the homemade cheese sauce.

5

The Main Event

All the other courses lead up to this: the entrée. Whether meat, poultry, or vegetarian options, these are dishes that exude the flavors of the state. In this chapter you'll find that these Jersey-inspired dishes — regardless if they come from a fancy restaurant, the boardwalk, a café, or your neighbor's kitchen — are easy to prepare, fun to make, and even better to eat.

Ancho and Ale Chili with Avocado Mousse

Hearty, with a kick of spice, this chili won first place in a local chili contest, and with good reason. Partnering with the Cape May Brewery, the Blue Rose Inn seasoned its chili with a generous glug of Scotch ale, which is malty sweet with a hint of smoke. Top this terrific chili with a cooling avocado mousse and watch your guests come back for more until the pot is empty.

THE CHILI

- 6 whole dried ancho chiles
- 2 tablespoons coriander seed
- 2 tablespoons cumin seed
- 3 tablespoons olive oil
- 3 pounds beef shoulder or beef short ribs, cut into large cubes
- Salt and freshly ground black pepper
- 2 chipotles in adobo sauce, minced
- 2 tablespoons smoked paprika
- 4 tablespoons tomato paste
- 18 ounces Cape May Brewery Scottish ale or similar beer
- 2 cups chicken stock
- Freshly squeezed lime juice
- 1 tomato, diced, for garnish

THE AVOCADO MOUSSE

- 4 avocados
- 1 garlic clove, minced
- 1 small jalapeño, seeded and sliced
- 1 small shallot, minced
- 1 teaspoon salt
- ½ cup water
- Juice of 4 limes
- 1 cup heavy cream

Makes 8 servings

1. Put the ancho chiles in a medium saucepan. Add enough water to just cover them and bring to a boil over high heat. Cover the pot and remove from the heat. Let the chiles steep until they are soft and tender, 1 hour. Remove the stems and seeds. Transfer the chiles and their soaking water to a blender and purée until smooth.

2. Toast the coriander and cumin seeds in a dry skillet over medium-high heat until fragrant, about 1 minute. Remove from the heat and let cool slightly, then transfer to a spice grinder; grind to a fine powder.

3. Heat the oil in a large pot over medium heat until shimmering. Season the beef with salt and pepper, and then sear the beef in the oil until browned on all sides, 3 to 4 minutes per side. Add the ground cumin and coriander, the chipotles, and the paprika; stir. Add the tomato paste, the ancho chile purée, and 12 ounces (1½ cups) of the ale. Bring to a boil, then reduce the heat and let simmer until the mixture thickens, about 20 minutes.

4. Add 1½ cups of the chicken stock and let simmer until the meat is tender, 2 hours, adding additional ale and stock as needed.

5. After 90 minutes, or at least 30 minutes before serving the chili, make the avocado mousse: Combine the avocados, garlic, jalapeño, shallot, and salt with the water and lime juice in a blender and purée until smooth. Switch the blender to low and slowly add the cream, whipping until the mixture is stiff. Transfer to a bowl and set aside.

6. Use a potato masher to mash the chili, breaking the meat apart until it separates into shreds. Season with salt, pepper, and lime juice to taste.

7. Scoop the chili into bowls and garnish each with the avocado mousse and a sprinkling of chopped tomato. Serve immediately.

Vegetarian Three-Bean Chili

There's a decent amount of chopping involved with this recipe, but once everything goes into the pot, all this chili needs is the occasional stir and several hours on the stovetop. In my family, this is a favorite autumn weekend dish. The aromas cover the house like a blanket, and when the final dish is topped with sour cream, shredded cheddar, and even some diced jalapeño, the all-day cooking will have been worth the wait.

Use the combination of vegetables listed here as a base and then build on it to make it your own. Perhaps you can find other root vegetables, like parsnips or rutabaga, at the farmers' market. Or maybe you'd prefer to add butternut squash or mushrooms. Pick up whatever moves you as you browse the local offerings.

2 tablespoons olive oil

5 garlic cloves, minced

4 stalks celery, peeled and diced

2 large carrots, diced

2 large green bell peppers, diced

2 large white or yellow
   onions, diced

2 jalapeños, diced

12 ounces stout ale

2 tablespoons ground cumin

1 tablespoon chili powder

2 teaspoons chipotle chile powder

1 teaspoon dried oregano

2 (28-ounce) cans
   stewed tomatoes

1 cup corn kernels

1 (15-ounce) can black beans,
   drained and rinsed

1 (15-ounce) can kidney beans,
   drained and rinsed

1 (15-ounce) can pinto beans,
   drained and rinsed

2 medium zucchini, diced

Sour cream, grated cheddar
   cheese, and tortilla chips,
   for serving

Makes about 20 servings

1. Heat the oil in a large pot over medium heat. Add the garlic, celery, carrots, bell peppers, and onions, along with half of the jalapeño, and cook until softened, about 7 minutes.

2. Add the ale, cumin, chili powder, chipotle powder, and oregano, and stir to combine. Stir in the stewed tomatoes. Bring to a simmer, and cook for 90 minutes, stirring occasionally.

3. Add the corn and black, kidney, and pinto beans, stir to combine, cover, and cook for an additional 90 minutes, stirring occasionally.

4. Add the zucchini just before serving. The almost-raw crunch is nice in the otherwise soft dish. Serve in bowls and top with sour cream, cheddar cheese, tortilla chips, and the remaining diced jalapeño.

North Jersey Venison Chili
with Cilantro Pesto

Butchers throughout the state will have venison on hand during hunting season, and they will ground your order if asked. This chili has a lot of deep flavors from the meat itself, the strong coffee, the beer with roasted notes, and the punch of cilantro. Topped with blueberries, a great state crop, this unusual chili is in a class by itself.

THE CHILI

- 8 poblano peppers
- 3 tablespoons olive oil
- 1 small white onion, diced
- 3 garlic cloves, minced
- 2½ pounds ground venison
- ½ cup porter beer
- 3 tablespoons ground coriander
- 2 tablespoons chili powder
- 1½ tablespoons ground cumin
- 1 teaspoon cayenne pepper
- 2 (14-ounce) cans great northern beans, or similar white bean, drained and rinsed
- 1 quart beef stock
- 1½ cups brewed dark roast coffee
- 1 (14-ounce) can diced tomatoes
- 1 (4-ounce) can tomato paste
- ½ cup chopped fresh cilantro
- Salt and freshly ground black pepper

THE CILANTRO PESTO

- 2 cups fresh cilantro
- 2 garlic cloves, roasted
- ½ cup shredded Pecorino Romano cheese
- ⅔ cup extra-virgin olive oil
- Salt and freshly ground black pepper

THE GARNISH

- 1½ cups shaved Manchego cheese
- ½ cup dried blueberries

Makes 4–6 servings

1. Char the poblano peppers over a medium-high grill flame until black. Place in a container and cover with plastic wrap to steam and allow to cool completely. Peel off the skins and remove the seeds, then chop into medium-sized pieces and set aside.

2. Heat a large soup pot or Dutch oven over medium heat and add the oil. Add the onions and sauté until translucent, about 5 minutes. Add the garlic and sauté until fragrant, about 1 minute. Add the ground venison and cook until browned, about 5 minutes. Add the beer to deglaze the pan (scrape up the browned bits), and cook for 2 minutes.

3. Add the coriander, chili powder, cumin, cayenne, beans, chopped poblano peppers, beef stock, coffee, diced tomatoes, and tomato paste, and stir together. Bring to a boil, then turn down to medium. Cook for 1 hour, stirring occasionally.

4. To make the pesto, combine the 2 cups cilantro, garlic, and Pecorino in a food processor. Add the oil and process until smooth. Season to taste with salt and pepper and set aside.

5. Add the ½ cup cilantro to the chili, stir to combine, and cook for 5 minutes. Season to taste with salt and pepper.

6. Serve in bowls and garnish with cilantro pesto, Manchego, and dried blueberries.

TEC (Taylor Ham, Egg, and Cheese) Soup

Take the flavors of the classic sandwich and liquefy them into a flavorful broth that celebrates all the elements Jerseyans hold dear. From chef Francesco Palmieri, owner of the Orange Squirrel Restaurant, this soup will play with your mind as you question why you never heard of it sooner.

6 tablespoons unsalted butter

1 stalk celery, finely diced

1 leek, finely chopped

1 onion, finely diced

¼ cup all-purpose flour

12 ounces golden ale

3 cups vegetable stock or water

1 cup shredded sharp
   cheddar cheese

Salt and freshly ground
   black pepper

⅛ teaspoon ground nutmeg

¼ cup black truffles, finely chopped

4 eggs

1 slice Taylor ham or pork roll, fried,
   cooled, and finely chopped

Makes 4 servings

1. Melt 4 tablespoons of the butter in a Dutch oven or soup pot over medium heat. Add the celery, leek, and onion, and cook until soft, 5 to 7 minutes.

2. Add the flour to the pan and stir to form a roux. Slowly whisk in the ale. When the ale is fully incorporated, stir in the stock. Bring to a boil, then reduce the heat and let simmer, covered, for 30 minutes.

3. Add the cheese to the soup and season with salt and pepper to taste. Add the nutmeg and stir until the cheese is melted. Remove from the heat. Using a stick blender, slowly blend the mixture until smooth. Fold in the black truffles.

4. Melt the remaining 2 tablespoons butter in a large skillet over medium heat. Fry the eggs sunny-side up.

5. Divide the soup among four bowls. Top each with an egg and garnish with a dusting of fried Taylor ham. Serve immediately.

Recipe from MANISCHEWITZ COMPANY, NEWARK

Chicken Thighs with Roasted Fall Fruit

The wonderful thing about skillet chicken is the crisp golden brown skin you get when you sear the bird on each side before finishing the cooking in the oven. Chef Jamie Geller — working with the Manischewitz Company to promote its products — says searing also locks in the juices so you have nice moist, flavorful chicken.

1 teaspoon olive oil

4 bone-in, skin-on chicken thighs (about 2 pounds)

2 tart apples, such as Pink Lady or Granny Smith, cored and sliced ½ inch thick

2 firm ripe pears, cored and sliced ½ inch thick

2 garlic cloves, minced

½ teaspoon ground cinnamon

½ teaspoon dry mustard

½ teaspoon kosher salt

½–¾ cup Manischewitz reduced-sodium chicken broth, or broth of your choice

1 cup red grapes

3 tablespoons balsamic vinegar

1 tablespoon fresh thyme leaves or 1 teaspoon dried thyme

Makes 4 servings

1. Preheat the oven to 400°F.

2. Heat the oil in a large ovenproof skillet over medium-high heat. Add the chicken and cook until nicely golden brown, 8 to 10 minutes per side. Remove and set aside.

3. If there are more than 2 tablespoons of grease in the skillet, drain the excess. Add the apples and pears and sauté until they are just beginning to brown, 4 to 6 minutes. Add the garlic, cinnamon, mustard, and salt, and sauté for 1 minute. Return the chicken thighs to the pan along with ½ cup of the chicken stock and bring to a boil. Transfer the skillet to the oven and bake for 15 minutes. Add the grapes, plus ¼ cup more chicken stock if the pan is dry, and return to the oven for 15 minutes.

4. Drizzle the vinegar over everything and garnish with the thyme. Serve each chicken thigh with about 1 cup of the roasted fruit.

THE MANISCHEWITZ COMPANY

Although founded in Ohio, the Manischewitz Company has been a part of New Jersey's culinary history since 1932. That's when the company, started by Rabbi Dov Behr Manischewitz, opened a state-of-the-art facility in Jersey City that used machines to make matzo (unleavened bread). The N.J. location was so successful, according to the company's history, that soon enough the Cincinnati kitchen was no longer needed.

While Manischewitz is certainly known for matzo, it's the wine that bears the company name that is likely the most famous. Manischewitz began to distribute its kosher wine in 1940, and 14 years later took over a plant in Vineland to process the company's jarred and canned goods, such as borscht and chicken soup.

The company closed the Jersey City facility in 2006, moving operations — both production and corporate headquarters — to Newark, and today it is the largest producer of kosher food products in the United States. Last year alone, the Manischewitz Company produced more than 37 million pounds of matzo.

Rabbi Yonah Hayum

Recipe from SPOON ME SOUPS, MORRISTOWN

Fall Vegetable Stew

Taking advantage of the local produce available in the state during autumn, Sarah Beattie of Spoon Me Soups has created this hearty vegetable and bean stew with a savory broth. *Read about Spoon Me Soups on page 128.*

2 tablespoons extra-virgin olive oil

½ yellow onion, diced

Salt

1 garlic clove, finely minced

3 small carrots, peeled and diced

1 small butternut squash, peeled, deseeded, and diced

2 small Yukon Gold potatoes, peeled and diced

1 (14.5-ounce) can diced tomatoes

1 teaspoon ground coriander

½ teaspoon ground cumin

1 teaspoon ground cinnamon

¼ teaspoon freshly ground black pepper

1 (14-ounce) can great northern beans, or similar white bean, drained and rinsed

6 cups low-sodium vegetable broth

4 large kale leaves, rinsed, stems removed, and roughly chopped

Makes 3½ quarts

1. Add the oil to a soup pot or Dutch oven and place over medium heat. Once heated, add the onion and a pinch of salt and cook, stirring occasionally until the onion starts to become translucent, about 5 minutes. Add the garlic and cook until the garlic starts to brown, about 1 minute.

2. Add the carrots and a pinch of salt and cook, stirring occasionally, until the carrots begin to soften, about 5 minutes. Add the butternut squash, potatoes, diced tomatoes, coriander, cumin, cinnamon, pinch of salt, and black pepper. Cook and stir until the spices become fragrant, about 2 minutes.

3. Add the beans, vegetable broth, and an additional pinch of salt, if desired. Bring the soup to a simmer, uncovered, and let cook until the vegetables are tender, about 20 minutes.

4. Turn off the heat and allow the soup to cool for 5 minutes. Stir in the chopped kale and serve warm. Any leftovers may be stored in freezer bags for up to 2 months.

SPOON ME SOUPS

Spoon Me Soups is on a mission to bring flavor, health, and excitement back to comfort food. Sarah Beattie, who worked in a variety of natural food businesses, founded the business, which sells soups at a growing number of farmers' markets throughout the state. Focusing on vegan and gluten-free options, Beattie strives to create flavorful soups for all to enjoy. She uses local produce and draws inspiration from a variety of food cultures. It's not uncommon to see customers stocking up on the prepackaged frozen soups every time she sets up shop.

Sarah Beattie

Recipe from UNIONVILLE VINEYARDS, RINGOES

Honey-Roasted Chicken

Honey mustard and chicken are a classic combination, but chef Emily Rogalsky suggests that rather than using honey mustard as a dipping sauce, simmer the chicken in it with fresh herbs and white wine. Serve with a side of rice and pair with a Unionville Vineyards' Marsanne Roussanne, a full-bodied white wine.

THE CHICKEN AND RUB

- 2 tablespoons olive oil
- 1 tablespoon whole-grain mustard
- Salt and freshly ground black pepper
- 4 bone-in, skin-on chicken thighs (about 2 pounds)
- 1 yellow onion, chopped
- 2 garlic cloves, minced
- ¼ cup Marsanne Roussanne or a similar full-bodied white wine
- 2 sprigs fresh thyme
- 2 sprigs fresh marjoram

THE HONEY MUSTARD SAUCE

- 3 tablespoons Dijon mustard
- 3 tablespoons whole-grain mustard or honey mustard of your choice
- 3 tablespoons honey
- 1 tablespoon olive oil
- ½ teaspoon grated fresh ginger

Makes 2–3 servings

1. Preheat the oven to 400°F.

2. For the rub, combine 1 tablespoon of the oil with the mustard and salt and pepper to taste in a small bowl. Using your fingers or a brush, work the rub all over the chicken and set aside.

3. Make the honey-mustard sauce: Whisk together the Dijon, whole-grain mustard, honey, 1 tablespoon oil, and ginger in a small bowl and set aside.

4. Heat the remaining 1 tablespoon oil in a cast-iron skillet over medium heat. Add the onion and garlic and cook until golden brown, about 5 minutes. Add the chicken and sear for 2 to 3 minutes on each side. Add the wine and the honey mustard sauce to the skillet. Nestle the fresh herbs around the chicken and place the skillet in the oven. Roast for 25 to 30 minutes, or until the chicken has cooked through to 165°F.

5. Allow the chicken to rest for 5 minutes before serving.

Recipe from MANISCHEWITZ COMPANY, NEWARK

Carrot, Quinoa, and Spinach Soup

The recipe, developed for the Manischewitz Company, is special enough for a holiday meal and hearty enough to serve anytime. Chef Jamie Geller says that if you want to add dairy, try adding ½ cup of whole milk when you stir in the spinach. It gives the dish a light, creamy flavor. *Read about the Manischewitz Company on page 124.*

2 tablespoons olive oil

8 carrots, cut into ¼-inch pieces

2 medium onions, chopped

3 garlic cloves, chopped

1 teaspoon ground cumin

1 teaspoon paprika

½ teaspoon ground coriander

¼ teaspoon ground ginger

1 cup quinoa, rinsed

6 cups Manischewitz vegetable broth, or broth of your choice

2 cups baby spinach (or frozen spinach, defrosted and drained)

2 teaspoons kosher salt

Freshly ground black pepper

Manischewitz gluten-free crackers, or crackers of your choice, for serving

Makes 6 servings

1. Heat the oil in a large pot over medium-high heat. Add the carrots, onions, and garlic, and sauté until the vegetables soften, 8 to 10 minutes.

2. Add the cumin, paprika, coriander, and ginger, and cook 1 minute longer. Add the quinoa and broth and stir to combine. Bring to a boil, then reduce the heat to a simmer and cook, covered, until the carrots are tender and the quinoa is cooked, 15 minutes.

3. Stir in the spinach and season to taste with salt and pepper. Serve hot, with gluten-free crackers on the side.

Classic Lawrenceville Mac and Cheese

Cherry Grove's tomme-style Toma Primavera and Herdsman cheeses are velvety and meltable — perfect for a classic like macaroni and cheese. This dish can be made ahead of time and stored in the fridge for up to 2 days, though you shouldn't add the breadcrumbs until you're ready to bake.

6 tablespoons unsalted butter, plus more to grease the baking dish

1 cup panko breadcrumbs

12 ounces Cherry Grove Herdsman or similar cheddar cheese, grated

12 ounces Cherry Grove Toma, or similar semisoft rind cheese, grated

1 pound elbow macaroni or your favorite shape of short pasta

3¼ cups whole milk

3 tablespoons all-purpose flour

1½ teaspoons dry mustard

1 teaspoon fine sea salt

½ teaspoon freshly ground black pepper

NOTE: For additional flavor, flake a can of tuna or salmon into your cheese mixture, or add your favorite green vegetables to the sauce. Tuna fish and broccoli together make a tuna tetrazzini!

Makes 4–6 servings

1. Preheat the oven to 350°F. Lightly butter a 9- by 13-inch baking dish.

2. Melt 3 tablespoons of the butter in a small saucepan over medium heat. Place the panko in a small bowl, drizzle with the melted butter, and toss to combine. Add a handful of the grated cheeses to the bowl, toss to combine, and set aside.

3. Bring a large pot of salted water to a boil. Add the pasta and cook until al dente. Drain the pasta and return them to the pot without rinsing.

4. Warm the milk in a small saucepan over moderate heat just until it starts to steam and form tiny bubbles around the edges, 3 to 5 minutes — be careful not to let the milk come to a boil. Remove from the heat.

5. Melt the remaining 3 tablespoons butter in a medium saucepan over medium heat. Add the flour and use a flat-edged wooden spoon or heat-safe rubber spatula to stir the mixture together, scraping the bottom of the pan to prevent burning, just until it starts to turn a light brown color, about 3 minutes. Remove from the heat and stir in the mustard, salt, and pepper. Add the warm milk. Add the rest of the grated cheeses and stir until completely melted. Adjust the seasoning to taste. Pour the cheese sauce over the cooked macaroni and gently stir to coat the pasta.

6. Pour the macaroni and cheese into the prepared baking dish and top with the panko-cheese mixture. Bake for about 30 minutes, or until light golden brown and bubbling. Serve hot.

CHERRY GROVE FARM

Listen carefully while out in the fields and you might be able to detect the faint din of traffic from I-95. But soon enough the sounds of the farm, a short drive from Princeton, will be all you can hear. Fields of cattle and hogs, chickens, and field insects, even the wind blowing through country grass, make you forget just how close you are to modern life.

At 480 acres, Cherry Grove is first and foremost a dairy farm and creamery, with the cheese shop visible from the country store at the edge of the property. The store contains all the farm's bounty and products, along with other artisanal items — from chocolate

and pickles to books and throws. Open to the public, it's a great opportunity to see the animals up close, to take a deep breath, and to reignite a relationship with nature.

Sautéed Ricotta Gnocchi
with Portobello Mushrooms, Tomato Confit, and Mushroom Butter Sauce

Chewy and satisfying, homemade gnocchi are a treat. Here, they are combined with the deep, earthy flavors of roasted portobellos and a rich, creamy sauce, making your kitchen worthy of the finest of white-linen restaurants. Note that the gnocchi dough has to chill in the refrigerator for at least 8 hours; you'll want to prepare it well ahead of time. Any leftover mushroom stock can be cooled and stored in a freezer bag until ready to use again.

THE GNOCCHI

- 1 cup ricotta cheese
- ½ cup grated Parmesan cheese
- 2 pinches of salt
- 1 egg, beaten
- ¾ cup all-purpose flour

THE TOMATO CONFIT

- 3 garlic cloves, minced
- 2 tablespoons minced fresh thyme
- ½ cup virgin olive oil
- 2 pints cherry tomatoes, halved
  Salt

THE PORTOBELLOS

- 4 large portobello mushrooms
- 2 garlic cloves, minced
- 1 tablespoon chopped fresh thyme
  Salt and freshly ground
    black pepper

Serves 4 as a light meal or appetizer

1. To make the gnocchi dough, combine the ricotta, Parmesan, and salt in a large bowl. Stir in the beaten egg. Add the flour and mix just to incorporate. Do not overmix. Cover the bowl with plastic wrap and let the dough sit in the refrigerator for at least 8 hours.

2. Preheat the oven to 200°F.

3. For the tomato confit, combine the garlic, thyme, and oil in a large bowl and mix well. Lay the tomatoes skin-side down on a rimmed baking sheet or roasting pan and drizzle with the oil. Season well with salt. Roast for 2 to 2½ hours, until the tomatoes are dried but not crispy. Remove from the oven and let cool.

4. For the portobellos, raise the oven temperature to 350°F. Remove and save the stems from the mushrooms. Place the mushrooms upside down on a rimmed baking sheet. Top each cap with garlic and thyme, and season well with salt and pepper. Roast for 25 minutes. Remove from the oven and let cool. When they're cool enough to handle, dice the portobellos.

5. For the butter sauce, begin with a mushroom stock: Heat the oil in a large pot over medium-high heat. Add the cremini mushrooms along with the portobello trimmings and sauté until deep brown, about 10 minutes. Add the carrots, celery, shallots, fennel, onion, garlic, thyme, bay leaves, and peppercorns, and cook for 5 minutes. Add the vegetable stock, bring to a simmer, and cook for 1½ hours. Then strain the stock, return the liquid to the pot, and cook until it is reduced by half.

THE MUSHROOM BUTTER SAUCE

- 2 tablespoons olive oil
- 8 cups cremini or button mushrooms
- 3 carrots, sliced
- 3 stalks celery, sliced
- 2 shallots, sliced
- 1 fennel bulb, sliced
- 1 white onion, sliced
- 1 garlic clove, minced
- 4 sprigs fresh thyme
- 2 bay leaves
- 12 peppercorns
- 1 gallon vegetable stock or water
- 1½ cups (3 sticks) chilled butter, cut into chunks

6. Measure out ½ cup of the mushroom stock. Bring to a simmer and slowly whisk in the butter.

7. Cut the gnocchi dough into rectangular 1-inch chunks. Flour a work surface and knead the gnocchi rectangles into rope-shaped pieces. Cut the ropes into pillow-shaped bite-size pieces and set on parchment paper until ready to cook. You should have about 40 gnocchi.

8. Bring a large pot of salted water to a boil and gently add the gnocchi. Cook until the gnocchi float to the top, 2 to 4 minutes.

9. Drain the gnocchi, divide among plates, and top with diced portobello, tomato confit, and then the butter sauce. Serve immediately.

Recipe from SÁTIS BISTRO, JERSEY CITY

Cheese Curd Poutine with Pork Shank Gravy

Basically, this is disco fries for the adult set. This recipe from Sátis Bistro's executive chef, Michael Fiorianti, puts a decidedly sophisticated kick on the traditional, usually more humble diner dish. Quality meat always makes a difference; Chef Fiorianti uses pork shanks from Mosefund Farms in Branchville. The gravy can be made a day in advance and reheated gently before serving. The pork, too, can be made a day or two in advance; in fact, it's even better that way. Homemade fries are outstanding, but if need be, you can substitute prepared frozen fries. This recipe requires some time, so if you're looking for disco fries in a flash, head to your local diner — but these are totally worth the wait.

THE GRAVY

- 2 pork shanks, bone-in (about 2½ pounds total)
- Salt and freshly ground black pepper
- 15 garlic cloves, minced
- 3 stalks celery, diced
- 2 carrots, diced
- 1 large onion, diced
- 2 cups white wine
- 1 tablespoon Dijon mustard
- 8 cups chicken stock or water
- 12 sprigs fresh thyme
- 2 tablespoons toasted mustard seed
- 2 tablespoons whole black peppercorns
- 1½ teaspoons toasted fennel seed
- 2 bay leaves
- 4 tablespoons butter
- 5 tablespoons all-purpose flour
- 1 tablespoon Worcestershire sauce
- 1 teaspoon malt vinegar

Makes 8–10 servings

1. To make the gravy, season the pork shanks with salt and pepper. Warm a Dutch oven or casserole pot over medium-high heat, add the pork shanks, and sear until golden brown on both sides, 3 to 4 minutes per side. Remove the shanks and set aside.

2. Add the garlic, celery, carrots, and onion to the pot and lower the heat to medium. Cook, stirring frequently, until the onions start to turn translucent, about 5 minutes.

3. Raise the heat to medium-high and add the white wine. Simmer until the liquid is reduced by half, being sure to scrape up the browned bits from the bottom of the pot. Stir in the mustard.

4. Return the pork shanks to the pot. Pour the chicken stock over everything. Bundle up the herbs and spices — the thyme, mustard seeds, peppercorns, fennel seeds, and bay leaves — in a square of cheesecloth, tie shut with twine. and add the bundle to the pot as well. Bring to a boil, then reduce the heat and let simmer, covered, until the meat just starts to fall off the bone, about 3 hours.

5. Remove the shanks from the pot and set aside to cool. Bring the cooking liquid back to a boil and let boil until it is reduced by 25 percent (roughly 1¾ cups). Strain the cooking liquid into a separate container and set aside.

Oil, for frying

3 Kennebec or Idaho russet potatoes

Salt

4 ounces cheddar cheese curds

2 scallions, thinly sliced

6. Add the butter to the now-empty pot and melt over low heat. Add the flour and whisk until golden brown and smooth, about 3 minutes. Pour 4 cups of the reserved cooking liquid into the pot and whisk until fully incorporated. Bring to a simmer.

7. While the gravy sauce is simmering, pull the meat off the shanks and chop into pieces. Add the pork to the gravy and season with the Worcestershire, vinegar, and salt and pepper as needed.

8. To make the poutine, heat 3 inches of oil in a deep fryer or pot to 315°F. Cut the potatoes into ¼-inch-thick French fries and fry in the oil for 4 minutes. Scoop them out and lay them on paper towels or wire racks to drain.

9. Heat the oil to 350°F. Return the potatoes to the oil and cook until crispy and golden, about 3 minutes. Remove from the oil, drain, and toss with salt to taste and the cheese curds. Heap the fries onto plates, top with the gravy, and garnish with sliced scallions.

NOTE: If you like your curds fried, combine ⅔ cup milk, ½ cup flour, ½ teaspoon baking powder, and 1 teaspoon salt in a mixing bowl. Coat the curds and deep-fry at 350°F until golden, about 4 minutes.

Recipe from MANISCHEWITZ COMPANY, NEWARK

Roasted Lamb with Pomegranate and Wine

Roasted rack of lamb is made extra-succulent by honey, which helps lock in the moisture. From chef Alessandra Rovati, the pomegranate-Syrah sauce makes this dish even more special. Accompanied by roasted butternut squash and sautéed greens, this makes a perfect holiday meal. *Read about the Manischewitz Company on page 124.*

1 (2½-pound) rack of lamb

5 tablespoons extra-virgin olive oil

1 tablespoon honey

Salt and freshly ground
black pepper

1 tablespoon chopped fresh thyme

1 tablespoon chopped
fresh marjoram

1 shallot or ½ onion, finely minced

½ cup pomegranate seeds

1 bottle Syrah or Pinot Noir

½ cup Manischewitz reduced-
sodium chicken broth, or broth
of your choice

Makes 4 servings

1. Preheat the oven to 350°F.

2. To prepare the lamb, trim off most of the fat. Combine 1½ tablespoons of the oil and the honey in a small bowl and mix well. Brush the mixture over the lamb. Season with salt and pepper and rub with the thyme and marjoram.

3. Heat another 1½ tablespoons of the oil in a large oven-safe skillet over medium-high heat. Add the lamb and brown all over, about 3 minutes per side. Transfer the skillet to the oven and roast for 20 minutes.

4. Heat the remaining 2 tablespoons oil in a saucepan over medium heat. Add the shallot and sauté until translucent, about 3 minutes. Add the pomegranate seeds and wine, turn the heat up to high, and cook for 3 minutes. Add the broth, lower the temperature to medium, and simmer until the sauce is reduced by half, about 10 minutes.

5. Serve the lamb with the sauce on the side.

Recipe from VILLAGE IDIOT BREWING COMPANY, MOUNT HOLLY

Pressure-Cooker Corned Beef

Using a pressure cooker saves time and energy and makes the corned beef tender and easy to cut. No more standing over a hot pot boiling this tough cut of meat for hours. The beer helps break down the meat and makes it even more flavorful and tender. Plus, you get to drink what you don't use! This recipe requires overnight preparation and is best served alongside cooked carrots, potatoes, and, of course, cabbage. Have good mustard and rye bread on hand for sandwiches.

1 (3-pound) piece packaged corned beef, with spice packet included

24 ounces dry Irish stout, such as Oud Dublin Dry Irish Stout from Village Idiot Brewing Company

1 large onion, peeled and quartered

Makes 8 servings

1. Rinse the corned beef well under cold water and pat dry. Place the corned beef in a large pot and pour in the beer; it should cover the meat. Add the pickling spice packet. Cover and let marinate in the refrigerator for 8 hours or overnight.

2. Remove the meat from the refrigerator about 2 hours before cooking time. When you're ready to cook, put the corned beef in a pressure cooker and add the onion. Discard the beer.

3. Cook, following the manufacturer's directions for your pressure cooker. Cooking times are generally based on weight, and a 3-pound cut should take about 45 minutes.

4. After the cooking time has elapsed and the cooker has depressurized, remove the corned beef. Let it rest for at least 10 minutes, then slice across the grain into serving pieces.

Whey-Fed Pork Chops
with Berry-Mustard Sauce

Taking advantage of farm-fresh ingredients — from the meat to the sauces — this terrific pork dish is one you won't soon forget. The piquant berry-mustard sauce is a beautiful complement to the sweetly succulent whey-fed chops. For the berry preserves, Cherry Grove suggests the product made by Eat This of Bucks County, Pennsylvania. *Read about Cherry Grove Farm on page 133.*

¼ cup tart, chunky blackberry or black currant preserves

1½ tablespoons Dijon mustard

6 center-cut whey-fed pork chops (like the ones produced at Cherry Grove Farm)

Salt and freshly ground black pepper

⅓ cup white wine vinegar

Makes 6 servings

1. Mix the preserves and mustard together in a small bowl.

2. Warm a nonstick skillet just large enough to hold the chops comfortably over medium-high heat. Add the chops and brown lightly on both sides, about 2 minutes per side. Season with salt and pepper to taste, then spoon the mustard mixture evenly over the chops.

3. Cover the skillet, reduce the heat to medium, and cook for 20 minutes, or until the chops are cooked through (the internal temperature should reach 160°F). Transfer the chops to a platter and keep warm.

4. Skim off any excess fat from the pan juices in the skillet. Stir in the vinegar and bring to a boil over medium-high heat, stirring and scraping up any browned bits from the bottom of the pan. Simmer until the sauce is reduced by about one-third, about 10 minutes. Then pour the sauce over the chops and serve.

Recipe from THE INN AT FERNBROOK FARMS, BORDENTOWN

Poached Chicken Meatballs in Pesto Cream

Chicken meatballs in pesto may sound almost too simple . . . there is, after all, only a handful of ingredients. But it's the care and attention they receive during cooking that makes them great, says chef Christine Wendland. Infused with fresh oregano and bathed in creamy pesto with demiglace, these meatballs are pillowy, succulent bites of chicken.

1 pound ground chicken

1 egg

½ cup stale breadcrumbs or panko

¼ cup chopped fresh oregano
  or marjoram

½ small onion, finely minced

1 garlic clove, finely minced

1 teaspoon salt

½ teaspoon freshly ground pepper

2 quarts chicken stock,
  preferably homemade

1 tablespoon olive oil

1½ cups heavy cream

½ cup basil pesto,
  preferably homemade

Makes 4 servings

1. With a gentle hand, combine the chicken, egg, breadcrumbs, oregano, onion, garlic, salt, and pepper, and mix until well combined. Keep chilled until ready to use.

2. Pour the stock into a large saucepan and bring to a rolling boil, then reduce to a low simmer.

3. With wet hands, form the chicken mixture into 1-inch meatballs, pressing and rolling them gently into shape (over-handling will compress the meat too much; the meatballs should be very soft).

4. Heat a cast-iron skillet over medium-high heat; swirl the oil over the skillet. Fill the skillet with meatballs, leaving at least ½ inch between them. You'll probably have to brown them in batches. Sear to golden brown on one side, about 1 minute, then roll around and sear another side. As soon as they are nicely colored all over, drop them into the simmering stock (they will still be raw inside).

5. Poach for about 4 minutes, then check a ball for doneness; if it is cooked through, there will be no trace of pink and it will be very juicy and tender. Transfer the cooked meatballs to a bowl to hold them. Repeat the browning and poaching with the remaining meatballs.

6. Meanwhile, bring the cream to a simmer in a small saucepan. Let simmer until it is reduced by half, about 10 minutes.

7. When all the meatballs are finished, bring the stock to a rapid boil and reduce until it becomes thick and syrupy, about 10 minutes. Stir the pesto into the reduced cream and season to taste with salt and white pepper. Pour over the meatballs and toss to coat. Drizzle with the reduced chicken stock. Serve at once.

THE INN AT FERNBROOK FARMS

The Kuser family has owned Fernbrook Farms since 1890, and has remained committed to its tranquil setting and the importance of sustainable environmental stewardship. The sprawling property actually houses several businesses. There is the inn, which dates back to 1752, and is used as an events space for parties, weddings, and more. Outfitted with a kitchen that relies on sustainable and local fare, the inn also hosts a dinner every other Thursday, with a menu announced only after those with reservations have arrived. There is also a community supported agriculture (CSA) component. There is a plant nursery that specializes in indigenous Jersey plants, and a summer camp for kids focusing on nature, food, and sustainability. Coming to the farm is like being transported to a different era far from the bustle of the rest of the state. In the words of a longtime visitor: "It's magical."

Firehouse Chicken

The familiar flavors of Lipton onion soup make this easy-to-prepare dinner a popular choice at firehouses, where the foil-wrapped chicken stays moist and tender even if the firefighters are called away suddenly. Serve with a side of garlic mashed potatoes and green beans and you have yourself a meal.

8 bone-in, skinless chicken breasts

1 (1-ounce) package Lipton onion soup mix

4 tablespoons butter

Makes 8 servings

1. Preheat the oven to 375°F. Pat the chicken dry with paper towels.

2. Pour the contents of the soup mix into a bowl. Press each chicken breast into the soup mixture, coating the chicken on all sides.

3. Place each breast in a piece of aluminum foil, top with ½ tablespoon butter, and wrap tightly. Set the packets on a baking sheet.

4. Bake for 45 minutes, or until the chicken reaches an internal temperature of 165°F. Unwrap and serve immediately.

Recipe from VILLAGE IDIOT BREWING COMPANY, MOUNT HOLLY

Beer-Braised Sausage and Peppers

Making sausage and peppers is a lot like making chili. You can follow the recipe and be rewarded with a delicious pot of food. Or you can start with the basic recipe and take off from there. You can cut the pepper and onions into strips, or chunks, or diced morsels. Use any kind of sausage that tickles your fancy. Spice it how you wish. Add tomato paste or crushed tomatoes if that's your heart's desire. Serve as a dish on its own, or get good sub rolls for sandwiches. Sausage and peppers are delicious no matter what you do.

¼ cup extra-virgin olive oil

2 large onions, sliced into strips

4 bell peppers, seeded and sliced

7 garlic cloves, chopped

2 pounds sausage, hot or sweet

1 (12-ounce) bottle blonde ale or rye beer

Makes 6–8 servings

1. Heat the oil in a large Dutch oven over medium heat; when shimmering, add the onions, peppers, and garlic. Cook until soft, 5 to 7 minutes. Remove the vegetables from the pot and set aside.

2. Raise the heat to high and add the sausage to the pot. Brown on all sides, about 6 minutes total. Return the vegetables to the pot, add the ale, and bring to a simmer; cook until the liquid has nearly evaporated, 20 minutes.

3. Serve immediately, or store in the refrigerator overnight to allow the flavors to deepen; reheat before serving.

Vegetarian Stuffed Peppers

Many recipes for stuffed peppers call for cutting off the tops, boiling the peppers, then packing them like cups. But slicing the peppers in half prevents the pepper from toppling over while it's cooking in the oven, and it allows for easier eating. And skipping the boiling step means that the peppers maintain some texture, rather than becoming mushy.

1 cup cooked quinoa, at room temperature

1 red onion, finely diced

1 zucchini, diced

12 ounces feta cheese

1 (14½-ounce) can diced tomatoes, juice reserved

Salt and freshly ground black pepper

4 bell peppers, halved lengthwise and seeded

Makes 4–6 servings

1. Preheat the oven to 400°F.

2. Combine the quinoa, onion, zucchini, and three-quarters of the feta in a bowl. Mix in the tomatoes and season with salt and pepper to taste.

3. Pour 1 cup water and the reserved tomato juice into a baking dish. Pack the pepper halves with the filling and set in the dish. Bake for 40 minutes, then scatter the remaining feta over the peppers and bake for 10 minutes longer. Serve hot.

Grilled Venison Sausage Hash
with Cider Jus

During certain times of the year — especially early autumn through midwinter, during hunting season — it's not hard to find fresh venison at specialty meat shops, or from a neighbor willing to share a fresh harvest. This recipe makes for a flavorful dinner, sure, but it's also a hearty breakfast. Serve alongside grilled asparagus with a spritz of fresh lemon to round out the meal.

THE SPICE RUB

- 2 tablespoons brown sugar
- 1 tablespoon salt
- 2 teaspoons freshly ground black pepper
- 1 teaspoon unsweetened cocoa powder
- 1 teaspoon dry mustard
- 1 teaspoon onion powder
- ½ teaspoon cayenne pepper
- ½ teaspoon garlic powder
- ½ teaspoon ground coriander

THE HASH

- ½ pound loose venison sausage
- 3 tablespoons salt
- 1 tablespoon cider vinegar
- 3 cups diced Yukon Gold potatoes (about 4 potatoes)
- 2 tablespoons butter
- 1½ cups diced red onion
- 4 sprigs fresh thyme, minced
- 1 sprig fresh rosemary, minced
- Salt and freshly ground black pepper
- 1½ cups diced tart apple such as Granny Smith
- 2 jalapeños, seeded and diced
- 12 ounces NJ-made Twisted Limb Original Hard Cider, or a similar dry hard cider

Makes 4–6 servings

1. Make the spice rub: Combine the sugar, salt, pepper, cocoa, mustard, onion powder, cayenne, garlic powder, and coriander in a small bowl and whisk together. Reserve 1 tablespoon of the rub for the final step, and rub the rest of it thoroughly over the sausage. Let sit for at least 1 hour and up to overnight, refrigerated.

2. Combine 2 quarts of water with the salt and vinegar in a large pot and bring to a boil. Add the potatoes and cook for 5 minutes; drain.

3. Preheat the oven to 425°F.

4. Put the sausage in a cast-iron skillet over medium-low heat. Cook until the fat is rendered, 10 to 15 minutes. Add the butter and increase the heat to medium; stir in the onion, and then add the blanched potatoes, along with the thyme, rosemary, and salt and pepper to taste. Sauté over medium-high heat for 5 minutes. Stir in the apples and jalapeños.

5. Transfer the skillet to the oven. Roast for 15 minutes, then remove from the oven, stir things up, and continue to roast for about 30 minutes, or until the potatoes start to brown and turn crisp.

6. Transfer the hash to a serving platter. Return the skillet to the stove and add the cider and the reserved spice rub. Cook over medium-high heat until reduced by one-third. Pour the cider reduction over the hash and serve hot.

Recipe from HAINES PORK SHOP, MICKLETON

Baked Ham with Bourbon Glaze

This is a feast for a large family. Fresh ham from the farm and a generous dash of that ol' brown spirit is the right meal for holiday gatherings. Smoked ham tastes best for this recipe; a good local butcher can provide the right cut. *Read about the Haines Pork Shop on page 151.*

1 cup honey

½ cup molasses

¼ cup orange juice

½ cup bourbon (or substitute more orange juice if you like)

2 tablespoons Dijon mustard

1 (6- to 8-pound) smoked fresh ham

Makes 12–14 servings

1. Place a rack in the lower third of the oven and preheat the oven to 325°F. Lightly grease a large roasting pan.

2. Combine the honey and molasses in a microwave-safe mixing bowl. Warm in the microwave until the mixture is soft, 1 minute. Whisk to combine and then add the orange juice, bourbon, and mustard.

3. Place the ham in the prepared pan. Make ¼-inch-deep cuts in the ham in a diamond pattern. Generously rub the glaze over the ham. Bake on the lower rack for 1½ to 2 hours, basting every 15 minutes, or until a meat thermometer inserted into the thickest portion of the ham registers 140°F.

4. Transfer the ham to a serving platter. Transfer the drippings to a small saucepan and bring to a boil. Boil until the mixture thickens, 1 to 2 minutes; serve with slices of the ham.

Recipe from HAINES PORK SHOP, MICKLETON

Crown Roast of Pork

Golden brown on the outside, juicy and white on the inside, a roast pork is a great pleasure. When it's combined with a slightly sweet and very savory stuffing, all you need for a wonderful autumn meal are harvest vegetables. If you're unfamiliar with how to make a crown roast, this is a great opportunity to learn. Most butchers will prepare the roast in advance, when you place your order.

1 (5- to 6-pound) pork crown rib roast (about 12 to 16 ribs)

Salt and freshly ground black pepper

1 pound ground pork or mild sausage

9 slices raisin bread, cut into ½-inch cubes

1 teaspoon ground cinnamon

¾ teaspoon salt

½ teaspoon ground cardamom

¼ teaspoon ground allspice

20 ounces canned sliced apples, juices reserved

Makes 12–16 servings

1. Preheat the oven to 325°F.

2. Place the roast, bone tips up, on a rack in a shallow roasting pan. Season with salt and pepper. Make a ball of aluminum foil and put it in the cavity to hold everything open. Wrap the bone tips in foil. Roast for 2½ hours.

3. Cook the ground pork in a skillet over medium heat until browned, 5 to 7 minutes. Drain off any excess fat and stir in the bread cubes, cinnamon, salt, cardamon, allspice, and apples. Add the apple liquid and toss to moisten.

4. Remove the roast from the oven and discard the foil ball. Pack the stuffing loosely into the center of the roast and cover the whole thing with foil to prevent overbrowning. Bake for 1 hour, or until the internal temperature reaches 160°F.

5. Let rest for 15 to 20 minutes before slicing and serving.

HAINES PORK SHOP

There are businesses born out of necessity that turn into institutions. Such is the story of the Haines Pork Shop. Rachael Haines, a widow, began seasonally processing neighbors' hogs for additional income in the late 1800s. Soon her recipes for scrapple and sausages drew a following, and the customers began arriving in droves. Her son Jeremiah expanded the business into Philadelphia, and later generations expanded the shop to offer a variety of products, as well as local processing for farmers.

Today customers come from all over the area to stock up on fresh cuts of pork, expertly prepared in the cozy white clapboard garage-like building. Order early for holidays, or risk being left out of the flavorful cuts that will impress your guests and taste buds.

Recipe from HAINES PORK SHOP, MICKLETON

Pork Loin with Sausage Stuffing

Pork inside of pork. A meal for a crowd and perfect for holiday gatherings, this impressive entrée is assembled with a few humble ingredients and a delicious cut of meat. Serve with your favorite roasted potatoes and plenty of fresh vegetables for sides. *Read about the Haines Pork Shop on page 151.*

1 cup chopped onion

¼ pound loose sweet Italian sausage

½ cup soft fresh breadcrumbs

½ cup chopped fresh parsley

½ cup raisins

1½ teaspoons chopped fresh thyme

¼ teaspoon freshly ground black pepper

1 (2½- to 3-pound) boneless pork roast

¼ cup apricot preserves

Makes 8–10 servings

1. Preheat the oven to 325°F.

2. Combine the onion and sausage in a skillet and cook over medium heat until the sausage is browned and the onion is tender, 5 to 7 minutes. Drain any fat or liquid from the skillet and then add the breadcrumbs, parsley, raisins, thyme, and black pepper. Toss to combine and add 2 tablespoons water to moisten the breadcrumbs.

3. Transfer the stuffing to the pocket of the roast. Place the roast on a rack in a shallow roasting pan. Roast for 1 to 1¼ hours, or until the internal temperature nears 160°F.

4. While the roast is cooking, warm the preserves in a small saucepan over medium heat until melted. About 15 minutes before the roast is going to be done, brush the preserves over the outside of the roast.

5. When the roast reaches 160°F, remove it from the oven. Let it rest for 15 minutes before slicing.

Recipe from DIANE HENDERIKS

Black Bean and Quinoa Pilaf

Chef Diane Henderiks offers this healthy and flavorful spin on a Spanish classic. It's hearty enough to stand on its own as a filling vegetarian entrée. *Read about chef Diane Henderiks on page 109.*

1 tablespoon olive oil

2 cups chopped onion

1 cup chopped celery

4 garlic cloves, thinly sliced

1½ cups quinoa, rinsed

1 tablespoon chili powder

2 teaspoons ground cumin

1 teaspoon dry mustard

2 cups low-sodium chicken or vegetable broth

1 cup tomato sauce

1 cup diced tomatoes

1 cup cooked corn kernels

1 (14½-ounce) can black beans, drained and rinsed

3 scallions, thinly sliced

¼ cup chopped fresh cilantro

1 tablespoon freshly squeezed lime juice

1 tablespoon rice wine vinegar

Salt and freshly ground black pepper

Makes 6–8 servings

1. Heat the oil in a large saucepan over medium heat. Add the onion, celery, and garlic, and cook until tender, about 5 minutes. Add the quinoa, chili powder, cumin, and mustard. Cook and stir until the quinoa begins to brown lightly, about 1 minute. Add the broth and tomato sauce and bring to a boil; reduce the heat and simmer, covered, until the liquid is absorbed, about 20 minutes.

2. Combine the tomatoes, corn, black beans, scallions, cilantro, lime juice, and vinegar in a large bowl. Stir together, then slowly add the quinoa mixture and gently fold everything together until fully combined. Season to taste with salt and pepper and serve.

6

Sandwiches, Sauces, and Spreads

Jerseyans know that you can take anything, put it between two slices of bread, and instantly make it better. But for a sandwich to be truly great, it needs the right topping. Whether you like yours hot or cold, in a wrap or on a roll, pita, or toast, get these into your hands and into your belly.

New Jersey Sloppy Joe

In certain parts of the Garden State, the term "sloppy Joe" does not refer to the sandwich made with ground beef and tomato sauce but, instead, a deli classic: a double-decker sandwich that combines two meats (usually beef tongue and oven-roasted turkey), Swiss cheese, coleslaw, and Russian dressing on rye bread. This recipe pays homage to the Town Hall Deli in South Orange, which claims to be the originator of the sandwich in this form. While some sandwiches benefit from haphazard, pile-it-on construction, with a Jersey sloppy Joe, uniformity and proper layering are key to keep it from falling apart. Use coleslaw and Russian dressing to taste, but a thin layer of each is really all you need.

3 (½-inch thick) slices fresh rye bread, crusts removed, cut lengthwise from a whole 9-inch loaf

6 thin slices Swiss cheese

4 ounces coleslaw

Russian dressing (see page 170)

4 thin slices beef tongue, corned beef, or pastrami, trimmed to fit the bread

4 thin slices oven-roasted turkey breast, trimmed to fit the bread

Serves 2–4

1. Lay three slices of cheese on one slice of bread and top with coleslaw, then Russian dressing, then tongue. Lay a second slice of rye bread over the tongue. Again, lay down three slices cheese, coleslaw, and Russian dressing, followed by the turkey. Top with the third slice of bread.

2. Slice the sandwich into three equal sections and then halve those sections lengthwise, creating six equal pieces.

Recipe from UNIONVILLE VINEYARDS, RINGOES

Marinated Eggplant Sandwich
with Soppressata and Mozzarella

Inspired by picnics in Italy, chef Emily Rogalsky created this simple yet flavorful sandwich to be enjoyed closer to home. She suggests that if you're taking these on a picnic of your own, wrap the sandwiches in butcher paper to avoid soggy bread. Then head out and find that perfect maple tree to sit under and enjoy.

2 sandwich rolls

1 tablespoon olive oil

4 ounces thinly sliced soppressata

6 slices fresh mozzarella

1 (8-ounce) jar marinated eggplant, drained, patted dry, and halved

1 (8-ounce) jar roasted red peppers, drained, patted dry, and halved

1 cup arugula

2 tablespoons balsamic vinegar

Makes 2 sandwiches

1. Preheat the oven to 350°F.

2. Cut the rolls in half and lightly drizzle with the oil. Bake on a small baking sheet for about 8 minutes, or until lightly toasted.

3. On the bottom half of each roll, layer half the soppressata, mozzarella, eggplant, red peppers, and arugula. Drizzle vinegar on the other half of the rolls. Place the two sides together and cut in half. Enjoy!

Tomato Sandwich

Simplicity between two slices of bread. During peak tomato season — July to September — I'll make these several times a week and never get palate fatigue. They're easy and delicious. Be sure to eat this sandwich quickly, while the bread is still warm and has a bit of crunch.

1 tablespoon mayonnaise

2 slices white sandwich bread, toasted

4 slices ripe heirloom tomato

¼ teaspoon kosher salt

Makes 1 sandwich

Spread mayonnaise on both slices of the toast. Place the tomato on one slice of bread and sprinkle with salt. Top with the second slice of bread. Cut diagonally and serve.

French Onion Sliders

Taking two favorite pub classics and mashing them into one, this recipe by Bob Leahy of the Outslider food truck calls for caramelized onions, which bring a rich, deep flavor to the sliders.

2 tablespoons butter

3 cups chopped Spanish onion

2 garlic cloves, chopped

2 cups sherry

½ cup beef stock

2 tablespoons finely chopped fresh parsley

1 teaspoon freshly ground black pepper

⅓ cup grated Parmesan cheese

10 slider-size burgers (approximately 1 ounce each)

10 slices provolone cheese

10 slider-size rolls

Ketchup (optional)

Makes 10 sliders

1. Melt the butter in a saucepan over medium heat. Add the onions and garlic and sauté, stirring often, until the onions caramelize and turn a deep brown, about 15 minutes. Turn down the heat if they're browning too fast.

2. Add the sherry and stock and cook down until the liquids are almost evaporated, 20 to 30 minutes. Add the parsley and pepper. Remove from the heat and stir in the Parmesan.

3. Prepare a hot fire in a gas or charcoal grill or heat a grill pan or skillet over high heat. Season the burgers with salt and pepper to taste. Cook the burgers for about 2 minutes on each side, or until you reach your preferred doneness. Top each burger with a slice of provolone and a spoonful of the onion mixture.

4. Place each burger on a bun, top with ketchup, if using, and serve.

THE OUTSLIDER. Following the devastation of Hurricane Sandy in 2012, Bob Leahy lost his job and was looking for a new inspiration. He found it in the form of a food truck, which he named the Outslider. It specializes in — you guessed it — sliders. While seemingly simple to make, Leahy's sliders go beyond just meat in a bun, with toppings — like blue cheese, bacon, Old Bay seasoning — that have evolved past lettuce and tomato. After operating the truck for several years, he opened up a restaurant attached to the well-known Olde Queens Tavern in New Brunswick, establishing a permanent location for his tiny creations.

The Fat Darrell

It was born from the famous grease trucks of Rutgers University in New Brunswick, and there is only one right time to eat this sandwich: after midnight, after a few rounds. Created by then student, now entrepreneur Darrell W. Butler, this is a crammed combination of frozen foods, fresh produce, and good marinara sauce (like the weeknight pasta sauce on page 196). This recipe makes one sandwich but can be easily scaled up for the buddies that came home with you from the bar. It's easy to assemble, and no joke, this sandwich name is trademarked.

1 (8-inch) sub roll

2 chicken fingers, cooked according to package instructions

2 mozzarella sticks, cooked according to package instructions

¼ cup marinara sauce

1 cup French fries, cooked according to package instructions

½ cup shredded lettuce

2 or 3 tomato slices

Makes 1 sandwich

Slice open the roll, but do not cut all the way through. Place the chicken fingers and mozzarella sticks inside. Cover with marinara sauce and top with French fries, tightly packing them into the sandwich. Top with lettuce and tomato. Serve immediately.

The Happy Waitress

The ubiquitous diner classic, this open-faced grilled cheese sandwich is easy to make at home. After mastering the basic model, try adding your own toppings, like sliced green onions, or experimenting with different cheeses. Honey mustard as a dipping sauce is a particular favorite of mine. This open-faced version is a diner staple using bacon and tomato. A side of fries is optional, but recommended.

2 tablespoons butter

2 slices white bread

6 strips bacon, cooked

4 slices American cheese

4 thin slices tomato

Salt and freshly ground black pepper

Makes 2 sandwiches

1. Melt the butter in a medium skillet over medium heat. Place both slices of the bread into the pan and immediately top each slice with bacon, cheese, and tomato, dividing each ingredient between the slices. Cook until the cheese is melted and the bread is crispy on the bottom, about 4 minutes.

2. Carefully remove the cheesy bread with a spatula and serve immediately.

Ripper Dog and Jersey Relish

Everyone has their preferred way of cooking a hot dog. Some like the boiled or steamed ballpark variety, others like them to a varying degree of doneness on the grill. Here in Jersey, we deep-fry them. A quality frankfurter — beef or pork — will have a tough casing that withstands the hot oil, to a point; the dogs are done when they rip open, hence the nickname "rippers." Served on a bun, with a heaping of Jersey-style relish, these dogs require only a side of onion rings or fries.

3 large cucumbers,
   roughly chopped

1 red bell pepper, roughly chopped

1 summer squash, roughly chopped

1 white onion, roughly chopped

4 garlic cloves

¼ cup apple cider vinegar

¼ cup prepared yellow mustard

1 tablespoon sugar

½ teaspoon mustard seed

½ teaspoon ground turmeric

   Kosher salt

   Oil, for frying

12 premium hot dogs (beef or pork),
   preferably from a local butcher

12 buns

Makes 12 servings, with some extra relish

1. Combine the cucumber, bell pepper, squash, onion, and garlic in the bowl of a food processor. Add the vinegar, mustard, sugar, mustard seed, turmeric, and salt to taste. Pulse until you have a finely chopped mixture, with the vegetables retaining some shape.

2. Transfer the relish to a saucepan and bring to a boil over medium-high heat. Reduce to a simmer and cook, partially covered, for 30 minutes, stirring frequently to prevent burning. Let cool in the pan, then strain the relish through a fine-mesh strainer to remove excess liquid. Refrigerate for at least 4 hours before serving. (The relish will keep for up to a week in the refrigerator.)

3. To prepare the hot dogs, heat 3 inches of the oil in a deep cast-iron pot or Dutch oven to 375°F. Working in batches if necessary, fry the hot dogs until the skin rips open, 3 to 4 minutes. Cook longer if you prefer a more done dog.

4. Remove the dogs from the oil, drain on paper towels, and place in buns. Top with relish and serve.

Recipe from THE FARM COOKING SCHOOL, STOCKTON

Country Wheat Bread

You'll need a grain mill to complete this recipe. Chef Ian Knauer explains: "You can find them freestanding, but I got an attachment to my stand mixer. I ground the grain as finely as I could and found that the aroma of the freshly ground grain was already leaps and bounds greater than any flour I could purchase. The resulting bread is practically a meal all by itself. It has a nutty flavor and a tight crumb. It's just the kind of bread I like to eat every day."

1 cup hard red wheat berries

1½ cups organic all-purpose flour

½ ounce fresh yeast, crumbled, or ¼ ounce active dry yeast

1½–1¾ cups warm water (about 110°F)

1 tablespoon kosher salt

Makes 1 loaf

1. Grind the wheat berries on the finest setting of the grain mill. Combine the resulting flour with the all-purpose flour, yeast, and 1½ cups of the water in a stand mixer fitted with a dough hook. Mix on low speed until combined. Add the remaining ¼ cup water if the dough seems dry and shaggy. Let the mixture sit at room temperature for 30 minutes.

2. Add the salt and mix the dough on high speed for 10 minutes. Transfer the dough to a floured work surface and form into a ball by pulling the edges of the dough up and into the center of the round, pressing down.

3. Place the dough, seam side down, into a floured bowl. Cover the bowl with plastic wrap and let rise at warm room temperature until it is doubled in size, about 2 hours.

4. Transfer the dough back to your floured work surface and form again into a ball as in step 2, and press down. Place the dough, seam side down, back into the floured bowl. Cover with plastic wrap and let rise at warm room temperature until it is doubled in size again, about 1 hour.

5. Preheat the oven to 450°F. Place a medium-size heavy pot or Dutch oven and its lid in the oven.

6. When the oven and the pot are hot, pour the dough into the pot and immediately cover with the lid. Bake until the loaf is set, about 30 minutes.

7. Uncover the pot and continue to bake until the loaf is browned, about 20 minutes longer. Remove the bread from the pot and let cool completely before slicing.

Recipe from VILLAGE IDIOT BREWING COMPANY, MOUNT HOLLY

Spent-Grain Bread Rolls

This recipe is easiest to prepare with a bread machine or a mixer with a dough hook. If you prefer more malt flavor, replace half or more of the water with a blonde ale, like the Bridgetown Blonde from Village Idiot Brewing Company. This dough can also be used for making pizza crust; just form the split dough into large rounds after the second rising.

3 cups unbleached all-purpose flour

¼ cup spent brewing grain (see note)

1 tablespoon plus ⅛ teaspoon salt

1 tablespoon sugar

2½ teaspoons active dry yeast

1 cup warm water (about 110°F)

2 tablespoons olive oil

1 egg white

1 tablespoon water

Makes a dozen rolls

1. Combine the flour, spent grain, 1 tablespoon salt, sugar, and yeast in a stand mixer fitted with a dough hook. With the mixer going at slow speed, slowly add the water. Work for 3 to 4 minutes. The dough should form an elastic yet smooth, thick ball. If it's too wet, sprinkle on more flour; if it's too dry, add water 1 tablespoon at a time. When the dough seems right, add the oil and knead for 2 minutes.

2. Place the dough in a lightly oiled bowl, cover, and set in a warm place to rise until it has doubled in size, roughly 15 minutes to an hour. Punch down the dough and split into two pieces. Place each piece in its own lightly oiled bowl, cover, and let rise until doubled in size, about 1 hour. At this point the dough is ready for immediate use.

3. Form the dough into 2- to 3-inch balls; you should get about 10 to 12 buns.

4. Preheat the oven to 400°F. Prepare an egg wash by mixing together the egg white, water, and remaining ⅛ teaspoon salt in a small bowl.

5. Place the buns on a parchment-lined baking sheet or silicone baking sheet. Brush with the egg wash. Bake for 15 minutes, or until golden brown. Allow to cool slightly before serving.

NOTE: Spent grain is the grain that brewers use to make beer. It adds a chewy, nutty consistency to the dough. Sourcing spent grain is not hard — ask a homebrewer friend, or call your local brewery and ask if they have any to spare.

THE FARM COOKING SCHOOL

Ian Knauer never wanted to run a restaurant. Once an avid home cook who found success with *Gourmet* magazine, a cookbook (*The Farm: Rustic Recipes for a Year of Incredible Food*), and a television show (*The Farm*, on PBS and Hulu), Knauer wanted to connect with like-minded food enthusiasts and pass on his own knowledge, while continuing to learn himself. So he founded the Farm Cooking School, a culinary work space on a working farm, where food enthusiasts of all stripes can gather to learn kitchen confidence.

"It's about opening the cabinets and cooking with what you have on hand, without worrying about a recipe or technique," he says. "A lot of students here want to become better cooks, but not necessarily do it for a living, just to have confidence in the kitchen. I want to help them build that."

From the working farm in Stockton Township, Knauer has an interesting vantage point for where the country is, food-wise. "We're living in the greatest time for American food culture," he says. "Some of that has to do with TV and magazines, but they were always there, so they could be a reaction to the trend. I think the understanding of where food comes from, and provenance, has stoked interest in food in the last 10 years. It's a fun and exciting time."

Ian Knauer

Russian Dressing

It's become common for the general public to be duped when they order salad dressing at restaurants. The culprit? Fake Russian dressing. People across America request Russian and are actually served Thousand Island. While many will have you believe that Russian and Thousand Island are one and the same, they are not. Russian dressing has a decisive spicy kick — lacking in Thousand Island — thanks to the addition of horseradish and fresh garlic.

Though Russian dressing was invented in New Hampshire (which you'd never guess from the name), it is popular on salads and sandwiches across the nation, not excepting New Jersey. It is essential, in fact, for the New Jersey Sloppy Joe (see page 156). There are many variations that call for chives, hot sauce, granulated onion, and more, but the recipe below is a solid start. Master this and then begin experimenting.

½ cup ketchup

½ cup mayonnaise

2 tablespoons finely chopped pickle or pickle relish

1 tablespoon prepared horseradish, patted dry

1 teaspoon paprika

1 garlic clove, finely grated

Makes 1 cup

Combine the ketchup, mayonnaise, pickle, horseradish, paprika, and garlic in a bowl or food processor and blend until everything is fully incorporated. Transfer to an airtight container and refrigerate for at least 2 hours before using. Leftover dressing will keep for up to 3 days in the refrigerator.

Recipe from MORE THAN Q, STOCKTON

MTQ BBQ Rub

Certain parts of the country do BBQ their own way. Since we don't have our own tradition here in Jersey, we're able to borrow from other parts of the country to suit our taste. Here's a rub — similar to rubs used in Kansas City — from Matt Martin of More Than Q that combines a little bit of sweet and a little bit of heat. Rub this on your ribs before putting them in the smoker or on the grill.

½ cup firmly packed dark
    brown sugar
¼ cup dark chili powder
¼ cup granulated garlic
¼ cup paprika
2 tablespoons granulated onion
2 tablespoons cayenne pepper
2 tablespoons ground cumin
2 tablespoons freshly ground
    black pepper
1 tablespoon kosher salt

Makes about 2 cups

Combine the sugar, chili powder, garlic, paprika, onion, cayenne, cumin, black pepper, and salt in a mixing bowl and whisk together. Store in an airtight container in a cool place, where the rub will keep for up to 4 months. Apply to ribs or other barbecue meats at least 4 hours and up to overnight before cooking.

Meat Marinade

Easy to prepare, this marinade is packed with flavors that will complement a fine cut of beef, lamb, or pork. The sugars in this sauce make it work. When the meat goes onto the grill, the sugars will caramelize just enough to add a bit of extra crust to the outside of the meat.

¾ cup cold coffee
2 tablespoons light soy sauce
2 tablespoons light brown sugar
1 garlic clove, minced
½ teaspoon kosher salt
1 teaspoon freshly ground black
    pepper
1½ pounds beef, lamb, or pork

Makes ¾ cup

1. Combine the coffee, soy sauce, sugar, garlic, salt, and pepper in a small bowl. Whisk until the sugar is completely dissolved.

2. Place the meat in an airtight container and pour the marinade on top. Cover and refrigerate for at least 2 hours or overnight before cooking.

Recipe from LANGOSTA LOUNGE, ASBURY PARK

Sweet and Sour Cucumber Dipping Sauce

This sauce is more proof of the versatility of the humble cucumber and its ability to absorb and enhance the ingredients it's paired with. This recipe comes from chef Marilyn Schlossbach and is a great complement to the Thai Fish Cakes on page 192.

1 small cucumber, very finely diced

1 small carrot, very finely diced

1 small onion, very finely chopped

2 red chiles or jalapeños, thinly sliced (optional)

4 ounces sugar

¼ cup white wine vinegar

4½ teaspoons water

2 teaspoons Thai fish sauce (nam pla)

1 tablespoon finely chopped peanuts

Makes about 2 cups

1. Combine the cucumber, carrot, onion, and chiles, if using, in a medium bowl and toss to mix. In a separate small bowl, whisk together the sugar, vinegar, water, and fish sauce. Pour over the cucumber mixture, mix well, and let sit for 20 minutes to allow the flavors to meld.

2. Garnish with the peanuts shortly before serving.

LANGOSTA LOUNGE

Marilyn Schlossbach comes from a creative family, but it wasn't until she was a young server at her brother's shore restaurant, on the day the chef failed to show up, that she found her calling. Familiar with the dishes and how they should look, she rolled up her sleves, went into the kitchen, and started cooking for guests. By the time the evening came to a close, she had found her intended career path. Now she is at the helm of a thriving group of restaurants that includes the Langosta Lounge, Labrador Lounge in Normandy Beach, and Pop's Garage, a Mexican restaurant in Asbury Park. There's also a café, a specialty goods shop, and a 20-acre Monmouth county farm that grows much of the produce used in the restaurants.

Langosta Lounge focuses on what Schlossbach calls "vacation cuisine," and the menu changes with each season so that it can focus on in-season ingredients. The beer, wine, and cocktail program also changes with the season.

Things had been going well for Schlossbach and her team until Hurricane Sandy in 2012 "trashed" them, forcing her to reevaluate where things were headed. She worked on and revealed a mission statement for all the businesses: "To share a plate of adventure, hospitality, and ebullience while enriching our local and global community." She also took the opportunity to form a 501(c) 3 called Food for Thought by the Sea, which helps youth through philanthropic endeavors.

Steak Sauce

A staple of fine steak houses throughout the state, this isn't the brown tangy sauce commonly found in bottles: this is slightly sweet and tomato based, with just the right amount of spice. It is best when made fresh and served quickly. At Barcade they put this atop a cold steak sandwich with thick tomato and white onion slices. Pair it with your favorite cut of red meat, however you like it.

1 tablespoon oil

6 shallots, minced

2 garlic cloves, minced

3 (6-ounce) cans tomato paste

3 (5½-ounce) cans tomato juice (about 2 cups)

1¼ cups Worcestershire sauce

1 cup brown sugar

¼ cup molasses

1½ cups grated horseradish

1½ cups ketchup

¼ cup red wine vinegar

1 tablespoon Tabasco sauce

Freshly ground black pepper

Makes about 3 cups

1. Warm the oil in a saucepan over medium heat. Add the shallots and garlic and cook, stirring occasionally, until soft and translucent, about 5 minutes. Add the tomato paste and cook for 5 minutes, stirring frequently.

2. Add the tomato juice and half of the Worcestershire and bring to a simmer. Let simmer for 5 minutes, stirring frequently. Whisk in the sugar and molasses, followed by the horseradish, ketchup, vinegar, Tabasco, the remaining Worcestershire, and pepper to taste. Simmer for 20 minutes, whisking occasionally.

3. Serve warm. Store leftovers in a tightly sealed container in the refrigerator, where they will keep for up to 2 weeks.

BARCADE. Beer and video games? Yes, please. Barcade is a bar for adults who love craft beer but are still kids at heart. Jersey City was the second location for cofounders Paul Kermizian and Kevin Beard, following a successful (and continuing) run in Brooklyn. A Philadelphia location is also in the mix, along with two locations in Manhattan. Featuring nearly 25 taps of nothing but American craft brews and old-school video games like Tapper, Ms. Pac-Man, Double Dragon, Mappy, Burger Time, and about 35 others (for just 25 cents per play), the bar has become a popular neighborhood hangout.

Steak sauce with cold roast beef sandwich

7

The Melting Pot

New York may have the Statue of Liberty, but Ellis Island is in Jersey. We were the country's entryway for scores of immigrants. Today Jerseyans of all stripes continue to celebrate our different ethnic heritages. From Italian to Irish, Cuban, Korean, Ukrainian, Polish, Chinese, Caribbean, Greek, Turkish, Indian, Mexican, Canadian, and every other conceivable background, New Jersey is the true melting pot. The recipes here are a reflection of the incredible diversity that permeates every corner of the state.

Ukrainian Holubtsi (Stuffed Cabbage Rolls)

Steaming and savory with just a touch of sweetness — impress your guests and yourself with this relatively-easy-but-looks-complicated traditional Ukrainian dish. The recipe comes from the kitchen of Daria Romankow of Berkeley Heights, who suggests that you use long-grain rice to ensure that it sticks properly to the meat during cooking. The cabbage rolls taste best when made a day in advance and reheated, allowing the flavors to infuse each other.

1 cup long-grain rice

2 tablespoons distilled white vinegar

2 small to medium heads cabbage, halved and cored

4 tablespoons salted butter

1 large onion, diced

2 pounds 80–85% lean ground beef

1 egg, lightly beaten

Salt and freshly ground black pepper

2 (28-ounce) cans crushed tomatoes

2 tablespoons brown sugar

Makes 6–8 servings

1. Prepare the rice according to the package instructions and let cool to room temperature.

2. Fill a large pot with water and bring to a boil over high heat. Add the vinegar. Add 2 halves of the cabbage to the pot and cook until softened, about 8 minutes. As the leaves soften, remove them from the water and drain, saving the first few large outer layers to line a casserole dish. Return water to a boil, add remaining 2 halves of the cabbage, and repeat the process.

3. Melt the butter in a skillet over medium heat. Add the onion and cook until translucent, 4 to 6 minutes.

4. Combine the ground beef, cooked rice, sautéed onion, and egg in a bowl. Season generously with salt and pepper and mix well.

5. To prepare the cabbage rolls, lay a cabbage leaf on a cutting board. Top with about ¼ cup of the meat mixture (depending on the size of the leaf). Roll up from the bottom a bit, flip the sides inward, and roll up the rest of the way to form the holubtsi. Do not overstuff; smaller rolls are just as tasty as big ones and easier to roll.

6. Preheat the oven to 350°F.

7. Line the bottom of a deep casserole dish or Dutch oven with the large cabbage leaves you set aside earlier. Spread a thin layer of crushed tomatoes on top of the leaves, followed by a sprinkling of the sugar. Set the finished cabbage rolls on top. When you've completely covered the bottom of the dish with a layer of cabbage rolls, top them with another layer of tomatoes and sugar, then set more cabbage rolls on top. Continue to layer in this fashion until you've used up all the cabbage and/or meat. Cover the top layer in the dish with tomatoes, a sprinkling of sugar, and any cabbage leaves you may have left over.

8. Cover the pot with a lid or aluminum foil. Bake for 3 to 3½ hours, until the sauce has thickened and the outer layers have developed a crust.

9. Let the holubtsi rest for at least 6 hours, and up to 1 day, before serving. Reheat by placing in a 350°F oven for 25 minutes.

Recipe from SEABRA'S MARISQUEIRA, NEWARK

Shrimp with Garlic Sauce

A staple at restaurants throughout the Ironbound section of Newark (an enclave for Central and South American cultures), this simple dish is big on flavor. It's quick to prepare and is always a crowd favorite. Make sure to have plenty of crusty Portuguese rolls on hand to sop up the sauce.

⅓ cup olive oil

4 garlic cloves, peeled and chopped

2 pounds large fresh shrimp, peeled and deveined

1¼ teaspoons salt

¼ teaspoon paprika

¼ cup dry white wine, preferably Portuguese

1 teaspoon hot pepper sauce (or to taste), preferably Red Devil brand

3 tablespoons chopped fresh parsley

Makes 4–6 servings

1. Heat the oil in a large skillet over medium heat. Add the garlic and cook, stirring occasionally, until lightly golden, 3 minutes.

2. Add the shrimp, salt, paprika, wine, and hot pepper sauce to the pan and stir to combine. Cook, stirring occasionally, until the shrimp are pink, 4 to 5 minutes. Transfer to a bowl, stir in the chopped parsley, and serve immediately.

SEABRA'S MARISQUEIRA. An institution in Newark's Ironbound section, Seabra's Marisqueira is part of a group of restaurants owned by the Seabra family. The Seabras have welcomed visitors from around the world to their traditional Portuguese restaurants. Established in 1989, Seabra's Marisqueira specializes in fresh seafood. To visit in person is to experience the vibrancy and true flavors of the Ironbound.

Recipe from THE FARM COOKING SCHOOL, STOCKTON

Dry Vegetarian Curry

There are many types of curries, and this recipe by Ian Knauer falls into the Karnataka category, from the southwest of India. This is a mostly dry curry that you scoop up with flatbread instead of slurping with a spoon. The vegetables are cooked with less liquid, and that liquid is allowed to evaporate, making for a more intensely spiced dish. This one-pot dinner has the kind of deep flavor that will get you through the brutal winters. *Read about the Farm Cooking School on page 168.*

¼ cup extra-virgin olive oil

1 large onion, chopped

1 head garlic, cloves separated, peeled, and sliced

2 tablespoons finely chopped fresh ginger

1 tablespoon black mustard seed

1 tablespoon coriander seed

1 tablespoon cumin seed

3 tablespoons harissa

4 cups puréed whole tomatoes in juice

2 cups water

1 pound carrots, sliced

1 pound potatoes, diced

½ pound turnips, diced

1 small head cabbage, cored and chopped

1 cup unsweetened dried coconut

2 teaspoons kosher salt

¾ teaspoon freshly ground black pepper

1 cup baby spinach

Makes 8 servings

1. Heat the oil in a large pot over medium-high heat. Add the onion, garlic, and ginger, and cook, stirring occasionally, until golden brown, about 8 minutes.

2. Stir in the mustard, coriander, and cumin seeds and cook, stirring, until the mustard seeds start to pop, about 2 minutes. Stir in the harissa and cook until fragrant, about 1 minute.

3. Stir in the tomatoes, water, carrots, potatoes, turnips, cabbage, coconut, salt, and pepper, and bring to a simmer. Simmer the curry, covered, until the vegetables are tender, about 20 minutes.

4. Uncover the pot and continue to simmer until most of the liquid has evaporated, about 15 minutes. Season with more salt and pepper to taste, then stir in the spinach and serve.

Tofu Tikka Masala

Even if you're largely unfamiliar with Indian cuisine, you're likely aware of tikka masala. Actually a British invention, it's a flavorful, creamy, spicy dish that usually comes with chicken (although other proteins are not uncommon). This recipe goes the vegetarian route by using tofu. Much like chili, it's hard to find one standard tikka masala recipe, so use this as a base and then add, subtract, or experiment over time and make this dish your own. Serve over a bed of rice and, if you're able to purchase or make, with fresh naan bread.

THE TOFU

1½ cups low-fat sour cream or whole milk yogurt

6 garlic cloves, grated

1 (1-inch) piece fresh ginger, peeled and grated

3 teaspoons garam masala

3 teaspoons ground turmeric

2 teaspoons ground coriander

1 (14-ounce) package extra-firm tofu, patted dry, cut into ½-inch slices, and dried again

2 tablespoons vegetable or peanut oil

THE SAUCE

1 small onion, finely diced

¼ teaspoon salt

¼ cup tomato paste

1 tablespoon ground cardamom

½ tablespoon red pepper flakes

1 (28-ounce) can diced tomatoes

1 cup light cream

2 cups Basmati rice

1 cup fresh peas (or frozen peas, defrosted)

Naan, for serving

Makes 6 servings

1. Combine the sour cream, garlic, ginger, garam masala, turmeric, and coriander in a large mixing bowl and whisk together until well mixed. Remove ½ cup of the mixture and set aside in the refrigerator.

2. Add the tofu to the mixing bowl and coat the pieces well with the sour creme mixture. Cover and refrigerate for 1 hour.

3. Preheat the oven to 200°F.

4. Heat 1 tablespoon of the oil in a large skillet over medium-high heat until shimmering. Remove the tofu from the sauce, shaking off any excess, and carefully add to the skillet. Cook until slightly crispy, about 3 minutes, then flip. Cook the other side until slightly crispy and cooked through, 3 minutes longer. Transfer the tofu to an oven-safe plate and place in the oven. Wipe down the skillet with paper towels to remove any residue.

5. To make the sauce, heat the remaining 1 tablespoon oil in the skillet over medium heat, and add the onion and salt. Cook, stirring often, until the onion becomes translucent, 2 minutes.

6. Add the tomato paste, cardamom, and pepper flakes and stir until the paste becomes browned and the spices are fragrant, about 3 minutes.

7. Add the diced tomatoes and cook for 10 minutes.

8. Add the cream and the ½ cup reserved sour creme mixture from step 1. Stir to combine. Bring to a simmer, then reduce the heat to medium-low. Cook for 30 minutes, stirring often.

9. Meanwhile, prepare the rice according to the package directions. Once cooked, add the peas to the rice and stir to combine.

10. Carefully remove the tofu from the oven and add to the sauce. Stir to combine. Place rice on each plate and top with Tofu Tikka Masala. Serve with naan.

Beef Empanadas

An empanada is a stuffed pastry typically filled with savory ingredients, though you will occasionally find sweet varieties. This is a recipe for traditional beef empanadas — firmly in the savory category — and it yields *a lot* of little pastries, so it's perfect for large parties. Serve with a side of white beans and rice and chimichurri sauce for dipping to round out the meal.

¼ cup extra-virgin olive oil

5 pounds 90% lean ground beef

10 garlic cloves, minced

2 stalks celery, diced

2 scallions, diced

1 green bell pepper, finely diced

1 red bell pepper, finely diced

1 Spanish onion, diced

1 jalapeño, diced

1 cup canned yams or sweet potato in light syrup, mashed

2 tomatoes, diced

1 cup minced fresh cilantro

3½ ounces chipotles in adobo sauce, minced

1 tablespoon freshly ground black pepper

1 tablespoon garlic powder

1 tablespoon ground cumin

1 tablespoon Spanish paprika

About 50 premade empanada shells

All-purpose flour, as needed

Vegetable oil, for frying

Makes about 50 empanadas

1. Heat the olive oil in a large skillet over medium heat. Add the beef and cook (working in batches if necessary) until no longer pink, 5 to 7 minutes. Drain the fat and transfer the meat to a large bowl to cool.

2. Return the skillet to the stovetop and add the garlic, celery, scallions, bell peppers, onion, and jalapeño, and cook for 5 minutes, stirring frequently. Add the yams, tomatoes, cilantro, chipotle, black pepper, garlic powder, cumin, and paprika, and cook for another 5 minutes, stirring often.

3. Transfer the vegetable mixture to the bowl with the beef and mix thoroughly. At this point you can pause in your preparations, if you like, and store the filling in the refrigerator, covered, for up to 1 day, or until you're ready to make the empanadas.

4. To prepare the empanadas, follow the preparatory instructions on the pastry packaging. Then, on a floured surface, lay out the shells. For each one, place 2 to 3 tablespoons of filling toward the edge on one side. Fold over the dough to create a half-circle and firmly crimp the edges with a fork or your fingers, ensuring the shell is closed.

5. Pour 4 inches of vegetable oil into a deep fryer or large cast-iron pot and heat to 375°F. Working in batches, fry the empanadas for about 5 minutes, until golden brown on the outside. Remove from the oil and transfer to a plate lined with paper towels to drain. Let rest for 1 minute before serving.

EMPANADA GUY

Carlos Serrano is living his dream. Though he worked in a number of different occupations, he has always been an avid home cook, specializing in empanadas. One day, while on the job, his then boss provided a spark of inspiration: what if Serrano took the Spanish-inspired dish he was so passionate about and sold them in the suburbs, the land of take-away pizza, Chinese food, and burgers? Surely, his boss said, he'd be welcomed with open arms.

Serrano agreed, soon made arrangements to get a food truck, and struck out on his own, making all kinds of empanadas and quickly gaining a loyal and growing following.

Now with a fleet of Empanada Guy trucks that traverse the state and a restaurant in Freehold, Serrano is able to bring the flavors and dishes he loves so much to more people than he ever imagined.

Recipe from VIET BISTRO, VINELAND

Chicken Lettuce Wraps with Avocado

Make this once and you'll be hooked. It is one of the most popular dishes prepared by chef Thuynhan Truong at her award-winning Viet Bistro. Better than anything you'll get from a chain restaurant, these lettuce wraps are bursting with flavor. They are also very easy to prepare.

SAUCE

4 tablespoons hoisin sauce

2 tablespoons sugar

2 tablespoons oyster sauce

2 teaspoons black soy sauce

½ teaspoon sesame oil

½ teaspoon white wine vinegar

WRAPS

1 pound boneless, skinless chicken breast

2 tablespoons olive oil

1 garlic clove, minced

½ cup chopped onion

⅓ cup chopped water chestnuts

¼ cup chopped scallions

¼ teaspoon freshly ground black pepper

¼ teaspoon ground fresh garlic

1 head iceberg lettuce

2 Haas avocados, finely chopped

Minced fresh cilantro (optional)

Sriracha hot sauce (optional)

Makes 4 servings

1. To make the sauce, combine the hoisin, sugar, oyster sauce, soy sauce, sesame oil, and white vinegar in a small bowl and mix well.

2. Place the chicken in a pot and cover with water. Bring to a boil over high heat then reduce heat to medium and cook until cooked through (165°F), 12 to 15 minutes. Remove the chicken from the water, allow to cool, and then finely chop.

3. Heat the olive oil in a skillet over medium heat. Add the minced garlic and stir until lightly browned, 2 to 3 minutes. Add the chicken to the skillet, along with the onion, water chestnuts, and scallions, and stir to combine. Cook for 3 minutes. Add the pepper and ground garlic and stir well.

4. To assemble the wraps, separate the iceberg lettuce into whole leaves. Scoop 2 tablespoons of the chicken mixture into the center of each leaf. Top with avocado. If desired, garnish with cilantro and hot sauce.

VIET BISTRO. The Viet Bistro is the reason to visit the mall for something other than shopping. Located in the food court of the Cumberland Mall, Viet Bistro offers dishes that are two steps above the fare that's usually served in that type of setting. With traditional and inventive Vietnamese-inspired dishes, chef Thuynhan Truong has gained a slew of awards and a loyal following. Visit in person; you won't be disappointed.

Recipe from LALA'S PUERTO RICAN KITCHEN, OLD BRIDGE

Crispy Chicken Chicharrones

Get on down with this classic Puerto Rican fried chicken. Get a good spice rub (LaLa's sells its own blend at the food truck and on its website), and serve the chicken alongside white rice with red beans or tostones (fried green plantains), with an avocado and tomato salad.

3 teaspoons LaLa's dry rub, or a similar adobo-based poultry rub of your choice

3 tablespoons garlic powder

3 tablespoons onion powder

1 tablespoon freshly ground black pepper

3 tablespoons kosher salt

2 tablespoons cider vinegar

2 pounds boneless, skinless chicken thighs, diced into 1-inch pieces

Canola oil, for frying

1 cup all-purpose flour

Makes 8–10 servings

1. In a small bowl, combine the dry rub, garlic power, onion powder, pepper, salt, and vinegar, and mix until combined. Apply to the chicken thighs until well coated. Let marinate for 30 minutes at room temperature, or for up to 1 day covered in the refrigerator.

2. Heat about 4 inches of oil to 350°F in a large heavy pot. While the oil is heating, pat the chicken dry and place the flour in a bowl. Dredge the chicken pieces in flour until well coated. Shake off any excess flour.

3. When the oil is ready, add the chicken to the pot (working in batches if necessary) and cook until golden brown and cooked through, about 4 minutes.

4. Remove the chicken with a slotted spoon and drain on paper towels. Serve immediately.

Recipe from VILLA MILAGRO VINEYARDS, FINESVILLE

Ropa Vieja

Ropa vieja means "old clothes," and indeed, this delicious Cuban slow-cooker stew looks like shreds of old torn clothing. Vineyard chef Audrey Gambino says it's best if made the day before it is eaten so that the flavors can marry. And to wash down this *sabroso* (delicious) dinner, she recommends a class of chilled Casi Dulce, a port-style wine from Villa Milagro Vineyards that is made of Cabernet Sauvignon, Merlot, and Cabernet Franc. Aged in oak, it carries the subtle smoky flavors of aged port.

½ cup all-purpose flour

1 teaspoon salt

1 teaspoon freshly ground black pepper

½ cup olive oil

2 pounds chuck roast, cut into ½-inch cubes

1 large onion, sliced into thin strips

2 stalks celery, chopped

1 green bell pepper, sliced into thin strips

2 garlic cloves, minced

3 cups diced fresh Jersey tomatoes

1 cup beef stock

2 tablespoons Casi Dulce or similar off-dry red wine

1 tablespoon ground cumin

2 bay leaves

1 cup chopped fresh cilantro, for serving

1 cup chopped iceberg lettuce, for serving

Corn tortillas, for serving

Makes 6–8 servings

1. Combine the flour, salt, and black pepper in a large bowl. Heat ¼ cup of the oil in a large cast-iron skillet over medium-high heat. Toss the meat cubes in the flour mixture until all the pieces are well coated, then sauté in the oil until browned on all sides, 2 to 3 minutes per side. Work in batches if necessary; do not crowd the beef in the skillet or it will "steam" instead of brown. As each batch is finished, toss the meat into a slow cooker.

2. Add the remaining ¼ cup oil to the skillet and reduce the heat to medium. Add the onion, celery, and bell pepper, and sauté until soft. Add the garlic and cook for 1 minute. Add the tomatoes, stock, wine, cumin, and bay leaves, and cook for 5 to 6 minutes. Pour the vegetable mixture over the meat in the slow cooker and cook on low heat until the meat begins to fall apart, 4 to 5 hours.

3. Serve in bowls, topped with cilantro and lettuce. Serve warm, soft corn tortillas on the side.

Recipe from LANGOSTA LOUNGE, ASBURY PARK

Tom Kha Ghai (Thai Chicken Coconut Soup)

Tom kha means "boiled galangal." But just what is galangal? Well, it's an Asian root similar to but slightly different from ginger — it has a woodier and spicier flavor. It's important to note that galangal has no real substitute. Some might suggest ginger, but it does a poor job in this recipe, so make sure you get the real thing. Marilyn Schlossbach makes up her own ketchup for this recipe, which you can buy at the Langosta Lounge, though of course plain ketchup will also do just fine. Serve with rice.

1 teaspoon sesame oil

6 garlic cloves, minced

4 scallions, sliced

2 cups good-quality Chinese chicken stock or vegetable stock

2 thin slices fresh galangal

1 (1-inch) piece fresh ginger, finely chopped

2 stalks fresh or dried lemongrass, thinly sliced

4 kaffir lime leaves, chopped

½ cup Thai sweet chili sauce, preferably the Mae Ploy brand, or ½ teaspoon sugar

3 Thai bird's-eye chiles or serrano chiles, thickly sliced, or 1–2 tablespoons sambal oelek

2 cups coconut milk

1 tablespoon fish sauce

8 shiitake or button mushrooms, sliced

½ cup diced carrots

½ cup sliced green beans

½ cup sliced snow peas or sugar snap peas

½ cup diced yellow bell pepper

¼ cup ketchup

1 cup diced chicken or ½ pound fresh shrimp (optional)

4 tablespoons chopped fresh cilantro

2 tablespoons freshly squeezed lime juice

Makes 6–8 servings

1. Warm a large stockpot or Dutch oven over medium heat. Add the oil, then the garlic and scallions, and cook for 3 minutes, stirring often. Add the stock and bring to a boil, then reduce the heat to a simmer and add the galangal, ginger, lemongrass, lime leaves, and sweet chili sauce. Let simmer for 5 minutes.

2. Add the chiles, coconut milk, and fish sauce, and simmer for another 5 minutes.

3. Add the mushrooms, carrots, beans, snow peas, bell pepper, ketchup, and, if using, your choice of chicken or shrimp, and simmer until the chicken is just cooked, 10 minutes.

4. Turn off the heat and add the cilantro and lime juice. Test for saltiness and sourness. You should get the earthy flavor of galangal, a noticeable amount of saltiness, sweetness from the coconut milk, and a fair bit of lime flavor, with a hint of chile in the background. If necessary, adjust the flavor with more fish sauce (salt) or lime juice (sour).

Thai Fish Cakes

In Thailand, fish cakes are common street food and tend to be much more flavorful than the Western varieties. They aren't battered, which chef Marilyn Schlossbach finds allows for more of the fresh taste of the fish, spices, and herbs to come through. These cakes are best eaten fresh out of the oil, while they're still very hot. Serve them with Thai sweet chili sauce, chopped cucumber, fresh cilantro, and a squeeze of lime juice. Simply delicious! *Read about Langosta Lounge on page 173.*

1 pound cod fillets or other mild white fish

3 tablespoons coconut milk

2 tablespoons fish sauce

1½ teaspoons chili powder

⅓ teaspoon ground cumin

½ teaspoon brown sugar

½ teaspoon shrimp paste

¼ teaspoon ground coriander

7 kaffir lime leaves, snipped into thin strips

3 scallions, sliced

3 garlic cloves

1 thumb-size piece fresh galangal or ginger, grated

1 red chile, sliced, or ½ teaspoon red pepper flakes

All-purpose flour or breadcrumbs, as needed

Vegetable oil, for frying

Chopped cilantro, for garnish

Lime wedges, for garnish

Makes 4–6 servings

1. Rinse the fish and pat dry (dry especially well if you're using frozen fish, which tends to be moister). Cut into chunks and place in a food processor.

2. Combine the coconut milk, fish sauce, chili powder, cumin, sugar, shrimp paste, and coriander in a bowl. Stir with a fork to combine and then pour into the processor over the fish. Add the lime leaf, scallions, garlic, galangal, and chile. Pulse to create a thick paste.

3. Scoop out a small amount of the paste (about the size of a golf ball), pat into a small cake, and set on a large plate. If your paste is too wet to easily form into a cake, add a little flour or breadcrumbs to the mix. Repeat until you've used up all the paste (you'll make 8 to 12 cakes). (If the paste sticks to your hands, just rinse them in cool water every so often.) Set the plate of cakes in the refrigerator for 10 minutes to firm up.

4. Pour at least 1 inch of oil into a small skillet or wok and heat until shimmering. Gently place the cakes in the oil, working in batches if necessary, and fry until golden brown, 30 to 60 seconds. Gently flip the cakes (they may stick a little to the pan) and fry until golden brown on the other side, 30 to 45 seconds. Drain on paper towels and serve hot, sprinkled with cilantro and with lime wedges on the side.

Amish-Style Beef Chili

This easy weeknight chili is often served at restaurants run by Amish in South Jersey. Just buy a pound of ground beef, add it to ingredients you most likely already have on hand, and dinner is served. It's the brown sugar that makes this such a special and flavorful dish — a hearty dash of sweet against the savory.

1 tablespoon olive oil

1 white onion, finely diced

4 stalks celery, finely diced

2 carrots, finely diced

1 pound 80% lean ground beef

3 tablespoons flour

¼ cup dark brown sugar

4½ cups tomato juice

¼ cup ketchup

1 (16-ounce) can kidney beans, drained and rinsed

1 tablespoon chili powder

Makes 6 servings

1. Heat the oil in a Dutch oven or soup pot over medium heat. Add the onion, celery, and carrots, and cook until softened, stirring often, about 5 minutes.

2. Add the beef to the pot and brown thoroughly, breaking the beef apart as it cooks, about 5 minutes. Add the flour to the mixture, stirring well to coat everything. Cook for 3 minutes, allowing the flour to brown a bit.

3. Add the sugar, mix well, and cook for 3 minutes. Add the tomato juice, ketchup, beans, and chili powder. Stir, bring to a simmer, and cook, covered, for 30 minutes. Serve hot.

Kielbasa and Sauerkraut

This is a family recipe, passed down from one generation to the next, with tweaks occurring along the way. It is currently residing with Melissa "Banacki" Lees, the wife of Jeremy "Flounder" Lees, the head brewer and founder of Flounder Brewing Co. — hence the addition of beer to the recipe. "It's great on the stove or on the grill and certainly celebrates our love for cooking with beer and our eastern European roots from our grandparents," says Jeremy. As for the kielbasa, he says, "the store-bought Hillshire Farms actually works the best because that kielbasa soaks up the beer and bacon and onion like a sponge." Serve with a good, crusty rye bread — it's excellent for soaking up the juices.

1 medium sweet onion, finely chopped

4 strips bacon, finely chopped

2 (13-ounce) packages kielbasa

1 (2-pound) package refrigerated sauerkraut

Freshly ground black pepper

1 (12-ounce) bottle dark beer, preferably Flounder Brewing Co. Murky Brown Ale

Beer mustard and rye bread, for serving

Makes 8–10 servings

1. Place a large, oven-safe pot or Dutch oven over medium heat. Add the onion and bacon and sauté until the onions are translucent, about 5 minutes.

2. Cut the kielbasa into small oval slices about ¼ inch thick. Add the kielbasa, sauerkraut, and pepper to taste to the onion mixture. Cook for 5 minutes, and then add half the bottle of beer. Bring to a simmer and let simmer for 30 minutes, stirring occasionally.

3. Add the rest of the beer and let simmer for another 30 minutes. Serve with beer mustard and rye bread.

FLOUNDER BREWING CO. When family members share a common interest, good things can happen. This is certainly the case with the three brothers behind Flounder Brewing Co. It started as a homebrewing hobby and quickly transformed into a small, award-winning Somerset County brewery. Along the way, Flounder — a nickname for brewer and owner Jeremy Lees — has had some big help, including two "experienceships" with the Boston Beer Company, makers of Samuel Adams. What started with three family members has grown considerably with the brewery's fan base. Everyone who walks through the door during the brewery's monthly open house tours is treated just like family.

Teresa Darcy's Weeknight Tomato Sauce and Pasta

With a quick sauce recipe this good, you'll never need to buy the jarred kind again. All you need are a few pantry staples, some fresh ingredients, and about 15 minutes. This is my mother-in-law's recipe, and her instructions are to use "enough garlic to kill a person," but you should tailor the garlic to suit your taste. Serve with your favorite pasta and freshly grated Parmigiano-Reggiano cheese.

2 tablespoons extra-virgin olive oil

15 garlic cloves, roughly chopped

1 teaspoon red pepper flakes

1 (28-ounce) can crushed tomatoes

Sea salt and freshly ground black pepper

1 teaspoon dried oregano

5 large fresh basil leaves, minced

1 pound pasta

Makes 4–6 servings

1. Heat the oil in a pot over medium heat. Add the garlic and stir until it becomes fragrant, about 30 seconds. Add the pepper flakes and stir for 30 seconds. Add the tomatoes, season with salt and pepper to taste, and stir. Bring to a simmer and cook for 10 minutes. Stir in the oregano and basil. Keep warm.

2. While the sauce is simmering, bring a large pot of salted water to a boil and cook the pasta according to the package directions. Drain the pasta and transfer to a serving bowl. Ladle two large scoops of sauce onto the pasta and mix well. Serve immediately, with additional sauce as desired.

Recipe from FONTANAROSA'S GOURMET SPECIALTY FOODS, TOTOWA

Fontanarosa's Eggless Pasta

It's easy to reach for a box of the dried pasta, but making it from scratch is (1) easier than you might expect and (2) so much better than the premade stuff. Perfect for a weeknight sauce (page 196) or a meat sauce (page 200). Once you have the ingredients in the pantry and master the preparation, you might be making this more often than not.

8 ounces semolina flour

8 ounces durum extra-fancy wheat flour (also known as macaroni wheat)

8 ounces warm water (about 110°F)

Additional flour, to prevent sticking

Makes 4-6 servings

1. On a clean surface, like a countertop, thoroughly mix together the flours and push into a pile, then create a well in the middle of the flour. Add the water in small increments (about an ounce at a time) and begin mixing by hand, slowing combining the water into the pasta. As the mixture thickens, continue to knead until the dough becomes thick and can be formed into a ball.

2. Knead the dough by hand by gently folding it. Start from the top of the ball and bring it toward you. Rotate the dough 90 degrees and fold again. Continue rotating clockwise and folding for 10 minutes, taking care not to rip the dough. At this point the ball should be firm enough that if you press your finger into it, it will bounce back. This is an indication that the gluten in the dough has been activated. Wrap the ball in plastic and let sit for 30 minutes on the counter.

3. Cut the dough into six equal parts. Using a rolling pin, roll out each section of the dough into a rectangle that's about $\frac{2}{16}$ inch thick (the pasta will expand during cooking). Fold each rectangle onto itself twice.

4. Orient the dough rectangles so that the long edge is at the bottom. Using a sharp knife, slice each folded rectangle into strips. For spaghetti, cut strips ⅛ inch wide; for fettuccini, cut into ½-inch-wide strips; for pappardelle, cut strips 1 inch wide.

5. Unfold the pasta strips and either hang on a dowel or put on a clean towel to lightly dry, about 15 minutes.

6. Bring a large pot of water to a boil. Place the pasta into the water and cook for 4 minutes. Remove and serve immediately with your favorite sauce.

FONTANAROSA'S GOURMET SPECIALTY FOODS

In certain parts of the state, the Fontanarosa family name is synonymous with pasta, specifically ravioli. Founded in 1982 by Italian immigrants Tony and Michelina, Fontanarosa's Gourmet Specialty Foods is now run by the couple's children, Anthony and Luciana. Today the business is a full-service deli and pasta shop, where Anthony works to create new ravioli flavors that go well beyond the traditional cheese, such as arugula, pear Gruyère, and eggplant rollatini. There are even dessert options, like peach and cannoli filling. A regular at Northern Jersey farmers' markets, Fontanarosa's pastas are like a taste of the old country with a modern twist, right in your home kitchen. For Anthony, it's more than a fun job, it's a calling.

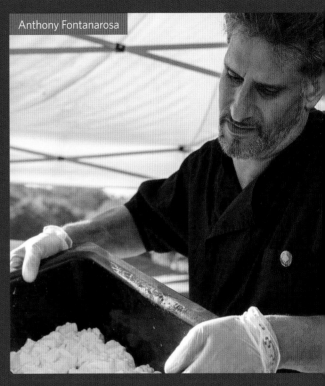

Anthony Fontanarosa

Unapologetic Carnivore's Slow-Cooker Sunday Sauce (North Jersey-Style)

Good things come to those who wait. Ask anyone who grew up in an Italian household waiting for Sunday dinner. As new ingredients are added and the hours slip by, the aromas build and everyone's hunger grows. Get this started in the morning (it takes upwards of 9 hours to cook), set the table, invite a lot of people over. Serve family-style on the dining-room table.

This recipe is from author and food enthusiast Jeff Cioletti and tastes even better the next day. There are rarely leftovers, but the sauce and extra meatballs can be frozen for up to 1 month in an airtight container.

THE SAUCE

- ⅓ cup extra-virgin olive oil
- 20 garlic cloves, chopped
- 1 tablespoon red pepper flakes
- 4 (28-ounce) cans whole San Marzano tomatoes (see note)
- 2 teaspoons sea salt
- 1 pound bone-in beef short ribs
- 1 pound bone-in pork spare ribs
- 3 links sweet Italian sausage, halved

THE MEATBALLS

- 4 cups torn-up ciabatta bread or baguette
- 2 cups water
- 2 pounds ground beef
- 2 pounds ground pork
- 10 garlic cloves, minced
- 1 medium red onion, minced
- ½ cup chopped fresh parsley
- 8 eggs
- ½ cup grated Pecorino cheese
- 3 teaspoons sea salt
- 2 teaspoons freshly ground black pepper
- 1 cup panko breadcrumbs
- ½ cup finely chopped walnuts
- 2–3 tablespoons olive oil

Makes about 20 meatballs
and roughly 10 cups of sauce

1. To start the sauce, pour the oil into a large skillet and warm over medium heat for 1 minute. Add the garlic and cook, stirring constantly, until browned, 6 to 8 minutes. Add the pepper flakes and cook for 1 minute, stirring frequently. Transfer the seasoned oil to a slow cooker. Add the tomatoes and their juices to the slow cooker, using a masher to crush and break them apart. Add the salt and stir. Turn the slow cooker to low and cook for 4 hours.

2. After about 3½ hours, heat a large skillet over medium-high heat and, working in batches, use it to brown the short ribs, spare ribs, and sausage. Add the short ribs and spare ribs to the sauce, reserving the sausage and any juices that have collected in the skillet. Keep the slow cooker on low and cook for 4 hours.

3. While the sauce is cooking, you can make the meatballs. Preheat the oven to 350°F.

4. Combine the bread and water in a large bowl and let soak for 1 minute. Drain the bread in a colander, pushing out any excess moisture and tearing the bread into smaller pieces. Then transfer the bread back to the bowl.

5. Add the ground beef and pork to the bowl and knead thoroughly by hand until fully incorporated. Add the garlic, onion, and parsley, and mix again until the ingredients are well blended.

6. Add four of the eggs and knead the mixture. Add the Pecorino, salt, pepper, and ⅓ cup of the panko. Knead that mixture. Add the remaining four eggs, another ⅓ cup of the panko, and the walnuts. Continue to knead, intermittently shaking in the remaining ⅓ cup panko; stop adding panko if it seems like the mixture might become too dry.

7. Lightly oil two baking sheets. Shape the meat mixture into racquetball- or tennis-ball-size spheres. Arrange in rows of three on the baking sheets. You should have about 20 meatballs.

8. Bake the meatballs for about 30 minutes. After 25 minutes, check them: they're done when they are firm and are forming a light crust. Don't leave them in the oven for more than 35 minutes or they will become too dry. When they're done, pull them out of the oven and let them cool.

9. Add the meatballs, sausage, and reserved drippings to the sauce and cook for another 60 to 90 minutes at the low setting. The sauce is done when the meat of the short ribs and spare ribs falls off the bone to become one with the sauce and create a carnivorous symphony.

NOTE: Cans advertising themselves as San Marzano tomatoes should be marked with D.O.P. (Denominazione d'Origine Protetta) certification. If they don't carry that certification, they're not true San Marzanos. Accept no domestically grown substitute, as authenticity is paramount to a recipe like this.

Recipe from FORMICA BROS. BAKERY, ATLANTIC CITY

Grandma Rosa's Tomato Pie

It's not really pizza, although the uninitiated can be forgiven for thinking otherwise. Dough and sauce, that's all you need for a tomato pie. No mozzarella, no toppings, just the flavors of fresh, crisp dough and bright tomato sauce. Most will eat it warm, but there's a certain pleasure that comes with eating it at room temperature or even cold from the fridge the next day.

THE DOUGH

1 cup warm water (about 110°F)

1 package active dry yeast

2½ cups all-purpose flour

2 tablespoons olive oil

½ teaspoon salt

THE SAUCE

1 cup marinara sauce

½ teaspoon dried basil

½ teaspoon dried oregano

½ teaspoon dried parsley

⅔ cup shredded Pecorino Romano cheese

Makes 6–8 servings

1. Combine the water, yeast, and 1½ cups of the flour in a large bowl. Mix well. Add the oil, salt, and another ½ cup of flour. Knead the dough with your hands (or use a stand mixer with the dough hook attachment) until the dough holds the shape of a ball and doesn't stick to the bowl, 4 to 6 minutes. If the dough is still very sticky, knead in the remaining ½ cup flour.

2. Place the dough on a lightly floured surface and knead until smooth and elastic, about 5 minutes. If the dough becomes sticky, sprinkle a bit more flour over it. Transfer the dough to a lightly oiled 2-quart bowl. Cover the bowl with a wet kitchen towel and let the dough rest in a warm spot until it has doubled in size, about 1 hour.

3. Place an oven rack in the lower third of the oven, set the oven to 450°F, and let it warm for 30 minutes.

4. Lightly oil and flour a 12- by 17-inch baking sheet. Place the dough on the sheet and spread the dough with your hands to cover the entire surface of the pan. Cover with a wet towel and let rest for 15 minutes.

5. Top the dough with the marinara sauce and sprinkle on the basil, oregano, and parsley, followed by the cheese. Reduce the oven temperature to 400°F and bake for 15 to 25 minutes, until the pie is cooked through and the edges are slightly browned.

6. Let the pie cool slightly, then cut into squares. Serve hot.

Bacon-Cheddar Boxty

A staple in Irish-American households and taverns, a boxty is a potato pancake. Not unlike similar dishes from other cultures, this version is served with sour cream on the side. The Irish twist is the bacon and cheddar topping.

2 pounds russet potatoes, peeled

1 medium yellow onion, grated

¾ cup all-purpose flour

2 eggs, beaten

1 tablespoon kosher salt

1 teaspoon freshly ground black pepper

2 tablespoons canola oil

8 ounces Irish cheddar cheese, shredded

½ pound bacon, cooked and chopped

2 teaspoons thinly sliced chives

1 cup sour cream

Makes 4–6 servings

1. Use a box grater to grate the potatoes into a colander. Squeeze the potatoes to drain out as much water as possible. Add the onion, flour, eggs, salt, and pepper, and mix well.

2. Preheat the oven to 450°F.

3. Heat the oil in a large skillet over high heat. Use a ¼-cup measuring cup to scoop up the potato mixture and transfer to the hot skillet. Work in batches, so that the pancakes are not crowded in the pan. Cook until golden brown on both sides, about 2 minutes per side. Remove to a plate lined with paper towels to drain the oil, and then transfer to a baking sheet.

4. Top each boxty with 1 tablespoon cheese and 1 tablespoon bacon. Bake for 2 minutes, or until the cheese is melted. Garnish with chives and serve immediately with a side of sour cream.

The Shannon Rose Irish Pub. You'll be forgiven for forgetting you're in Jersey. The Irish pub concept is ubiquitous in the Garden State, where many of our ancestors from the Emerald Isle settled after coming through Ellis Island. Pubs, with pints of Guinness, shots of whiskey, hearty meat and potato dishes, live music, and loud conversation, popped up in nearly every town where the eyes smiled. The Shannon Rose — with two locations in the state — is the embodiment of all the traditions that make a pub great. It's why locals come back again and again and why first-time visitors immediately feel at home.

Mary Gibbons-Holl's Irish Soda Bread

Soda bread is taken seriously in my family. So much so that when my mother was growing up in the Bronx, various family members would bring their own versions to parties, trying to unseat the then current champion, Aunt Sally. My mother, Mary, received a recipe from a neighbor, Mrs. Rynne, and over time made a few adjustments. When she brought a loaf to the next family party, this recipe became the family favorite. It's been shared inside and outside of our family for years, and I'm so happy to carry on my mother's memory by sharing this recipe with you.

4½ cups all-purpose flour

¾ cup sugar

2 teaspoons baking powder

1 teaspoon baking soda

2 cups milk

1 egg, beaten

2 tablespoons sour cream

½ cup raisins

3 tablespoons caraway seeds, or to taste

Cream cheese or butter, for serving (optional)

Makes 1 loaf

1. Preheat the oven to 350°F. Grease a loaf pan.

2. Whisk together the flour, sugar, baking powder, and baking soda in a large bowl. Add the milk, egg, sour cream, raisins, and caraway seeds. Mix by hand until thoroughly combined; the dough should be sticky.

3. Transfer the dough to the prepared pan and bake for 75 minutes, until the top is golden brown and a toothpick inserted into the center comes out clean.

4. Let cool in the pan. Then slice and serve with cream cheese or butter, or simply on its own.

Tzatziki

This is the cool, thick, refreshing white sauce most commonly found in Mediterranean dishes, such as gyro sandwiches or falafel. It can also be used as a vegetable dip and is a great condiment for sweet potato fries.

1 English cucumber, peeled, seeded, and chopped

1 teaspoon kosher salt

2 garlic cloves

2 tablespoons freshly squeezed lemon juice

1 tablespoon extra-virgin olive oil

2 cups Greek yogurt

2 teaspoons minced fresh dill

2 teaspoons minced fresh mint

Freshly ground black pepper

Makes about 3 cups

1. Place the cucumber in a colander and sprinkle with the salt. Toss to combine and let drain for 1 hour. Then remove from the colander and pat dry with paper towels.

2. Transfer the cucumber to a food processor and add the garlic, lemon juice, and oil. Pulse several times until well blended.

3. Transfer the mixture to a medium bowl and stir in the yogurt, dill, mint, and pepper to taste. Mix well to combine, then cover and refrigerate for at least 1 hour. Drain any excess liquid before serving.

Vegetable Fried Rice

It's the indulgence many of us get when ordering Chinese takeout. We know that brown rice is healthier, but hey, fried rice has vegetables in it. How bad can it be? Well, we know the answer, of course. This recipe is a healthier at-home version and comes in handy when you have leftover rice. The vegetables used here are just a suggestion; add your own as you see fit. The key to remember is small pieces — finely dice all the vegetables to ensure easy forkfuls and quick cooking.

2 tablespoons peanut oil

1 garlic clove, grated

1 teaspoon grated fresh ginger

2 cups cooked white rice

1 small onion, finely diced

1 green bell pepper, seeded and finely diced

1 red bell pepper, seeded and finely diced

½ cup fresh peas or frozen and defrosted

½ cup fresh baby corn or frozen and defrosted (or canned, in a pinch)

1 egg, lightly beaten

2 scallions, minced

Makes 4 servings

1. Add the oil to a wok or large skillet over medium-high heat. When the oil is shimmering, add the garlic and ginger and cook for 30 seconds. Immediately add the rice and cook, stirring frequently, for 2 minutes.

2. Add the onion, bell peppers, peas, and corn, and cook, stirring frequently, for 4 minutes.

3. Add the egg to the top of the rice mixture and cook until hardened, 1 to 2 minutes, stirring to incorporate the egg into the mixture. Add the scallions and cook for 1 minute longer, stirring frequently. Serve immediately.

Lamb-Stuffed Eggplant

Keeping the Greek tradition of diner food alive, this farm-to-table dish will delight with its fresh flavor and stunning presentation. This is a perfect weekend meal, because as the lamb slowly cooks, your home will fill with rich, savory aromas. Serve with a simple arugula salad.

1 (3-pound) leg of lamb

1 large onion, sliced lengthwise

4 garlic cloves, thinly sliced

8 ounces canned peeled tomatoes, crushed

½ cup red wine

1 cinnamon stick

1 tablespoon chopped fresh rosemary

3 medium eggplants, sliced in half lengthwise

1 tablespoon extra-virgin olive oil

Salt and freshly ground black pepper

2 ounces feta cheese

2 ounces grated Pecorino Romano cheese

2 ounces grated cheddar cheese

Makes 6 servings

1. Preheat the oven to 300°F.

2. Combine the lamb, onion, garlic, tomatoes, wine, cinnamon, and rosemary in a Dutch oven. Cover and bake for 2 to 2½ hours, or until the meat is cooked through and can be removed easily from the bone with a fork. Remove the lamb from the oven, and raise the temperature to 325°F.

3. Place the eggplant, skin side down, on a baking sheet. Drizzle with the oil, coating thoroughly, and season with salt and pepper. Place in the oven for 15 to 20 minutes, or until the eggplant becomes soft. Remove from the oven and set aside. In a small bowl, combine the feta, Pecorino, and cheddar cheeses.

4. Remove the meat from the pot and shred with forks. Remove the cinnamon stick from the liquid. Spoon the sauce over the shredded lamb to keep it moist.

5. Turn on the broiler and place a rack in the middle of the oven. Place heaping forkfuls of the lamb on top of each eggplant half and top each with 1 ounce of the cheese mixture, spreading evenly across the meat.

6. Place the stuffed eggplant in the oven and broil for 2 to 5 minutes, or until the cheese is bubbly and lightly browned. Remove from the oven and serve immediately.

AMERICANA DINER

Healthy. Organic. Fresh. These are not words usually associated with diners in New Jersey. What we usually get are short-order items, hot off a griddle with the unmistakable taste of oil and butter, along with all the other flavors. When Constantine Katsifis took over the Americana Diner, he sought to change the status quo and announced this to his customers on the menu with three simple words: "eat better food."

Of course he offers the diner classics, but with a bent toward local and sustainable, such as cage-free eggs, multigrain toast, and fresh-squeezed organic lemonade. Fries are available with the grass-fed burgers, but you can also get apple and celery salad, or chickpea and red bean salad. Much is made in-house, from the kimchi to the hand-battered onion rings. It's a diner for the modern era, and a model that others across the state should embrace.

Nancy Friedman's Amazing Chopped Liver

The name of this recipe is not an exaggeration. After enjoying chicken liver pâté for years and feeling satisfied with our own recipe, my family was fortunate to be introduced to Nancy Friedman and her amazing chopped liver. Our lives (and family gatherings) have never been the same. Note that you should make this dish at least a day in advance. Serve with crackers.

3 cups canola oil

3 large sweet onions, sliced into ½-inch rings

6 eggs

1 pound chicken livers

Salt and freshly ground white pepper

½ teaspoon agave nectar (optional)

Makes 5 cups

1. Heat 2 cups of the oil in a large deep skillet over medium-low heat until it reaches a slow simmer. Add the onions, reduce the heat to low, and poach slowly for about 1 hour, stirring for about 15 seconds every 10 minutes, until the onions are soft, caramelized (light golden), and translucent. Let the onions cool to room temperature in the pan. The key, says Friedman, is to not overstir the onions and to heat them slowly — the longer they take to caramelize, the better the end result.

2. While the onions are caramelizing, place the eggs in a pot in a single layer. Cover the eggs with at least 2 inches of cold water and bring to a full boil over high heat. Boil for 1 minute, then turn off the heat, cover the pot, and let sit for 12 minutes. Remove the eggs and plunge them into ice water to stop the cooking. When the eggs are cool enough to handle, peel them.

3. If the chicken livers are packaged in a container of liquid, take them out of the liquid, rinse with water, and pat dry. Heat the remaining 1 cup oil in a large skillet over medium-low heat. Place the chicken livers in a single layer in the skillet; the oil should rise up to about the halfway point for them. Be careful of spattering, especially if the livers are not completely dry. Let the livers poach for 10 minutes; lower the heat if it sounds like they are deep-frying. Then turn them over very carefully with a slotted spoon — they tend to fall apart easily, so try to be gentle — and poach on the other side for 5 to 6 minutes. Then check to see if they're cooked: Cut open one liver to inspect the inside. If it is still bloody, they are not done. If it looks dry, they are overcooked. If tender, they are just right. Remove from the heat and let stand in the pan with the oil until the livers cool down, about 20 minutes.

4. Using a slotted spoon, remove the livers from the oil and place them in a blender. Add 2½ cups (almost all) of the onion-oil mixture to the blender. Add the hard-boiled eggs. Season with salt and pepper to taste. Pulse the ingredients in the blender five to ten times, until it reaches a slightly chunky but almost smooth consistency, sort of like cottage cheese.

5. Taste, and add more salt and pepper to your liking. If there is any metallic taste, add the agave nectar and pulse for 2 to 3 seconds.

6. Transfer the chopped liver to a covered container and refrigerate. For best flavor, serve at room temperature. Chopped liver always seems to taste best the day after it has been made. Leftovers keep for up to 5 days.

Sweet Treats

Whether behind a display case, in a specialty aisle, hidden in the kitchen cabinet, tucked into the freezer, or on full display on the counter, sweets enjoy a place of honor in this state — we have an undeniable sweet tooth. Grab a fork (or spoon) and dive into these delectable desserts.

Recipe from THE BENT SPOON, PRINCETON

Strawberry-Basil Sorbet

This is one of the more popular sorbet flavors at the Bent Spoon. It's simply bursting with flavor, and light-years better than any mass-marketed concoction you'll find in grocery-store freezers. Strawberries and basil, of course, are simply amazing when they're fresh from the garden or farmers' market, so this sorbet is a true summer highlight — something to dream about in the dark cold of winter.

¾ cup sugar

6 tablespoons water

¼ teaspoon salt

3 pints (about 1½ pounds) fresh-picked strawberries, preferably organic, hulled

½ cup loosely packed fresh basil leaves

3 tablespoons freshly squeezed lemon juice

1 large egg white, preferably farm-fresh (optional)

Makes 1 quart

1. Make a simple syrup: Combine the sugar, water, and salt in a saucepan and cook, stirring, over medium heat until the sugar and salt have dissolved, about 3 minutes. Remove from the heat and let cool for 15 minutes.

2. Combine the simple syrup with the strawberries, basil, and lemon juice in a blender and purée until very smooth. *Note:* You may need to divide this mixture into several batches if your blender is not extra-large. Don't strain; the texture from the pulp and seeds really highlights the fruit and creates a nice creaminess. Cover and refrigerate until chilled, at least 4 hours and up to overnight.

3. Churn in an ice cream maker according to the manufacturer's directions. Add the egg white, if using, during the last 2 to 3 minutes of churning. (Egg white acts as a stabilizer if you won't be eating the sorbet right away; it will keep in the freezer for up to 2 weeks.)

THE BENT SPOON

The Bent Spoon is a Princeton institution. Owned and operated by Gabrielle Carbone and Matthew Errico (along with employees known as "spoonies"), it's the best place in town for ice cream and sorbet. Have a big sweet tooth? They also make cupcakes, cookies, and ice cream cakes. The Bent Spoon is the reason you save room for after dinner.

Gabrielle Carbone

new Jersey Terroir

"terroir" — loosely translated in french "a sense of place" or, as we like to say: "the taste of a place". we are so lucky in this area to have so many people growing & producing such amazing & wonderful things that you just can't get anywhere else. that's where being able to make ice creams & sorbets out of just about anything really comes in handy !! supporting local farmers & producers help to keep the land they farm on free from overdevelopment ! open for all of us to admire, enjoy & sustain ourselves isn't it wonderful in the face of threatened resources to get food that hasn't traveled miles & miles? it supports our local economy, is fresher & in turn, supports all of us in this community. we choose to support local farmers/producers for lots of reasons — first, & if they are also organic (like so many here are)-then WOW! all the better! this isn't just "yada-yada organic" & "yada-yada local" — THIS IS REAL! anyway, the point is next time you're enjoying some local ice cream or sorbet, know that whether you're tasting a farm-fresh jersey cheese, heirloom fruit or vegetable, organically grown herb, or a locally produced product like beer, coffee or honey,

YOU ARE REALLY tasting & EXPERIENCING the ESSENCE of this place — a taste you'll find no where else !!

~ support local stuff !

know your farmer & where your stuff comes from

Blueberry-Apple Crumb Pie

Delicious New Jersey blueberries are available at many farmers' markets in the summertime. Buy as many as you can while they're available, because blueberries freeze beautifully, which is great because you can save some for when the apple crop comes in during late summer and autumn. You and your family will be able to enjoy Jersey blueberries year-round in muffins, jams, and pies like this one, created by baker Jen Carson. *Read about LiLLiPiES Bakey on page 222.*

THE CRUST

- 2 cups all-purpose flour
- ¼ cup granulated sugar
- ½ teaspoon salt
- 1 cup (2 sticks) unsalted butter, ice cold and cut into ½-inch cubes
- 4-6 tablespoons ice-cold water

THE FILLING

- 4 baking apples (like Staymans, Granny Smiths, or Golden Delicious)
- 1 pint blueberries
- ¼ cup granulated sugar
- 3-4 tablespoons all-purpose flour
- 2 tablespoons butter
- Juice of ½ lemon
- 1 teaspoon ground cinnamon
- ¼ teaspoon ground nutmeg

THE STREUSEL TOPPING

- ½ cup all-purpose flour
- ½ cup brown sugar
- 4 tablespoons butter, cubed
- ½ teaspoon ground cinnamon
- ½ teaspoon ground nutmeg
- ⅛ teaspoon salt

Makes 1 pie

1. Make the crust: Combine the flour, granulated sugar, salt, and butter in a food processor and pulse to mix. (You can also cut the butter into the dry ingredients by hand with a pastry cutter.) When the butter pieces are the size of small peas, add 4 tablespoons ice-cold water. Pulse until combined. Squeeze a handful of dough. If the dough holds together, you have enough water. If not, add more water, 1 tablespoon at a time, pulse to mix, and check again. When it's ready, shape the dough into a disk, wrap in plastic, and chill in the refrigerator for at least 30 minutes.

2. For the filling, peel, core, and dice the apples. Rinse and pat dry the berries. Combine the apples, granulated sugar, 3 tablespoons flour (or 4 tablespoons if the apples and berries are super juicy), butter, lemon juice, cinnamon, and nutmeg in a skillet and cook over medium heat just until the butter is melted. This prebaking step allows the apples to cook perfectly in your pie.

3. Take the apples off the heat, stir in the blueberries, and allow the mixture to cool completely. (You can speed up this process by removing the filling from the hot pan and spreading it out on a cool baking sheet.)

4. Preheat the oven to 400°F.

5. On a well-floured surface, roll out the dough into a round about ⅛ inch thick. Lay the dough into an ungreased 8- or 9-inch pie pan. Tuck the edges under and crimp as desired. Chill the crust in the refrigerator until you're ready to pre-bake it (see step 7).

6. Make the streusel topping: Combine the flour, brown sugar, butter, cinnamon, nutmeg, and salt in a food processor and pulse until combined. (You can also cut the butter into the dry ingredients by hand with a pastry cutter.) Keep the streusel topping chilled in the refrigerator until you're ready to use it.

7. Line the chilled piecrust with parchment, then fill the cavity with pie weights, dried beans, or uncooked rice. Bake the crust for 15 minutes. (Blind baking ensures that the finished crust will be golden brown and crisp.) Remove the pie weights and parchment and fill the pie shell with the blueberry-apple filling. Top with the streusel, squeezing the crumbly topping into clumps if possible (clumped streusel is delicious on the finished pie).

8. Bake the filled pie for 30 to 35 minutes, or until the crust and streusel have browned and the filling is bubbling. Allow the pie to rest for 20 minutes. Serve warm.

NOTE: You can save yourself some cleanup by placing your pie pan on a parchment-lined half sheet pan before baking. When your topping bubbles over (and it will), it will bubble onto your parchment-lined baking sheet, and not your oven floor.

Recipe from LILLIPIES BAKERY, PRINCETON

Peach-Habanero Pocket Pies

You might be surprised by this combination, but let me tell you, this recipe by Jen Carson is absolutely delicious. The heat of the habanero is tamed by the sugar and sweet peaches, though the fruitiness of the chile remains. *Read about LiLLiPiES Bakey on page 222.*

THE DOUGH

2 cups all-purpose flour
¼ cup granulated sugar
½ teaspoon salt
1 cup (2 sticks) cold butter, cubed
4–6 tablespoons cold water

THE FILLING

3 large peaches
½ habanero chile, minced
¼ cup granulated sugar
Juice from ½ lemon
1 tablespoon cornstarch

FOR ASSEMBLY

1 egg
2 tablespoons water
Coarse sugar

Makes 6 pocket pies

1. Make the dough: Combine the flour, granulated sugar, salt, and butter in a food processor and pulse to mix. (You can also cut the butter into the dry ingredients by hand with a pastry cutter.) When the butter pieces are the size of small peas, add 4 tablespoons ice-cold water. Pulse until combined. Squeeze a handful of dough. If it holds together, you've added enough water. If not, add more water, 1 tablespoon at a time, pulse to mix, and check again. When it's ready, shape the dough into a disk, wrap in plastic, and chill in the refrigerator for at least 30 minutes.

2. Make the peach-habanero filling: Peel the peaches and remove their pits, then slice and dice them into ½-inch cubes. Combine the peaches in a medium bowl with the habanero, granulated sugar, lemon juice, and cornstarch, and mix well.

3. On a well-floured surface, roll out the pie dough to about ⅛-inch thickness. Cut out twelve 4-inch circles. (A circle-shaped cookie cutter works well for this.) Set the dough circles on a parchment-lined baking sheet; if you're not going to fill and bake them right away, set them in the refrigerator to chill.

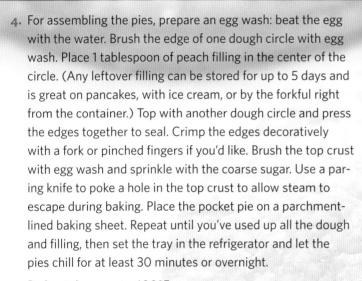

4. For assembling the pies, prepare an egg wash: beat the egg with the water. Brush the edge of one dough circle with egg wash. Place 1 tablespoon of peach filling in the center of the circle. (Any leftover filling can be stored for up to 5 days and is great on pancakes, with ice cream, or by the forkful right from the container.) Top with another dough circle and press the edges together to seal. Crimp the edges decoratively with a fork or pinched fingers if you'd like. Brush the top crust with egg wash and sprinkle with the coarse sugar. Use a paring knife to poke a hole in the top crust to allow steam to escape during baking. Place the pocket pie on a parchment-lined baking sheet. Repeat until you've used up all the dough and filling, then set the tray in the refrigerator and let the pies chill for at least 30 minutes or overnight.

5. Preheat the oven to 400°F.

6. Bake the pies for 20 minutes, or until deep golden brown. Cool slightly before serving.

NOTE: When you're making pie dough, the amount of water you need for the dough to hold together can depend on the weather, the time of year you are baking, how your flour was stored, et cetera. Adding too much water will yield a sticky dough (and a tough crust later). Adding too little water will cause the dough to fall apart as you are rolling. After a few tries, you'll get a feel for it.

LILLIPIES BAKERY

LiLLiPiES Bakery was founded in 2007 by chef/owner Jen Carson. This from-scratch bakery prides itself on using locally grown New Jersey produce and products, from fruits and vegetables to honey, eggs, cheese, and bacon.

The bakery, originally named "Jen's Cakes & Pastries," quickly earned a following at local farmers' markets as well as at Small World Coffee in Princeton. LiLLiPiES (single-serving sweet pies, filled with seasonal fruit) became the bakery's signature menu item. After many years of hearing market-goers call her bakery (and her) "LiLLiPiES," Jen chose to embrace the title and renamed the bakery after her now-famous hand pies.

LiLLiPiES is a bake-to-order bakery, sharing a commercial production kitchen with four other food producers in Princeton. LiLLiPiES' products can be ordered by individual clients and caterers but are also found at farmers' markets throughout the region and in various coffee shops and other retail venues in northern New Jersey.

BAKED CAKE DONUTS

CHOCOLATE
VANILLA BEAN
BANANA WITH COCONUT

wheat flour, butter, canola oil, sour cream, sugar, eggs, vanilla bean, cocoa, Small World coffee, bananas, coconut

$1.50 EACH

Jen Carson

Recipe from MUIRHEAD FOODS, TRENTON

Cranberry Pie

Sauces and jellies are fine, but to get the true tang and sweet potential of cranberries, try baking them in a pie. This is a straightforward recipe by Barbara Simpson of Muirhead Foods that bursts with rustic flavor and is sure to be a hit for autumn and winter dinners. *Read about Muirhead Foods on page 57.*

2 premade piecrusts, sized for a 9-inch pie

3 cups fresh cranberries

1 cup dark or golden raisins

1 cup water

1½ cups sugar

¼ cup all-purpose flour

Zest of 1 orange

2 tablespoons milk

Makes 1 pie

1. Preheat the oven to 400°F.

2. Roll out one crust and fit into a 9-inch pie plate. Roll out the second crust and, using a pastry cutter, cut into ten ½-inch strips. Set aside.

3. Combine the cranberries, raisins, and water in a medium saucepan and bring to a boil over medium-high heat; boil for 3 minutes.

4. Combine the sugar and flour in a small bowl. Stir the flour mixture into the hot cranberry mixture. Cook and stir until thick and bubbly, about 5 minutes. Stir in the orange zest.

5. Spoon the hot pie filling into the prepared piecrust. Top with the strips of piecrust to form a lattice (placing one strip vertically and one horizontally, working from the center of the plate outward). Brush the lattice strips with the milk.

6. Bake for 30 to 35 minutes, until the filling is bubbling and the crust is slightly browned. Cover the edges with aluminum foil to prevent overbrowning, if necessary. Remove and allow the pie to cool slightly before serving.

Funnel Cake at Home

Even those folks who claim not to like sweets are tempted by the warm sugary smell of deep-fried batter coming from the boardwalk kiosks each summer. Funnel cake is a messy sharable treat, served with an unreasonable (but welcome) amount of confectioners' sugar on a flimsy paper plate and often with napkins not strong enough to handle sticky fingers. But what about funnel cake at home? Is such a thing possible, and is it even worth it? Yes and yes. This is great for kids' birthday parties and sleepovers, backyard cookouts, and really anytime you want a shore-minded treat but can't make it there in person. The only special equipment you'll need is a squeeze bottle.

Vegetable or peanut oil, for frying

2 cups instant pancake mix, like Bisquick

1 large egg

1 cup milk

1 teaspoon vanilla extract

Confectioners' sugar

Makes 12–18 funnel cakes, depending on size

1. Add 2 inches of oil to a deep-bottomed pot or Dutch oven and heat to 350°F.

2. Combine the pancake mix, egg, milk, and vanilla extract in a large mixing bowl and stir until fully incorporated and the consistency of cake batter.

3. Transfer the mix to a squeeze bottle and carefully squeeze the batter into the oil, working in a circular and sideways motion, to create your desired shape. If you want smaller cakes, you can fry two at a time, but don't overcrowd the pot. Cook for 30 seconds, and carefully flip the cake using a wire spider or tongs. Cook until the cake is deep golden brown, an additional 30 seconds. Remove from the oil, transfer the cake to a plate lined with paper towels, and cool slightly. Work in batches until the batter is gone, taking time to let the oil return to 350°F between frying.

4. Pour confectioners' sugar into a fine-mesh strainer and hold it above each cake, gently tapping the side of the strainer to release the sugar. Serve immediately.

Summer Berries and Biscuits
(Featuring the Jersey Blueberry)

These look so good on the plate, expect your guests to whip out the cell phone and snap a picture to post on social media before digging in. Sweet, fluffy, and with a generous helping of fresh blueberries, this might be the only dessert you need all summer long.

THE BISCUITS

2 cups all-purpose flour

¼ cup plus 2 tablespoons granulated sugar

1 tablespoon lemon zest

2 teaspoons baking powder

½ teaspoon baking soda

¼ teaspoon salt

⅛ cup (¼ stick) chilled butter, diced

½ cup buttermilk

1 teaspoon water

1 egg white

THE FILLING

3 cups fresh blueberries

½ cup granulated sugar

2 tablespoons fresh lemon juice

2 teaspoons cornstarch

2 cups fresh blackberries

THE WHIPPED CREAM

2 cups heavy cream

2 teaspoons vanilla extract

¼ cup confectioners' sugar

Makes 8–10 servings

1. Preheat the oven to 400°F. Line a baking sheet with parchment paper or grease with cooking spray or shortening.

2. Make the biscuits: In a mixing bowl, combine the flour, ¼ cup granulated sugar, lemon zest, baking powder, baking soda, and salt, and stir with a whisk. Cut in the chilled butter with two knives or a pastry cutter until the mixture looks coarse and crumbly. Add the buttermilk and stir until moistened throughout. You may need slightly more buttermilk if the mixture is too dry.

3. Turn the mixture out onto a floured surface, knead lightly, and pat the dough to a ½-inch thickness. Cut the dough with a 3-inch biscuit cutter or a small juice glass into 8 to 10 rounds. (If using a juice glass, be sure to flour the rim well between each cut.)

4. Place the rounds on the prepared baking sheet and bake for 12 to 15 minutes, or until the tops are golden.

5. In a small bowl, combine the water and egg white and beat lightly. Using a pastry brush, coat the top of the biscuits with the egg wash, and sprinkle the tops liberally with the remaining 2 tablespoons granulated sugar.

6. To prepare the filling, combine 1¼ cups of the blueberries, the sugar, lemon juice, and cornstarch in a small saucepan. Bring to a boil, reduce the heat, and simmer for 5 to 7 minutes, stirring constantly so as not to burn the bottom. The berries will melt away into a beautiful, slightly thick sauce. Pour the sauce into a medium bowl and fold in the remaining 1¾ cups blueberries and the blackberries to coat. Chill in the refrigerator, covered, for 1 hour or overnight.

7. To make the whipped cream, chill a metal bowl and electric mixer beaters in the freezer for at least 10 minutes. Add the heavy cream and vanilla to the bowl and beat until soft peaks form, about 1 minute. Add the confectioners' sugar and beat until medium peaks start to form, about 30 seconds. Be careful not to overbeat! Overbeating will turn your whipped cream into butter.

8. Cut the biscuits in half, spoon a generous ½ cup of filling on each bottom half, add a dollop of whipped cream, and place the remaining biscuit half on top.

NOTE: If you are preparing this dessert ahead of time, hold off on making the whipped cream until just before you are ready to serve.

Boardwalk Fudge

This sweet beach-vacation staple is thick, chewy, and satisfying. For decades vacationers have been coming to Jenkinson's on the Point Pleasant boardwalk, and it's a good bet that most of them, at some point, succumbed to the sugary cocoa aroma of freshly made fudge. While not the original recipe found in the shop, this fudge is easy and fun to make at home and will bring back memories of a great shore visit.

½ cup (1 stick) butter, softened
1 cup semisweet chocolate chips
1 teaspoon vanilla extract
2 cups sugar
1 (5-ounce) can evaporated milk
10 large marshmallows
1 cup chopped walnuts

Makes 15–20 servings

1. Butter an 8-inch square baking dish.

2. Combine the butter, chocolate chips, and vanilla in a mixing bowl until fully incorporated. Set aside.

3. Combine the sugar, evaporated milk, and marshmallows in a medium saucepan over medium heat. Bring to a boil, stirring frequently. Reduce the heat to low and let simmer for 6 minutes, stirring constantly.

4. Pour the marshmallow mixture over the chocolate chip mixture. Beat the fudge until it thickens and loses its gloss. Quickly fold in the nuts and pour into the prepared baking dish.

5. Refrigerate the fudge for several hours, until firm. Slice into bite-size pieces and serve.

JENKINSON'S SWEET SHOP

Willy Wonka ain't got nothin' on Jenkinson's Sweet Shop — it's a sugar lover's dream come to life, with all the favorites made in-house. Peanut butter cups, truffles, almond bark, fudge, jumbo caramel apples the size of softballs — whatever you bring home, it won't last long.

Chocolate Espresso Hazelnut Bark

Here is proof that a few ingredients can go a long way in the flavor department. For crisp, glossy bark, you'll need to temper the chocolate; if you're unfamiliar with how to do that, this recipe by Kathleen Hernandez is a great introduction. Just keep your eye on the thermometer and have all the tools you'll need laid out in advance. Once the bark is cooled, grab a bite, because there'll be many hands reaching for this one.

8 ounces hazelnuts, without skins
1 pound dark chocolate, chopped
6 tablespoons ground espresso

Makes 8–12 servings

1. Preheat the oven to 350°F.

2. Spread the hazelnuts on a parchment-lined baking sheet and bake until they smell nutty and are lightly browned, 10 to 12 minutes. Check frequently and stir with a wooden spoon to toast evenly. Let cool for about 15 minutes and then roughly chop.

3. Line a rimmed baking sheet with parchment or a silicone mat. Set up a double boiler, or make one by fitting a stainless-steel bowl into a saucepan. The bowl should nestle into the pan without sinking down too far. You want water to simmer in the pan without touching the bottom of the bowl.

4. Put two-thirds of the chocolate in the bowl and set aside; fill the saucepan about one-third full with water. Bring the water to a boil and then remove from the heat and place the bowl of chocolate over the pan. Stir the chocolate while it melts, checking frequently with a thermometer to make sure that the temperature does not exceed 125°F. When the chocolate is melted, remove the bowl from the pan and wipe the bottom of the bowl with a towel, making sure that no water is mixed into the chocolate. Stir in the remaining chocolate and the ground espresso and let cool, stirring frequently, until it reaches 85°F, which will be the tempered state, 5 to 12 minutes.

5. Quickly pour the tempered chocolate onto the prepared baking sheet and spread with a cake frosting spatula, making sure the surface is even. Quickly sprinkle the toasted hazelnuts evenly over the top. Transfer to the refrigerator and let cool for about 5 minutes.

6. Break up the bark with your hands into candy-size pieces. If you don't intend to eat it right away, place the bark in an airtight container and store in a cool, dry place. This keeps for up to 1 week.

Recipe from CHOCODIEM, CLINTON

Grand Marnier Truffles

Save these candies for after the kids go to bed. A good shot of the orange liqueur goes a long way flavor-wise, especially with the help of the candied citrus.

THE FILLING

18 ounces dark chocolate
(64% cocoa)

2 tablespoons butter, softened

3 ounces Grand Marnier

10 ounces heavy cream

3 ounces corn syrup

2 ounces orange zest

FOR DIPPING

1½ pounds dark chocolate
(64% cocoa)

4 ounces candied orange peel,
diced into ¼-inch squares

Makes approximately 80 truffles

1. Line three baking sheets with parchment paper or silicone mats and set out a candy thermometer, heatproof spatula, wire whisk, and piping bag with a small piping tip, such as Wilton #1A.

2. To make the filling, melt the chocolate in the microwave or in a double boiler. Combine the melted chocolate, butter, and Grand Marnier in a stainless-steel mixing bowl and whisk together. The butter should melt during this step thanks to the heated chocolate.

3. Stir together the cream, corn syrup, and orange zest in a saucepan and bring to a boil. Pour the mixture over the chocolate. Let stand 1 to 2 minutes, then whisk until all the ingredients are smooth and well emulsified. Pour this ganache mixture onto one of the prepared baking sheets and let cool to 75°F.

4. Use a spatula to scoop the ganache into the piping bag with the attached tip. Pipe small balls of ganache onto the second baking sheet. The balls can be anywhere in size between marbles and golf balls. When you're done, transfer the baking sheet to the refrigerator to chill while you temper the dipping chocolate.

5. Set up a double boiler or make one by fitting a stainless-steel bowl into a saucepan. The bowl should nestle into the pan without sinking down too far. You want water to simmer in the pan without touching the bottom of the bowl.

RECIPE CONTINUES ON PAGE 234

6. Put two-thirds of the dipping chocolate in the bowl and set aside; fill the saucepan about one-third full with water. Bring the water to a boil and then remove from the heat and place the bowl of chocolate over the pan. Stir the chocolate while it melts, checking frequently with a thermometer to make sure that the temperature does not exceed 125°F. When the chocolate is melted, remove the bowl from the pan and wipe the bottom of the bowl with a towel, making sure that no water is mixed into the chocolate. Stir in the remaining chocolate and let cool, stirring frequently, until it reaches 85°F, which will be the tempered state, 5 to 12 minutes. The chocolate is now ready for dipping your piped truffles.

7. Remove the chilled truffle fillings from the refrigerator. Using a small fork to hold each ball of truffle filling, dip it into the tempered chocolate. Place the dipped truffles onto the third prepared baking sheet, and quickly — before the chocolate sets — place a few pieces of diced candied orange zest on top.

8. Let the truffles set for 20 minutes before serving. If you don't plan to eat them all immediately, store the truffles in an airtight container in the refrigerator, where they will keep for 3 to 5 days.

NOTE: If the chocolate loses its tempered state — by becoming too hard — while you are dipping the truffles, you can set the bowl with the chocolate back over the pan of hot water for 3 to 5 seconds at a time until it reaches 87° to 91°F. If the temperature exceeds this limit, however, you will have to repeat the tempering process.

Recipe from THE CARRIAGE HOUSE BISTRO AND BAR, MILLBURN

Warm Black and Blue Cobbler

Celebrating the best sweet treats of the New Jersey summer, this old-fashioned dessert is relatively simple to prepare and infinitely delicious. It comes from the files of Holly Guber, executive chef at the Carriage House Bistro of the Paper Mill Playhouse in Millburn. Serve with — what else? — fresh vanilla bean ice cream.

THE FILLING

- 4 cups fresh blackberries
- 4 cups fresh blueberries
- ¾ cup granulated sugar
- 2 tablespoons all-purpose flour
- ⅛ teaspoon salt
- Zest and juice of 1 lemon

THE TOPPING

- 1⅔ cups all-purpose flour
- ⅓ cup granulated sugar
- 1 tablespoon baking powder
- 6 tablespoons cold unsalted butter, cut into small pieces
- ¾ cup sour cream
- 3 tablespoons milk
- 2 tablespoons demerera sugar
- ½ teaspoon cinnamon

Makes 8–10 servings

1. Prepare the filling: Butter a 9- by 13-inch baking dish. Combine the blackberries, blueberries, granulated sugar, flour, salt, and lemon zest and juice in a large bowl; toss together gently. Transfer to the prepared baking dish and set aside.

2. Preheat the oven to 350°F.

3. For the topping, combine the flour, granulated sugar, and baking powder in a large bowl. Cut in the butter, using two sharp paring knives to slice the butter into very fine pieces. Blend until the mixture resembles coarse meal.

4. In a separate bowl, whisk together the sour cream and milk until smooth. Add the sour cream mixture gently to the flour mixture, tossing with a rubber spatula until the mixture comes together in featherlike shreds.

5. Gently spread the topping over the berry filling, covering evenly. Combine the demerara sugar with the cinnamon in a small bowl, mix well, and sprinkle over the top of the cobbler.

6. Bake for 50 to 60 minutes, until the juices are bubbling and the topping is browned. Let cool for at least 20 minutes before serving.

Recipe from MECHA ARTISAN CHOCOLATE, HADDON TOWNSHIP

Honey-Thyme Caramels

Here's yet another use for that thyme growing in your garden, and this time it's for something sweet, not savory. Caramel can seem daunting to make the first time, but once you get the hang of it, you'll likely appreciate the attention it requires and, of course, the taste. Just make sure you have a candy or digital thermometer on hand. This recipe is also a great use for local honey, the kind found at farmers' markets or roadside stands. Stock up on cellophane or candy wrappers in advance of making this recipe.

Cooking spray
½ teaspoon sea salt
1 cup heavy cream
1 bundle fresh thyme
1½ cups sugar
¼ cup wildflower honey
2 tablespoons light corn syrup
1 tablespoon butter
4 ounces dark chocolate
1 tablespoon bee pollen (optional)

Makes about 60 caramels

1. Spray an 8-inch square baking dish with cooking spray, line it with plastic wrap (pressing to take the shape of the pan), and then spray the plastic wrap. Sprinkle the salt evenly over the bottom of the pan and set aside.

2. Heat the cream and thyme in small pot over medium heat until just beginning to boil; turn off the heat and set aside, removing the thyme sprigs.

3. Warm a slightly larger pot over medium-high heat. Add ½ cup of the sugar and melt while swirling the pan. *Do not stir.* The sugar will take on a light amber color after about 2 minutes. Add another ½ cup of the sugar and swirl the pan until that sugar has melted, 1 to 2 minutes. Again, *do not stir.* Add the remaining ½ cup sugar and resume the swirling process until it's melted, 1 to 2 minutes. Add the honey and cook for 2 minutes longer, until the sugar has taken on a medium amber color.

4. Turn off the heat, add the light corn syrup, and stir with a wooden spoon; the mixture will bubble up, so be careful. Very slowly, add the thyme-infused cream to the sugar mixture and stir to combine.

5. Clip a candy thermometer to the pot and bring to a boil over medium heat, without disturbing the contents. Once the bubbling starts to subside or the temperature is at a steady 230°F, stir gently until the caramel reaches 250°F. Remove from the heat and stir in the butter.

6. Pour the caramel into the prepared baking dish and set aside to cool at room temperature for at least 4 hours, but preferably overnight.

7. When the caramel is set, melt half of the chocolate by using a double boiler or the microwave. Coat the top of the caramel with the melted chocolate. Let the chocolate set (you can hurry up that process by placing the pan in the fridge).

8. Flip the pan over onto a cutting board lined with parchment paper. Pull on the plastic wrap to remove the caramel from the pan, then peel off the plastic wrap. Melt the rest of the chocolate and coat the exposed side of the caramel with more melted chocolate and sprinkle with bee pollen, if desired. Let the chocolate set.

9. Use a chef's knife to cut the caramel into 1-inch squares; you should end up with 55 to 60 caramels. Once cut, the caramels will slowly lose their shape, so it's important to wrap them right away in cellophane or other candy wrappers. Store the caramels in the refrigerator in an airtight container, where they will keep for about 4 weeks.

Blueberry Caramels

You won't be able to have just one. Rich with the flavors of fresh blueberry and dark chocolate, plus the subtle depth of honey, these are worth the preparation time. You'll need silicone candy molds and a candy thermometer, but it's a good bet you'll make these again and again. This recipe, by Diane Pinder, yields nearly 100 caramels.

Cooking spray
1 cup heavy cream
4 tablespoons butter
1 cup prepared blueberry purée
3 cups sugar
2 tablespoons honey
2 cups (1 pound) dark
    melting chocolate

Makes roughly 96 caramels

1. Spray a 9- by 13-inch rimmed baking sheet with cooking spray.

2. Warm the cream with 2 tablespoons of the butter in a small saucepan over low heat. When the butter is melted, add the blueberry purée, stir to combine, and remove from the heat.

3. Affix a candy thermometer to a heavy-bottomed pot. Combine the sugar and honey in the pot and cook until the mixture reaches 300°F. Slowly add the warmed cream and blueberry mixture, stirring to fully combine. Cook, stirring often, until the mixture reaches 258°F and then remove from the heat. Add the remaining 2 tablespoons butter and stir to combine.

4. Pour the caramel onto the prepared baking sheet and allow to cool. Using a paring knife, cut into ½-inch squares.

5. Use a double boiler or make one by fitting a stainless-steel bowl into a saucepan. The bowl should nestle into the pan without sinking down too far. You want water to simmer in the pan without touching the bottom of the bowl.

6. Put two-thirds of the chocolate in the bowl and set aside; fill the saucepan about one-third full with water. Bring the water to a boil and then remove from the heat and place the bowl of chocolate over the pan. Stir the chocolate while it melts, checking frequently with a thermometer to make sure that the temperature does not exceed 125°F. When the chocolate is melted, remove the bowl from the pan and wipe the bottom of the bowl with a towel, making sure no water is mixed into the chocolate. Stir in the remaining chocolate and let cool, stirring frequently, until it reaches 85°F, which will be the tempered state, 5 to 12 minutes. The chocolate is now ready for dipping your caramels.

7. Line a baking sheet with parchment paper. Dip each piece of caramel into the melted chocolate to coat it completely. Transfer to the lined sheet to cool.

8. Once they're cooled and set, store the caramels in the refrigerator. They'll keep for about 6 months.

Recipe from L'ARTE DELLA PASTICCERIA, RAMSEY

Limoncello Cheesecake

Have this once and crave it forever. The zip and punch of citrus blends nicely with the creamy texture and tangy cheese flavor to create a one-of-a-kind cheesecake. For the cookie crumb base, the chef at L'Arte della Pasticceria uses ground cornmeal cookie crumbs but says almost any cookie crumbs will do, including graham cracker crumbs. To complete this recipe, you'll need eight individual 4-ounce molds, rings, or pans. *Read about L'Arte della Pasticceria on page 242.*

THE CRUST

- 1 cup cookie crumbs
- ¼ cup (½ stick) melted butter

THE CHEESECAKE

- ½ cup sugar
- Zest of 1 lemon
- Zest of 1 orange
- 1 cup cream cheese
- ½ cup fresh ricotta cheese
- 2 eggs
- 3 tablespoons sour cream
- 2 tablespoons limoncello
- 1½ tablespoons fresh lemon juice
- 1½ tablespoons fresh orange juice
- 1 teaspoon cornstarch
- Fresh berries, for garnish

Makes 8 individual cheesecakes

1. Preheat the oven to 350°F and place eight molds, rings, or pans on a baking sheet. To make the crust, combine the cookie crumbs and the melted butter in a medium mixing bowl and mix together.

2. Place 2 heaping tablespoons of the crust into each mold and press the crumbs into the bottom of the molds. Place the baking sheet in the oven and cook for 10 minutes, remove from the oven, and let cool. Raise the oven temperature to 400°F.

3. To make the cheesecake, combine the sugar, lemon zest, and orange zest in the bowl of a stand mixer. Add the cream cheese and ricotta. Using the paddle attachment, beat the mixture on the medium setting until very light and fluffy, about 5 minutes.

4. Add the eggs one at a time, beating for 30 seconds after each egg. Scrape down the sides of the bowl several times.

5. Add the sour cream, limoncello, lemon juice, and orange juice, and beat well. Switch from the paddle to the whip and beat until smooth, about 1 minute. Add the cornstarch and beat for an additional 30 seconds.

6. Fill the crust-lined molds with the batter, dividing evenly. Bake at 400°F for about 12 minutes, or until the cheesecakes are beginning to brown and have a "set" surface but are still somewhat jiggly underneath. Remove from the oven and let cool, about 20 minutes. Chill and freeze them for 2 hours or overnight.

7. Before serving, unmold the cheesecakes and garnish with fresh berries. Frozen cheesecakes will defrost quickly (about 15 minutes at room temperature or 30 minutes in the refrigerator).

241

L'ARTE DELLA PASTICCERIA

Inspired by the bakeries of Europe, especially the ones found in small Italian villages, the owners of L'Arte della Pasticceria wanted to bring the sense of community and freshness to their neighbors in North Jersey, not far from the New York state line. It's artisanal in every sense of the word. Everything is made from scratch, and it offers more than just fresh bread and pastry. It fills any meal you might have from breakfast treats to soups and paninis, salads, pizza, hand-dipped chocolates and truffles, and more, most featuring Italian or Mediterranean ingredients. The menu changes with the seasons, and thanks to its commitment to fresh and flavorful, in the few short years since it opened, the bakery has become a favorite go-to for residents.

Chef Vicki Wells

Vanilla Mascarpone Truffles

MILK CHOCOLATE ALMOND

Recipe from THE INN AT FERNBROOK FARMS, BORDENTOWN

Rosemary–Black Pepper Shortbreads

There are a lot of reasons to visit the Inn at Fernbrook Farms, and these shortbreads are one of them. Created by chef Christine Wendland, they became a *sensation* when they first appeared on the menu, and now they sell out in mere minutes when stocked in the inn's store. They are salty, a bit sweet, homey but upscale at the same time, and they feature the herb Larry "Farmer Q" Kuser grows for the inn in abundance — fresh rosemary. Says Wendland, "If any food I make can be defined as 'Fernbrook,' it's these." *Read about the Inn at Fernbrook Farms on page 143.*

1 cup (2 sticks) unsalted butter, softened

⅔ cup sugar

2 tablespoons finely chopped fresh rosemary

2 cups all-purpose flour

½ teaspoon salt

½ teaspoon freshly ground black pepper

Cooking spray

1 tablespoon coarse black or pink sea salt

Makes about 60 (1-inch-square) shortbreads

1. Preheat the oven to 325°F. Line a rimmed baking sheet with parchment paper.

2. Combine the butter, sugar, and rosemary in the bowl of a stand mixer and mix on low speed until fluffy. Add the flour, salt, and ¼ teaspoon of the black pepper, and mix on low until just combined into a thick, dense dough. Turn out onto plastic wrap, form into a flat disk, and chill in the refrigerator for 10 minutes.

3. Lightly flour the disk of dough and roll it out on the prepared baking sheet until it reaches all four corners evenly; this will take some pressing and effort and a good deal of flour for your rolling pin. Don't give up!

4. When the dough is evenly distributed on the pan, spray lightly all over with cooking spray and sprinkle the remaining ¼ teaspoon pepper and the coarse salt evenly over the dough. Press in gently with the rolling pin.

5. Bake for 12 minutes, then remove and quickly score into the desired cookie size (Wendland suggests 1-inch squares) with a sharp chef's knife. Rotate the pan and return to the oven for another 10 minutes. Remove and let cool before breaking on the score lines into cookies. The cookies store well, wrapped tightly, for about 2 weeks.

Recipe from TERHUNE ORCHARDS, PRINCETON

Mama's Apple Cake

This recipe is proof that baking doesn't have to be complicated or overthought. Just a few flavorful ingredients and an hour in the oven and you have one of the state's signature baked desserts. Use the apples that suit you, and over time try different varieties until you find the one (or blend) that you like best. The same is true with the nuts and raisins — find a topping that suits your taste, and soon enough this cake will be of your own design.

1 cup cooking oil

2 cups sugar

2 eggs, beaten until foamy

1 teaspoon vanilla extract

2 cups all-purpose flour

1 teaspoon baking soda

1 teaspoon ground cinnamon

½ teaspoon salt

4 cups apples, peeled, cored, and chopped

½ cup chopped nuts chopped or raisins, for garnish (optional)

Makes 6–8 servings

1. Preheat the oven to 350°F. Grease a Bundt pan.

2. Combine the oil and sugar in a large bowl until well mixed. Add the eggs and vanilla and whisk together.

3. In a separate bowl, sift together the flour, baking soda, cinnamon, and salt. Fold the dry ingredients into the oil mixture and mix thoroughly. Fold in the apples. Pour the batter into the prepared pan and bake for 1 hour.

4. Let cool completely before removing the cake from the pan. Garnish with nuts or raisins, if desired.

Cocktails

Walk into just about any bar these days and you'll likely find a specialty house cocktail, which is a drink conceived by a trained bartender that plays off the flavors of local spirits and liqueurs as well as garden-fresh ingredients. Shake up one of these for yourself and guests to get the party started. The cocktails in this chapter highlight the best of New Jersey's farms, orchards, and vineyards, while underscoring the great diversity of flavors, cultures, and talents that come together in the Garden State.

Red Sangria

Fruity yet rich, sangria is as much a thirst quencher as a perfect pairing for the many Portuguese-inspired dishes it is served alongside at restaurants throughout Newark's Ironbound. It's easy to make and suitable for any time of year, but it feels a bit more indulgent when the weather is warm. Keep multiple servings of fruit on hand for additional pitchers, or scale up the recipe for larger servings.

1 apple

1 orange

½ (750-milliliter) bottle dry red wine (preferably Spanish Tempranillo)

4 ounces freshly squeezed orange juice

4 ounces triple sec

4 ounces peach schnapps

4 ounces brandy

Makes 2–4 servings

1. Set the apple, orange, wine, and orange juice in the refrigerator to chill for at least 1 hour.

2. Chop the apple and slice the orange. Fill a large pitcher half-full with ice. Add the wine, orange juice, triple sec, schnapps, and brandy, and stir thoroughly. Add the chopped apple and the sliced orange and stir again.

3. The longer the sangria steeps, the more the flavors will develop and deepen. Give it at least 30 minutes in the refrigerator to rest. Pour into glasses and serve, adding ice and/or additional fruit to taste.

MOMPOU. Mompou opened in 2005 and quickly became an institution in the Ironbound. The restaurant offers an inventive and flavorful menu that veers toward the small-plate tapas style. It's not uncommon to see a line forming down Ferry Street for diners and drinkers waiting for their chance at a table or a spot on the rear garden patio.

Gunnison Beach Fizz

Here's a cocktail that celebrates bright citrus flavors with a warm tropical kick. Created by Jersey native Warren Bobrow, a renowned author and cocktail creator, it's perfect for backyard barbecues. When it comes to the fruit juices, freshly squeezed is always suggested, but prepackaged can work in a pinch. For the rum, check out Busted Barrel Silver, from Jersey Artisan Distilling, for a local option.

2 ounces light rum

1 ounce cream of coconut liqueur

1 ounce freshly squeezed grapefruit juice

1 ounce freshly squeezed lemon juice

1 ounce freshly squeezed lime juice

1 ounce freshly squeezed orange juice

1–2 spritzes absinthe (from an atomizer)

4 ounces natural grapefruit soda

Makes 2 cocktails

1. Fill a Boston shaker three-quarters full with ice and add rum, coconut liqueur, grapefruit juice, lemon juice, lime juice, and orange juice. Shake well for 10 seconds.

2. Add a few cubes of ice to two tall collins glasses and spritz each with the absinthe. Split the contents of the shaker between the two glasses. Top with the soda.

The Blue Jersey

A Garden State spin on the classic martini, this version uses farm-fresh berries. Drinks enthusiast Oswin Cruz suggests serving it straight up at your next midsummer cocktail party.

6-12 fresh blueberries

2 ounces Hendrick's gin

¾ ounce Carpano Antica Formula or similar sweet vermouth

4 dashes lemon bitters

Makes 1 cocktail

Muddle the blueberries (using as many as you like, depending on their size and your preference) in a Boston shaker. Fill the shaker with ice; add the gin, vermouth, and bitters; and stir. Strain into a fresh rocks glass and garnish with a few blueberries.

At Danube, Turn Left

Here's another from the Warren Bobrow cocktail collection, and it's perfect for those frozen winter nights spent in front of the fireplace. A bit of rum (the particular one used in this recipe yields a soft butterscotch flavor) in your rich hot chocolate is a wonderful indulgence.

1.25 cups prepared hot chocolate beverage or 10 ounces bittersweet chocolate

3 ounces Stroh 80 spiced rum (160 proof)

4 tablespoons fresh whipped cream

Aromatic bitters

Makes 2 cocktails

1. Heat the hot chocolate according to the package directions, or melt the solid bittersweet chocolate over medium-low heat in a saucepan until smooth, taking care not to burn.

2. Divide the hot chocolate between two mugs. Carefully float 1½ ounces of rum over the hot chocolate in each mug. Top each with 2 tablespoons of whipped cream and give each a dash of the bitters. Serve immediately.

The Ironbound Amazon

While sangria is the national drink of Newark's Ironbound neighborhood (see the recipe on page 248), drinks enthusiast Oswin Cruz created this ode to the Brazilian community that also calls "Down Neck" home.

2 sprigs fresh mint leaves

2 ounces strong yerba maté tea (use 2 teabags per cup)

1½ ounces Ypioca Ouro cachaça

¾ ounce green Chartreuse liqueur

¼ ounce freshly squeezed lime juice

4 dashes Angostura bitters

Makes 1 cocktail

Muddle 1 sprig of the mint in a Boston shaker and then fill with ice. Pour in the tea, cachaça, Chartreuse, lime juice, and bitters. Shake well, strain into a glass with fresh ice, and garnish with a small sprig of mint.

Recipe from AMERICANA DINER, EAST WINDSOR

The Formal

Taking many of the flavors of the warm weather — citrus, flower, and herb, — this cocktail is sunshine in a glass. It's the perfect sipper for summer afternoons spent lazing in the backyard. *Read about the Americana Diner on page 209.*

4 mint leaves

2 ounces Titos or similar premium vodka

2 ounces juice from freshly pressed red grapes

1 ounce St-Germain or similar elderflower liqueur

1 teaspoon freshly squeezed lemon juice

Makes 1 cocktail

Muddle three of the mint leaves in a Boston shaker. Fill with ice and then add the vodka, grape juice, St-Germain, and lemon juice. Shake well. Strain into a rocks glass and serve straight up with the remaining mint leaf as garnish.

Garden State Guanaco

As a drinks enthusiast, Oswin Cruz is of the (apparently slightly controversial) opinion that — with all due respect to those who drink it — vodka is too much of a neutral spirit and brings nothing to the table other than booze. Following a conversation with friends, he decided to try and prove a point, and his answer to the now-trendy Moscow Mule was the Vermont Llama: 1½ ounces Barr Hill Tom Cat barrel-aged gin (in lieu of vodka), 4 ounces ginger beer, ⅛ ounce lime juice, and hop bitters. It worked, so he improved upon it further and created the Garden State Guanaco.

1½ ounces Farmer's Botanical gin

¾ ounce St-Germain or similar elderflower liqueur

½ ounce cucumber juice (can be purchased, or mince and press out ¼ fresh peeled cucumber)

¼ ounce freshly squeezed lime juice

6 drops hop bitters

2 ounces ginger beer

Lime wheel, for garnish

Makes 1 cocktail

Combine the gin, St-Germain, cucumber juice, lime juice, and bitters in a Boston shaker with ice. Shake well to combine and pour into a rocks glass. Top with the ginger beer and garnish with a lime wheel.

Red Delicious Manhattan

Here's a modern spin on the classic Manhattan. The moonshine and apple-flavored liqueur are a sweet complement to the bourbon — in this case a modern craft whiskey. While this cocktail calls for specific brands, feel free to substitute your own favorites.

2 ounces Clyde May's Alabama Style whiskey

1 ounce Carpano Antica Formula sweet vermouth

½ ounce Dekuyper Red Apple schnapps

½ ounce cinnamon apple moonshine

Dash of Angostura bitters

Maraschino cherry, for garnish

Makes 1 cocktail

1. Fill a Boston shaker with ice, then add the whiskey, vermouth, schnapps, moonshine, and bitters. With the spirits in the stainless-steel half of the shaker, stir gently until the shaker begins to sweat.

2. Pour into a cocktail glass and garnish with a cherry.

PINT. While it's had a few names over the years, the bar now known as Pint opened its doors to Jersey City in 1911. Located just one block from city hall, it was reportedly once owned by Jersey City's infamous mayor Frank Hague (himself a teetotaler) and operated as a speakeasy during Prohibition. In 2008 Pint became the first bar in Jersey City to specialize in exclusively American craft beer, with a rotating menu featuring more than 50 brews from across the country. Pint has been awarded the coveted Good Beer Seal by an independent panel of bar owners and drinks professionals.

Boardwalk Bar and Grill Margarita

Countless glasses of this classic cocktail are shaken and served each summer down the shore. It's the go-to drink for pairing with seafood, burgers, and good times as the sun sets on another perfect beach day. The salt on the rim is key, as it balances out the sweetness of the lime juice and triple sec. *Read about Jenkinson's Boardwalk Bar & Grill on page 60.*

Kosher salt
1½ ounces tequila
¾ ounce triple sec
¾ ounce Rose's lime juice
4 ounces sour mix
Lime wedge, for garnish

Makes 1 cocktail

1. Line the rim of a margarita glass with salt: Place salt on a small plate, rub the rim of the glass with a wet paper towel, and then place the rim into the salt. The salt will adhere to the moist rim.

2. Fill a Boston shaker with ice. Add the tequila, triple sec, lime juice, and sour mix. Shake well.

3. Pour into the prepared glass and garnish with a lime wedge. Sit back, relax, and enjoy.

Homemade Irish Cream Liqueur

Popular as an after-dinner drink, this creamy liqueur with a boozy kick is most often associated with an Irish family name beginning with the letter *B*. A friend, Anne Frawley, gave me a bottle of her homemade version as a Christmas present a few years back, and it was quickly put to good use. After getting the recipe from Anne, I've taken on the tradition of whipping up batches every holiday season. I package the liqueur in cleaned wine or whiskey bottles and give them out as presents, always keeping a few on hand at the house.

1 cup light cream

1 teaspoon instant coffee

4 eggs, whisked

1¾ cups Irish whiskey

1 (14-ounce) can sweetened
    condensed milk

2 tablespoons chocolate syrup

1 teaspoon vanilla extract

½ teaspoon almond extract

Makes about 20 ounces

1. Heat the cream and instant coffee in a small saucepan over medium heat until warm, stirring until the grains are fully dissolved, 2 to 3 minutes.

2. Transfer the coffee mixture to the blender. Add the eggs, whiskey, condensed milk, chocolate syrup, vanilla, and almond extract. Blend until fully combined, about 1 minute.

3. Run the liquid through a fine-mesh strainer, chill, and serve or bottle. It can be kept refrigerated for up to 1 week.

RESOURCES

Festivals

No matter the time of year, New Jersey is full of events that celebrate food, culture, and ingredients. Some are held in locations that are off the beaten path, giving you the chance to visit new corners of the state. Festivals also give you the chance to meet like-minded foodies, chefs, artisans, and restaurateurs. Here is a list of some of the festivals worth putting on your calendar.

The Chatsworth Cranberry Festival
Chatsworth
www.cranfest.org
Held each October for the past three decades, this is a celebration of the state's strong cranberry crop as well as the culture of the Pine Barrens. In addition to featuring the autumnal fruit, the weekend-long event also provides a showcase for local craftspeople and artists.

Garden State Craft Brewers Guild Festival
Camden
http://njbeer.org
Held on the decks of the battleship *New Jersey* on the Camden waterfront, with sweeping views of the Philly skyline, this is an annual gathering of the state's breweries. Take a tour of the historic destroyer and meet the brewers behind the state's best beer. This is a chance to support local beer makers and maybe even find a new favorite.

Great Tomato Tasting
Clifford E. & Melda C. Snyder Research and
  Extension Farm
Pittstown
www.snyderfarm.rutgers.edu/snyder-events.html
Every summer the Snyder Research and Extension Farm hosts an educational event and tasting for the state's most famous fruit. Taste more than 60 heirloom tomato varieties, get gardening tips from pros, and learn about the research and hard work that Rutgers gives to state farmers.

Jazzy Scallop & Seafood Festival
Viking Village
Barnegat Light
http://vikingvillage.homestead.com/Jazzy-Scallop-Festival.html
A musical celebration of the sea held at Viking Village on Long Beach Island, this summer event combines dishes prepared by local restaurants (as well as many a raw bar) and live music. It's a warm-weather chance to eat, dance, and be merry.

Jersey Fresh Wine Festival
Garden State Wine Growers Association
Columbus
www.newjerseywines.com
Sponsored by the Garden State Wine Growers Association, this September showcase for Jersey vino is a must for oenophiles and casual fans alike. Held at the Burlington County Fairgrounds (there's a farmers' market, too), you can taste vintages, learn about the wine-making process, and meet the artisans putting their passion into bottles.

Jersey Shore Food Truck Festival
Oceanport
www.monmouthpark.com
A three-day festival featuring more than two dozen of the area's best and inventive food trucks, this is a must-visit for any serious street eater. Held at Monmouth Park, you can sample bites from different cuisines and meet the dedicated cooks and chefs who toil away in tiny hot kitchens to bring you the very best flavors.

Michael Arnone's Crawfish Fest
Augusta
www.crawfishfest.com
Here's a taste of the bayou in Jersey. Three decades after a crawfish boil for friends turned into an epic event, this is now a three-day camping and music festival. With national acts on the stage and the best Cajun food north of Louisiana, this is an annual pilgrimage for many.

New Jersey State Fair
Augusta
http://njstatefair.org
Deep-fried everything, along with sugary and salty delights, await you at the annual event held at the fairgrounds in Sussex County. Agricultural, farming, and gardening seminars and exhibits are featured along with local artisans of all stripes. Make the annual summer pilgrimage and celebrate all things Jersey.

Pork Roll Festival
Trenton
www.porkrollfestival.com
The state's "official" meat has an annual May event in the city of its creation. With historical lectures, live music, recipes showcasing pork roll, and the crowning of a Pork Roll Queen, it's an event not to be missed (just get your cardiologist's approval first).

St. Ann's Italian Festival
Hoboken
For more than a century, the faithful have gathered on 7th Street and Jefferson in the mile-square city for a festival that brings a needed dose of the old world to a quickly changing city. Food vendors, games, faith, and community all converge on the street for the four-day event that also features live music and a pizza contest.

Restaurant Weeks of Note

Asbury Park Restaurant Tour
www.loveasbury.com

Downtown Westfield Restaurant Week
www.westfieldtoday.com/Restaurantweek

Edible Jersey's Eat Drink Local Week
http://ediblejersey.com

Hudson Restaurant Week
http://hudsonrestaurantweek.com

Jersey Shore Restaurant Week
http://jerseyshorerestaurantweek.com

Wildwood Restaurant Week
Wildwood Restaurant Association
http://wildwoodbythesearestaurantweek.com

Restaurants, Farms, and Families by County

ATLANTIC COUNTY

Formica Bros. Bakery
2310 Arctic Avenue
Atlantic City, NJ 08401
609-344-2732
www.formicabrosbakery.com
Frank D. Formica, chef
Grandma Rosa's Tomato Pie, page 202

BERGEN COUNTY

L'Arte della Pasticceria
107–109 East Main Street
Ramsey, NJ 07446
201-934-3211
http://larte.biz
@LartePastry
Limoncello Cheesecake, page 240

BURLINGTON COUNTY

The Inn at Fernbrook Farms
142 Bordentown-Georgetown Road
Bordentown, NJ 08505
609-298-3868
www.innatfernbrookfarms.com
Christine Wendland, chef
Poached Chicken Meatballs in Pesto Cream, page 142
Rosemary–Black Pepper Shortbreads, page 244

Village Idiot Brewing Company
42 High Street
Mount Holly, NJ 08060
609-975-9270
http://villageidiotbrewing.com
@VillageIdiotNJ
Rich Palmay, chef
Beer-Braised Sausage and Peppers, page 145
Pressure-Cooker Corned Beef, page 139
Spent-Grain Bread Rolls, page 167

CAMDEN COUNTY

Mecha Artisan Chocolate
1001 White Horse Pike
SoHa Arts Building
Haddon Township, NJ 08107
609-410-2738
www.mechachocolate.com
@Mecha_Chocolate
Melissa Crandley, chef
Honey-Thyme Caramels, page 236

CAPE MAY COUNTY

The Blue Rose Inn and Restaurant
653 Washington Street
Cape May, NJ 08204
609-435-5458
www.blueroseinn.com
@blueroseinn
Michael Keating, chef
Ancho and Ale Chili with Avocado Mousse, page 118
Cape May Salt Oyster and IPA Chowder, page 94

Saltwater Café
at South Jersey Marina
1231 Route 109
Cape May, NJ 08204
609-884-2403
http://saltwatercafecapemay.com
Crab and Corn Chowder, page 96

CUMBERLAND COUNTY

Flaim Farms
Vineland, New Jersey
856-691-2970
rrflaimproduce.com
Baked Cauliflower Casserole, page 74
Farm-Fresh Beet Salad, page 54

Viet Bistro
in the Cumberland Mall
3849 South Delsea Drive, Storey F28
Vineland, NJ 08360
856-825-5001
http://vietbistronj.com
Thuynhan Truong, chef
Chicken Lettuce Wraps with Avocado, page 186

ESSEX COUNTY

The Carriage House Bistro & Bar
in the F. M. Kirby Carriage House at Paper Mill Playhouse
22 Brookside Drive
Millburn, NJ 07041
973-376-4343
http://papermill.org/restaurant.html
@Paper_Mill
Holly Guber, chef
Warm Black and Blue Cobbler, page 235

Hobby's Delicatessen and Restaurant
32 Brandford Place
Newark, NJ 07102
973-623-0410
http://hobbysdeli.com
Cheese Blintzes, page 24

Manischewitz Company
80 Avenue K
Newark, NJ 07105
201-553-1100
http://manischewitz.com
@ManischewitzCo
Shifra Klein, chef
Jamie Geller, chef
Alessandra Rovati, chef
Apple, Fennel, and Tarragon Slaw, page 75
Carrot, Quinoa, and Spinach Soup, page 130
Chicken Thighs with Roasted Fall Fruit, page 123
Roasted Lamb with Pomegranate and Wine, page 138

Mompou Tapas Wine Bar and Lounge
77 Ferry Street
Newark, NJ 07105
973-578-8114
www.mompoutapas.com
@MompouTapas
Red Sangria, page 248

The Orange Squirrel Restaurant
412 Bloomfield Avenue
Bloomfield, NJ 07003
973-337-6421
www.theorangesquirrel.com
@orangesquirrel
Francesco Palmieri, chef
TEC (Taylor Ham, Egg, and Cheese) Soup, page 122

Seabra's Marisqueira
87 Madison Street
Newark, NJ 07105
973-465-1250
http://seabras-marisqueira.com
Shrimp with Garlic Sauce, page 180

Haines Pork Shop
521 Kings Highway
Mickleton, NJ 08056
856-423-1192
http://hainesporkshop.com
Baked Ham with Bourbon Glaze, page 149
Crown Roast of Pork, page 150
Pork Loin with Sausage Stuffing, page 152

Anthony David's Gourmet Specialties
953 Bloomfield Street
Hoboken, NJ 07030
201-222-8399
http://anthonydavids.com
@Anthony_Davids
Anthony Pino, chef
Lamb Tartare, page 46

Barcade
163 Newark Avenue
Jersey City, NJ 07302
201-332-4555
http://barcadejerseycity.com
@barcadejersey
Larry Brinkman, chef
Steak Sauce, page 174

Busy Bee Organics
Grove Street Path Station
Jersey City, New Jersey
908-219-9066
http://busybeeorganics.com
Almond-Cherry Pancakes with Coconut Flakes,
    page 16
Cucumber Gazpacho with Crabmeat, page 84

Pint
34 Wayne Street
Jersey City, NJ 07302
201-367-1222
www.pintbar.com
Tommy DeMaio, chef
Red Delicious Manhattan, page 254

Sam a.m.
112 Morris Street
Jersey City, NJ 07302
201-432-2233
http://sam-am.com
Francis Samu, chef
Chicken and Waffles, page 20

Sátis Bistro
212 Washington Street
Jersey City, NJ 07302
201-435-5151
www.satisbistro.com
@satisbistro
Michael Fiorianti, chef
Cheese Curd Poutine with Pork Shank Gravy, page 136

Chocodiem
49 Main Street
Clinton, NJ 08809
908-200-7044
www.chocodiem.com
@chocodiem
Kathleen Hernandez, chef
Chocolate Espresso Hazelnut Bark, page 230
Grand Marnier Truffles, page 232

The Farm Cooking School
Tullamore Farms
1998 Daniel Bray Highway
Stockton, NJ 08559
http://thefarmcookingschool.com
@TheFarmCooks
Ian Knauer, chef
Country Wheat Bread, page 166
Dry Vegetarian Curry, page 181

More Than Q
Stockton Farm Market
19 West Bridge Street
Stockton, NJ 08559
215-512-7636
http://morethanq.com
MTQ BBQ Rub, page 171

Pudgy's Street Food
1100 County Road 523
Flemington, NJ 08822
732-684-4297
www.pudgysstreetfood.com
@pudgystreetfood
Garlic Knot Fries, page 38

Unionville Vineyards
9 Rocktown Road
Ringoes, NJ 08551
908-788-0400
http://unionvillevineyards.com
@unionvillewines
Emily Rogalsky, chef
Honey-Roasted Chicken, page 129
Marinated Eggplant Sandwich with Soppressata and
    Mozzarella, page 158

12 Farms Restaurant
120 North Main Street
Hightstown, NJ 08520
609-336-7746
www.12farms.com
@12farms
Rennie DiLorenzo, chef
Honey-Balsamic Roasted Beet Salad, page 53

Americana Diner
359 US Highway 130
East Windsor, NJ 08520
609-448-4477
www.americanadiner.com
@Americanadiner
Lamb-Stuffed Eggplant, page 208
The Formal, page 253

The Bent Spoon
35 Palmer Square West
Princeton, NJ 08542
609-924-2368
http://thebentspoon.net
@thebentspoon
Gabrielle Carbone and Matthew Errico, chefs
Strawberry-Basil Sorbet, page 214

Cherry Grove Farm
Lawrenceville Road (Route 206 North)
Lawrenceville, NJ 08648
609-219-0053
www.cherrygrovefarm.com
@cherrygrovefarm
Classic Lawrenceville Mac and Cheese, page 132
Whey-Fed Pork Chops with Berry-Mustard Sauce,
    page 140

LiLLiPiES
1225 State Road, #206
Princeton, NJ 08540
609-240-7738
http://lillipies.com
@lillipies
Jen Carson, chef
Blueberry-Apple Crumb Pie, page 218
Peach-Habanero Pocket Pies, page 220

Muirhead Foods
1040 Pennsylvania Avenue
Trenton, NJ 08638
800-782-7803
http://muirheadfoods.com
Barbara Simpson, chef
Autumnal Brown Rice Salad, page 56
Cranberry Pie, page 224

The Peacock Inn
20 Bayard Lane
Princeton, NJ 08540
609-924-1707
www.peacockinn.com
Sautéed Ricotta Gnocchi with Portobello Mushrooms,
    Tomato Confit, and Mushroom Butter Sauce,
    page 134

Rat's Restaurant
at Grounds for Sculpture
16 Fairground Road
Hamilton, NJ 08619
609-584-7800
www.ratsrestaurant.com
@gfsnj
Grilled Octopus with Romesco Sauce, Frisée, and
Marcona Almonds, page 98

Small World Coffee
Multiple locations; see website for details.
http://smallworldcoffee.com
@swcoffee
Rosemary-Citrus Soda Syrup, page 86

Terhune Orchards
330 Cold Soil Road
Princeton, NJ 08540
609-924-2310
http://terhuneorchards.com
Mama's Apple Cake, page 245

Tre Piani
Princeton Forrestal Village
120 Rockingham Row
Princeton, NJ 08540
609-452-1515
http://trepiani.com
@TrePiani
Jim Weaver, chef
Pignolia-Crusted Sea Scallops with Honey-Lemon
Beurre Blanc, page 100

Wildflour Bakery/Café
2691 Main Street
Lawrenceville, NJ 08648
609-620-1100
www.wildflourbakery-cafe.com
@wildflourNJ
Marilyn Besner, baker
Fresh Jersey Corn Cakes with Avocado Crème and
Tomato Salsa, page 64

MIDDLESEX COUNTY
Heirloom Kitchen
3853 Route 516
Old Bridge, NJ 08857
732-727-9444
http://ourheirloomkitchen.com
@HeirloomK
James Avery, chef
Jersey Green Clam Chowder, page 95

LaLa's Puerto Rican Kitchen
2854 Route 9 South
Old Bridge, NJ 08857
201-223-5252
www.lalasprkitchen.com
@lisalalaloca
Crispy Chicken Chicharrones, page 188

MONMOUTH COUNTY
Asbury Festhalle & Biergarten
527 Lake Avenue
Asbury Park, NJ 07712
732-997-8767
www.asburybiergarten.com
@APBiergarten
James Avery, chef
Oysters Braten, page 90

Carton Brewing Co.
6 East Washington Avenue
Atlantic Highlands, NJ 07716
732-654-2337
http://cartonbrewing.com
@cartonbrewing
The "Health Be Damned Tonight" Jersey Disco Fries,
page 115
The Heal-Your-Liver Paleo Salad, page 62

The Cinnamon Snail
862-246-6431
www.cinnamonsnail.com
@VeganLunchTruck
Adam Sobel, chef
Cauliflower Buffalo Wings with Roasted Garlic Ranch
Dip, page 34
Chocolate Cashew Milk, page 19

Confections of a Rock$tar
550 Cookman Avenue, Unit 104
Asbury Park, NJ 07712
732-455-3510
www.coarock.com
@cakindrummer
Kimmee Masi, chef
Fresh Doughnuts with Beer Glaze and Chocolate-
Covered Potato Chip Crumbles, page 12

Empanada Guy
Multiple locations; see website for details.
888-623-7765
www.empanadaguy.com
@EmpanadaGuy1
Carlos Serrano, chef
Beef Empanadas, page 184

Langosta Lounge
1000 Ocean Avenue
Asbury Park, NJ 07712
732-455-3275
http://langostalounge.com
@langostalounge
Marilyn Schlossbach, chef
Sweet and Sour Cucumber Dipping Sauce, page 172
Tom Kha Ghai (Thai Chicken Coconut Soup), page 190
Thai Fish Cakes, page 192

McLoone's Restaurants
Multiple locations; see website for details.
http://mcloones.com
@McLoones
Evan Victor, chef
Black Pepper Tuna Tataki with Edamame Succotash,
    Marinated Cabbage, and Grapefruit Ponzu, page 110
Grilled Swordfish Panzanella with Cherry Tomatoes,
    Cucumbers, and Baby Kale, page 106

The Outslider
Freehold, New Jersey
609-670-0970
http://theoutslider.com
@theoutslider
Bob Leahy, chef
French Onion Sliders, page 160

Talula's Pizza
550 Cookman Avenue #108
Asbury Park, NJ 07712
732-455-3003
http://talulaspizza.com
@TalulasDTAP
Swiss Chard and Poached Egg Toast, page 80

MORRIS COUNTY
Spoon Me Soups
Morristown, NJ
973-207-6909
www.spoonmesoups.com
Sarah Beattie, chef
Fall Vegetable Stew, page 126

OCEAN COUNTY
Jenkinson's Boardwalk Bar & Grill
401 Boardwalk
Point Pleasant Beach, NJ 08742
732-714-2241
http://jenkinsons.com/dining/boardwalk-bar-grill
@JenksBoardwalk
Paul Prudhomme, chef
Boardwalk Bar and Grill Margarita, page 256
Crab Cakes, page 112
Summer Strawberry-Avocado Salad with Broiled
    Scallops, page 60

Jenkinson's Sweet Shop
300 Ocean Avenue
Point Pleasant Beach, NJ 08742
732-892-7576
http://jenkinsons.com/sweet-shop
Boardwalk Fudge, page 228

The Ohana Grill
65 Grand Central Avenue
Lavallette, NJ 08735
732-830-4040
www.ohanagrill.com
@ohanagrilllava
James Costello, chef
Pan-Seared Lobster Tail over Corn and Asparagus
    Risotto, page 104

PASSAIC COUNTY
Fontanarosa's Gourmet Specialty Foods
86 Lincoln Avenue
Totowa, NJ 07512
973-942-7784
www.fontanarosas.com
Fontanarosa's Eggless Pasta, page 198

The Shannon Rose Irish Pub
Multiple locations; see website for details.
www.theshannonrose.com
@ShannonRose_C and @ShannonRose_R
Bacon-Cheddar Boxty, page 203
Short Rib Poutine, page 40

SALEM COUNTY
Running Deer Golf Club
1111 Parvin Mill Road
Pittsgrove, NJ 08318
856-358-2000
http://runningdeergolfclub.com
Stephen Pennese, chef
Stuffed French Toast, page 10
Cracked Black Pepper–Salmon Pinwheel Salad, page 68

SOMERSET COUNTY
The Bernards Inn
27 Mine Brook Road
Bernardsville, NJ 07924
888-766-0002
www.bernardsinn.com
Corey Heyer, chef
@bernardsinn
Barnegat Inlet Scallops with Charred Corn, Jalapeño,
    Cherry Tomatoes, Cilantro, and Lime, page 102

Flounder Brewing Co.
1 Ilene Court, Building 8, Suite 16
Hillsborough, NJ 08844
908-396-6166
http://flounderbrewing.com
Melissa Banacki Lees, chef
Kielbasa and Sauerkraut, page 195

Olde Mill Inn and Grain House Restaurant
225 Route 202
Basking Ridge, NJ 07920
800-585-4461
www.oldemillinn.com
Luca Carvello, chef
Stuffed Zucchini Blossoms with Heirloom Cherry
    Tomato Salad, page 58

Tapastre
1 West High Street
Somerville, NJ 08876
908-526-0505
www.tapastre.com
@Tapastre
Carlton Greenawalt, chef
Drunken Clams on Fire, page 41

SUSSEX COUNTY
Wheelhouse Craft Kitchen & Bar
94 Championship Place
Augusta, NJ 07822
973-459-4277
http://wheelhousekitchenbar.com
North Jersey Venison Chili with Cilantro Pesto,
    page 121

UNION COUNTY
Abeles & Heymann
739 Ramsey Avenue
Hillside, NJ 07205
908-206-8886
http://abeles-heymann.com
@abeles_
Chani Apfelbaum, chef
Sweet and BBQ Salami, page 42

Community FoodBank of New Jersey
31 Evans Terminal
Hillside, NJ 07205
908-355-3663
www.cfbnj.org
@cfbnj
Paul Kapner, chef
Acorn and Butternut Squash Soup, page 55

WARREN COUNTY
Jersey Girl Brewing Company
426 Shore Sand Road
Hackettstown, NJ 07840
www.jerseygirlbrewing.com
@Jerseygirlbeer
Grilled Shrimp and Sausage Skewers, page 36
Jersey Tomato and Corn Salsa, page 66

Marley's Gotham Grill
169 Main Street
Hackettstown, NJ 07840
908-852-2446
www.marleysgothamgrill.net
Bruno Pascale, chef
Fried Chicken Wings with Sauce Two Ways, page 30

Villa Milagro Vineyards
33 Warren Glen Road
Finesville, NJ 08865
908-995-2072
www.villamilagrovineyards.com
@VillaMilagroNJ
Audrey Gambino, chef
Ropa Vieja, page 189

Individual Recipe Contributors

Warren Bobrow
At Danube, Turn Left, page 252
Gunnison Beach Fizz, page 249

Darrell W. Butler
The Fat Darrell, page 162

John Cifelli
7 Fishes Caesar Salad, page 52

Jeff Cioletti
Unapologetic Carnivore's Slow-Cooker Sunday Sauce
    (North Jersey–Style), page 200

Oswin Cruz
The Blue Jersey, page 250
Garden State Guanaco, page 253
The Ironbound Amazon, page 252

Anne Frawley
Homemade Irish Cream Liqueur, page 258

Nancy Friedman
Nancy Friedman's Amazing Chopped Liver, page 210

Jessica García-Agullo
Caramelized Shallots, page 85

Diane Henderiks
Arugula and Papaya Salad with Pomegranate-Lime
    Vinaigrette, page 59
Asian Slaw, page 76
Backyard Clambake, page 109
Black Bean and Quinoa Pilaf, page 153

John Holl
Amish-Style Beef Chili, page 194
Buffalo Chicken Dip, page 33
Buttered Roll, page 6
Cantaloupe and Prosciutto, page 33
Cider Fondue, page 43
Classic Pork Roll, Egg, and Cheese Sandwich,
    page 8
Corned Beef Hash, page 23
Crunchy Broccoli Salad, page 70
Cucumber Dill Salad, page 72
Deep-Fried Salami Chips, page 44
Deviled Eggs, page 47
Escarole and Sun-Dried Tomato Salad, page 63
Funnel Cake at Home, page 225
The Happy Waitress, page 163
Hash Browns, page 11

Mary Gibbons-Holl's Irish Soda Bread, page 204
Meat Marinade, page 171
New Jersey Iced Tea, page 27
New Jersey Sloppy Joe, page 156
Radish Bread, page 50
Raspberry Tartar Sauce, page 114
Ripper Dog and Jersey Relish, page 164
Russian Dressing, page 170
Summer Berries and Biscuits (Featuring the Jersey
    Blueberry), page 226
Tofu Tikka Masala, page 182
Tomato and Mozzarella Salad, page 78
Tomato and Onion Salad, page 56
Tomato Sandwich, page 158
Tzatziki, page 206
Vegetarian Three-Bean Chili, page 120
Vegetable Fried Rice, page 207
Teresa Darcy's Weeknight Tomato Sauce and Pasta,
    page 196

Thomas Holl
Vegetarian Stuffed Peppers, page 146

Diane Pinder
Blueberry Caramels, page 238

Daria Romankow
Ukrainian Holubtsi (Stuffed Cabbage Rolls), page 178

Robert M. Rossetti and Anthony McDonald
Pork Roll Surprise, page 7

Matt Steinberg
Grilled Venison Sausage Hash with Cider Jus, page 148

Peter Stoffers
Firehouse Chicken, page 144

INDEX

Page numbers in *italic* indicate photos; page numbers in **bold** indicate charts.

A

Acorn and Butternut Squash Soup, 55

ale. *See* beer

almond(s)

Asian Slaw, 76, 77

Grilled Octopus with Romesco Sauce, Frisée, and Marcona Almonds, 98–99

almond flour/meal

Almond-Cherry Pancakes with Coconut Flakes, 16, *17*

Americana Diner, 209

Amish-Style Beef Chili, 194

ancho chiles

Ancho and Ale Chili with Avocado Mousse, 118–19, *119*

anchovies

7 Fishes Caesar Salad, 52

Heal-Your-Liver Paleo Salad, The, 62

Anthony David's, 46

apple(s)

Apple, Fennel, and Tarragon Slaw, 75

Blueberry-Apple Crumb Pie, 218–19

Crown Roast of Pork, 150

Mama's Apple Cake, 245

apple cider

Cider Fondue, 43

arugula

Arugula and Papaya Salad with Pomegranate-Lime Vinaigrette, 59

Asbury Festhalle & Biergarten, 92–93, *92, 93*

Asian Slaw, 76, 77

Asparagus Risotto, Pan-Seared Lobster Tail over Corn and, 104–5, *105*

At Danube, Turn Left, 252

Autumnal Brown Rice Salad, 56

Avery, James, 92, *92*

avocadoes

Ancho and Ale Chili with Avocado Mousse, 118–19, *119*

Chicken Lettuce Wraps with Avocado, 186, *187*

Fresh Jersey Corn Cakes with Avocado Crème and Tomato Salsa, 64, *65*

Summer Strawberry-Avocado Salad with Broiled Scallops, 60, *61*

B

Backyard Clambake, 109

bacon, 163

Bacon-Cheddar Boxty, 203

Cape May Salt Oyster and IPA Chowder, 94

Happy Waitress, The, 163

Pork Roll Surprise, 7

Baked Cauliflower Casserole, 74

Baked Ham with Bourbon Glaze, 149

bakeries

Confections of a Rock$tar, 15, *15*

L'Arte della Pasticceria, 242, *242–43*

LiLLiPiES Bakery, 222, *222–23*

balsamic vinegar

Honey-Balsamic Roasted Beet Salad, 53

Kung Foo Sauce, "a Bruce Lee Favorite," 32

Bang Bang Sauce, 32

Barcade, 174

Barnegat Inlet Scallops with Charred Corn, Jalapeño, Cherry Tomatoes, Cilantro, and Lime, 102–3

bars/pubs

Asbury Festhalle & Biergarten, 92, *92*, 93

Jenkinson's Boardwalk Bar & Grill, 60

Mompou [Tapas Wine Bar & Lounge], 248

Pint, 254

Shannon Rose Irish pub, 203

basil

Poached Chicken Meatballs in Pesto Cream, 142

Strawberry-Basil Sorbet, 214, *215*

Stuffed Zucchini Blossoms with Heirloom Cherry Tomato Salad, 58

Tomato and Mozzarella Salad, 78, *79*

BBQ Rub, MTQ, 171

BBQ Salami, Sweet and, 42

beans, canned

Amish-Style Beef Chili, 194

Black Bean and Quinoa Pilaf, 153

Fall Vegetable Stew, 126, *127*

North Jersey Venison Chili with Cilantro Pesto, 121

Vegetarian Three-Bean Chili, 120

Beattie, Sarah, 128, *128*

beef. *See also* corned beef

Amish-Style Beef Chili, 194

Ancho and Ale Chili with Avocado Mousse, 118–19, *119*

Beef Empanadas, 184, *185*

French Onion Sliders, 160, *161*

Meat Marinade, 171

New Jersey Sloppy Joe, 156, *157*

Ropa Vieja, 189

Short Rib Poutine, 40

Ukrainian Holubtsi (Stuffed Cabbage Rolls), 178–79, *179*

Unapologetic Carnivore's Slow-Cooker Sunday Sauce (North Jersey–Style), 200–201

beer

Ancho and Ale Chili with Avocado Mousse, 118–19, *119*

Beer-Braised Sausage and Peppers, 145

Cape May Salt Oyster and IPA Chowder, 94

Deep-Fried Salami Chips, 44, *45*

Drunken Clams on Fire, 41

Fresh Doughnuts with Beer Glaze and Chocolate-Covered Potato Chip Crumbles, 12–14, *13*

Kielbasa and Sauerkraut, 195

Pressure-Cooker Corned Beef, 139

Vegetarian Three-Bean Chili, 120

beets

    Farm-Fresh Beet Salad, 54

    Honey-Balsamic Roasted Beet Salad, 53

Behr, Dov, 124

bell peppers

    Beer-Braised Sausage and Peppers, 145

    Cucumber Gazpacho with Crabmeat, 84

    Grilled Shrimp and Sausage Skewers, 36, *37*

    Grilled Swordfish Panzanella with Cherry Tomatoes, Cucumbers, and Baby Kale, 106–8, *107*

    Vegetarian Stuffed Peppers, 146, *147*

Bent Spoon, the, 215–17, *216*

Berckes, Michelle, 18, *18*

Bernards Inn, the, 103

berries, **3**. See also specific type

beverages. See also cocktails

    Chocolate Cashew Milk, 19

    New Jersey Iced Tea, 27

Bigger, Charles Aaron and Mike, 36

Biscuits, Summer Berries and, 226–27, *227*

blackberries/blackberry preserves

    Warm Black and Blue Cobbler, 235

    Whey-Fed Pork Chops with Berry-Mustard Sauce, 140, *141*

black pepper

    Black Pepper Tuna Tataki with Edamame Succotash, Marinated Cabbage, and Grapefruit Ponzu, 110–11, *111*

    Cracked Black Pepper–Salmon Pinwheel Salad, 68–69

    Rosemary–Black Pepper Shortbreads, 244

Blintzes, Cheese, 24, *25*

blueberries

    Blueberry-Apple Crumb Pie, 218–19

    Blueberry Caramels, 238–39

    Blue Jersey, The, 250, *251*

    Summer Berries and Biscuits, 226–27, *227*

Boardwalk Bar and Grill Margarita, 256, *257*

Boardwalk Fudge, 228, *228*

bourbon

    Baked Ham with Bourbon Glaze, 149

Boxty, Bacon-Cheddar, 203

bread. See also rolls; sandwiches

    Country Wheat Bread, 166

    Crown Roast of Pork, 150

    Grilled Swordfish Panzanella with Cherry Tomatoes, Cucumbers, and Baby Kale, 106, *107*

    Mary Gibbons-Holl's Irish Soda Bread, 204, *205*

    matzo, 124, *124, 125*

    Radish Bread, 50, *51*

    Stuffed French Toast, 10

    Swiss Chard and Poached Egg Toast, 80, *81*

    Unapologetic Carnivore's Slow-Cooker Sunday Sauce (North Jersey–Style), 200–201

Broccoli Salad, Crunchy, 70, *71*

Buffalo Chicken Dip, 33

Busy Bee Organics, 18, *18*

Buttered Roll, 6

buttermilk

    Deep-Fried Salami Chips, 44, *45*

    Summer Berries and Biscuits (Featuring the Jersey Blueberry), 126, *127*

C

cabbage

    Asian Slaw, 76, *77*

    Black Pepper Tuna Tataki with Edamame Succotash, Marinated Cabbage, and Grapefruit Ponzu, 110–11, *111*

    Dry Vegetarian Curry, 181

    Ukrainian Holubtsi (Stuffed Cabbage Rolls), 178–179, *179*

Caesar Salad, 7 Fishes, 52

cafés. See restaurants/cafés

cake

    Funnel Cake at Home, 225

    Limoncello Cheesecake, 240, 241

    Mama's Apple Cake, 245

candies

    Blueberry Caramels, 238–39

    Grand Marnier Truffles, 232–34, 233

    Honey-Thyme Caramels, 226–27

Cantaloupe and Prosciutto, 33

Cape May Salt Oyster and IPA Chowder, 94

Caramelized Shallots, 85

caramels

    Blueberry Caramels, 238–39

    Honey-Thyme Caramels, 236–37

Carbone, Gabrielle, 216, *216*

carrots

    Asian Slaw, 76, *77*

    Carrot, Quinoa, and Spinach Soup, 130

    Dry Vegetarian Curry, 181

Carson, Jen, 222, *222*

cashews

    Chocolate Cashew Milk, 19

cauliflower

    Baked Cauliflower Casserole, 74

    Cauliflower Buffalo Wings with Roasted Garlic Ranch Dip, 34–35

chard. See Swiss chard

cheddar cheese

    Bacon-Cheddar Boxty, 203

    Cheese Curd Poutine with Pork Shank Gravy, 136–37

    Cider Fondue, 43

    "Health Be Damned Tonight" Jersey Disco Fries, The, 115

    TEC (Taylor Ham, Egg, and Cheese) Soup, 122

cheese. See also specific type

    Buffalo Chicken Dip, 33

    Cheese Blintzes, 24, *25*

    Cider Fondue, 43

    Classic Lawrenceville Mac and Cheese, 132

    Classic Pork Roll, Egg, and Cheese Sandwich, 8, *9*

    French Onion Sliders, 160, *161*

    Happy Waitress, The, 163

    Lamb-Stuffed Eggplant, 208

    Limoncello Cheesecake, 240, *241*

    Pork Roll Surprise, 7

    Sautéed Ricotta Gnocchi with Portobello Mushrooms, Tomato Confit, and Mushroom Butter Sauce, 134–35

cherries, frozen
  Almond-Cherry Pancakes with Coconut Flakes, 16, *17*
Cherry Grove Farm, 133, *133*
chicken
  Buffalo Chicken Dip, 33
  Cauliflower Buffalo Wings with Roasted Garlic Ranch Dip, 34–35
  Chicken and Waffles, 20–21, *21*
  Chicken Lettuce Wraps with Avocado, 186, *187*
  Chicken Thighs with Roasted Fall Fruit, 123
  Crispy Chicken Chicharrones, 188
  Firehouse Chicken, 144
  Fried Chicken Wings with Sauce Two Ways, 30, *31*
  Honey-Roasted Chicken, 129
  Poached Chicken Meatballs in Pesto Cream, 142
  Tom Kha Ghai (Thai Chicken Coconut Soup), 190, *191*
chicken fingers
  Fat Darrell, The, 162
chicken livers
  Nancy Friedman's Amazing Chopped Liver, 210–11
chili
  Amish-Style Beef Chili, 194
  Ancho and Ale Chili with Avocado Mousse, 118–19, *119*
  North Jersey Venison Chili with Cilantro Pesto, 121
  Vegetarian Three-Bean Chili, 120
Chips, Deep-Fried Salami, 44, *45*
chocolate
  Blueberry Caramels, 238–39
  Boardwalk Fudge, 228, *228*
  Chocolate Cashew Milk, 19
  Chocolate Espresso Hazelnut Bark, 230–31, *231*
  At Danube, Turn Left, 252
  Fresh Doughnuts with Beer Glaze and Chocolate-Covered Potato Chip Crumbles, 12–14, *13*
  Grand Marnier Truffles, 232–234, *233*
  Honey-Thyme Caramels, 236–37
Chopped Liver, Nancy Friedman's Amazing, 210–11

chowder
  Cape May Salt Oyster and IPA Chowder, 94
  Crab and Corn Chowder, 96, *97*
  Jersey Green Clam Chowder, 95
Church, Shanti, 83, *83*
Cider Fondue, 43
cilantro
  Barnegat Inlet Scallops with Charred Corn, Jalapeño, Cherry Tomatoes, Cilantro, and Lime, 102–3
  North Jersey Venison Chili with Cilantro Pesto, 121
clams
  Backyard Clambake, 109
  Drunken Clams on Fire, 41
  Jersey Green Clam Chowder, 95
Classic Lawrenceville Mac and Cheese, 132
Classic Pork Roll, Egg, and Cheese Sandwich, 8
Cobbler, Warm Black and Blue, 235
cocktails
  Blue Jersey, The, 250, *251*
  Boardwalk Bar and Grill Margarita, 254, *255*
  At Danube, Turn Left, 252
  Formal, The, 253
  Garden State Guanaco, 253
  Gunnison Beach Fizz, 249
  Homemade Irish Cream Liqueur, 258, *259*
  Ironbound Amazon, The, 252
  Red Delicious Manhattan, 254, *255*
  Red Sangria, 248
coconut, unsweetened dry
  Almond-Cherry Pancakes with Coconut Flakes, 16, *17*
  Dry Vegetarian Curry, 181
coconut milk
  Tom Kha Ghai (Thai Chicken Coconut Soup), 191, *191*
coffee
  Chocolate Espresso Hazelnut Bark, 230–31, *231*
  Homemade Irish Cream Liqueur, 258
  Meat Marinade, 171

North Jersey Venison Chili with Cilantro Pesto, 121
coleslaw
  Apple, Fennel, and Tarragon Slaw, 75
  Asian Slaw, 76, *77*
Confections of a Rock$tar, 15, *15*
cookies
  Rosemary–Black Pepper Shortbreads, 244
corn
  Backyard Clambake, 109
  Barnegat Inlet Scallops with Charred Corn, Jalapeño, Cherry Tomatoes, Cilantro, and Lime, 102–3
  Black Pepper Tuna Tataki with Edamame Succotash, Marinated Cabbage, and Grapefruit Ponzu, 110–11, *111*
  Crab and Corn Chowder, 96, *97*
  Fresh Jersey Corn Cakes with Avocado Crème and Tomato Salsa, 64, *65*
  Jersey Tomato and Corn Salsa, 66, *67*
  Pan-Seared Lobster Tail over Corn and Asparagus Risotto, 104–5, *105*
corned beef
  Corned Beef Hash, 23
  Pressure-Cooker Corned Beef, 139
Cosaboom, Brant, 86
Country Wheat Bread, 166
crabmeat
  Crab and Corn Chowder, 96, *97*
  Crab Cakes, 112, *113*
  Cucumber Gazpacho with Crabmeat, 84
Cracked Black Pepper–Salmon Pinwheel Salad, 68–69
cranberries
  Autumnal Brown Rice Salad, 56
  Chicken and Waffles, 20–21, *21*
  Cranberry Pie, 224
Crispy Chicken Chicharrones, 188
Crown Roast of Pork, 150
Crunchy Broccoli Salad, 70, *71*
cucumbers
  Cucumber Dill Salad, 72, *73*

cucumbers *(continued)*

    Cucumber Gazpacho with Crabmeat, 84

    Garden State Guanaco, 253

    Grilled Swordfish Panzanella with Cherry Tomatoes, Cucumbers, and Baby Kale, 106, *107*

    Ripper Dog and Jersey Relish, 164, *165*

    Sweet and Sour Cucumber Dipping Sauce, 172

    Tzatziki, 206

Curry, Dry Vegetarian, 181

D

dandelion greens

    Heal-Your-Liver Paleo Salad, The, 62

Deep-Fried Salami Chips, 44, *45*

Deviled Eggs, 47

dill

    Cucumber Dill Salad, 72, *73*

dips and spreads

    Buffalo Chicken Dip, 33

    Roasted Garlic Ranch Dip, 34

    Tzatziki, 206

Doughnuts with Beer Glaze and Chocolate-Covered Potato Chip Crumbles, Fresh, 12–14, *13*

Dressing, Russian, 170

Drunken Clams on Fire, 41

Dry Vegetarian Curry, 181

Durrie, Jessica, 86

E

edamame

    Black Pepper Tuna Tataki with Edamame Succotash, Marinated Cabbage, and Grapefruit Ponzu, 110–11, *111*

Eggless Pasta, Fontanarosa's, 198

eggplant

    Lamb-Stuffed Eggplant, 208

    Marinated Eggplant Sandwich with Soppressata and Mozzarella, 158

eggs

    Cheese Blintzes, 24, *25*

    Classic Pork Roll, Egg, and Cheese Sandwich, 8, *9*

    Deviled Eggs, 47

Homemade Irish Cream Liqueur, 258, *259*

Nancy Friedman's Amazing Chopped Liver, 210–11

Stuffed French Toast, 10

Swiss Chard and Poached Egg Toast, 80, *81*

TEC (Taylor Ham, Egg, and Cheese) Soup, 122

Unapologetic Carnivore's Slow-Cooker Sunday Sauce (North Jersey–Style), 200–201

Empanada Guy, 185

Empanadas, Beef, 184, *185*

Errico, Matthew, 216

escarole

    Escarole and Sun-Dried Tomato Salad, 63

Espresso Hazelnut Bark, Chocolate, 230–31, *231*

F

Fall Vegetable Stew, 126, *127*

Farm Cooking School, the, 168, *168–69*

farm(s), 49

    Cherry Grove Farm, 133, *133*

    Fernbrook Farms, 143, *143*

    Flaim Farms, 74

farmer cheese

    Cheese Blintzes, 24, *25*

Farm-Fresh Beet Salad, 54

Fat Darrell, The, 162

fennel bulb

    Apple, Fennel, and Tarragon Slaw, 75

    Sautéed Ricotta Gnocchi with Portobello Mushrooms, Tomato Confit, and Mushroom Butter Sauce, 134–35

feta cheese

    Vegetarian Stuffed Peppers, 146, *147*

Firehouse Chicken, 144

fish. *See also specific type*

    Thai Fish Cakes, 192, *193*

Flaim, Robert Jr. and Kevin, 74

Flaim Farms, 74

Flounder Brewing Company, 195

Fondue, Cider, 43

Fontanarosa, Anthony, 199, *199*

Fontanarosa's Eggless Pasta, 198

Fontanarosa's Gourmet Specialty Foods, 199, *199*

food trucks

    Empanada Guy, 185

    Outslider, The, 160

    Pudgy's Street Food, 39

Formal, The, 253

French fries

    Fat Darrell, The, 162

    Garlic Knot Fries, 38

    "Health Be Damned Tonight" Jersey Disco Fries, The, 115

    Short Rib Poutine, 40

French Onion Sliders, 160, *161*

French Toast, Stuffed, 10

Fresh Doughnuts with Beer Glaze and Chocolate-Covered Potato Chip Crumbles, 12–14, *13*

Fresh Jersey Corn Cakes with Avocado Crème and Tomato Salsa, 64, *65*

Fried Rice, Vegetable, 207

frisée

    Grilled Octopus with Romesco Sauce, Frisée, and Marcona Almonds, 98–99

fruit, fresh, **3**. *See also specific type*

    Chicken Thighs with Roasted Fall Fruit, 123

    Stuffed French Toast, 10

Fudge, Boardwalk, 228, *228*

Funnel Cake at Home, 225

G

Garden State Guanaco, 253

garlic

    Cauliflower Buffalo Wings with Roasted Garlic Ranch Dip, 34–35

    Cheese Curd Poutine with Pork Shank Gravy, 136

    Garlic Knot Fries, 38

    Heal-Your-Liver Paleo Salad, The, 62

    Roasted Garlic Ranch Dip, 34

    Shrimp with Garlic Sauce, 180

    Unapologetic Carnivore's Slow-Cooker Sunday Sauce (North Jersey–Style), 200–201

Gazpacho with Crabmeat, Cucumber, 84

Gnocchi with Portobello Mushrooms, Tomato Confit, and Mushroom Butter Sauce, Sautéed Ricotta, 134–35

Grand Marnier Truffles, 232, *233*, 234

Grandma Rosa's Tomato Pie, 202

grapefruit/grapefruit juice

Black Pepper Tuna Tataki with Edamame Succotash, Marinated Cabbage, and Grapefruit Ponzu, 110–11, *111*

greens. *See* arugula; cabbage; dandelion greens; escarole; kale; lettuce; spinach

Grilled Octopus with Romesco Sauce, Frisée, and Marcona Almonds, 98–99

Grilled Shrimp and Sausage Skewers, 36, *37*

Grilled Swordfish Panzanella with Cherry Tomatoes, Cucumbers, and Baby Kale, 106, *107*

Grilled Venison Sausage Hash with Cider Jus, 148

Gunnison Beach Fizz, 249

H

Haines, Rachael, 151

Haines Pork Shop, the, 151, *151*

ham

Baked Ham with Bourbon Glaze, 149

Classic Pork Roll, Egg, and Cheese Sandwich, 8, *9*

Taylor ham, 9, *9*

TEC (Taylor Ham, Egg, and Cheese) Soup, 122

Happy Waitress, The, 163

hard cider

Grilled Venison Sausage Hash with Cider Jus, 148

hash

Corned Beef Hash, 23

Grilled Venison Sausage Hash with Cider Jus, 148

Hash Browns, 11

Hayum, Yonah, 125

hazelnuts

Chocolate Espresso Hazelnut Bark, 230–31, *231*

"Health Be Damned Tonight" Jersey Disco Fries, The, 115

Heal-Your-Liver Paleo Salad, The, 62

Henderiks, Diane, 109

Heyer, Corey W., 103

Hobby's [Delicatessen and Restaurant], 26, *26*

Holubtsi, Ukrainian, 178–79, *179*

Homemade Irish Cream Liqueur, 258, *259*

honey

Baked Ham with Bourbon Glaze, 149

Honey-Balsamic Roasted Beet Salad, 53

Honey-Roasted Chicken, 129

Honey-Thyme Caramels, 236–37

Kung Foo Sauce, "a Bruce Lee Favorite," 32

Pignolia-Crusted Sea Scallops with Honey-Lemon Beurre Blanc, 100, *101*

hot dogs

Ripper Dog and Jersey Relish, 164, *165*

I

Iced Tea, New Jersey, 27

Inn at Fernbrook Farms, the, 143, *143*

Irish Cream Liqueur, Homemade, 258, *259*

Irish Soda Bread, Mary Gibbons-Holl's, 204, *205*

Ironbound Amazon, The, 252

J

jalapeños

Barnegat Inlet Scallops with Charred Corn, Jalapeño, Cherry Tomatoes, Cilantro, and Lime, 102–3

Jenkinson's Boardwalk Bar & Grill, 60

Jenkinson's Sweet Shop, 229, *229*

Jersey Girl Brewing Company, 36

Jersey Green Clam Chowder, 95

Jersey Tomato and Corn Salsa, 66

K

kale

Asian Slaw, 76, *77*

Fall Vegetable Stew, 126, *127*

Grilled Swordfish Panzanella with Cherry Tomatoes, Cucumbers, and Baby Kale, 106, *107*

Katsifis, Constantine, 209

Kielbasa and Sauerkraut, 195

Knauer, Ian, 168, *169*

Kung Foo Sauce, "a Bruce Lee Favorite," 32

Kuser family, 143

L

lamb

Lamb-Stuffed Eggplant, 208

Lamb Tartare, 46

Meat Marinade, 171

Roasted Lamb with Pomegranate and Wine, 138

Langosta Lounge, 173, *173*

L'Arte della Pasticceria, 242, *242–43*

Lawrenceville Mac and Cheese, Classic, 132

Leahy, Bob, 160

leeks

Farm-Fresh Beet Salad, 54

Oysters Braten, 90, *91*

Lees, Jeremy, 195

lemons/lemon juice/lemon zest

Backyard Clambake, 109

Pignolia-Crusted Sea Scallops with Honey-Lemon Beurre Blanc, 100, *101*

Rosemary-Citrus Soda Syrup, 86, *87*

lettuce

7 Fishes Caesar Salad, 52

Chicken Lettuce Wraps with Avocado, 186, *187*

Summer Strawberry-Avocado Salad with Broiled Scallops, 60, *61*

LiLLiPiES Bakery, 222, *222–23*

limes/lime juice/lime zest

Arugula and Papaya Salad with Pomegranate-Lime Vinaigrette, 59

Barnegat Inlet Scallops with Charred Corn, Jalapeño, Cherry Tomatoes, Cilantro, and Lime, 102–3

Garden State Guanaco, 253

Ironbound Amazon, The, 252

Limoncello Cheesecake, 240, *241*

Liqueur, Homemade Irish Cream, 258, *259*

Liver, Nancy Friedman's Amazing Chopped, 210–11

lobster

    Backyard Clambake, 109

    Pan-Seared Lobster Tail over Corn and Asparagus Risotto, 104–5, *105*

M

Mac and Cheese, Classic Lawrenceville, 132

Mama's Apple Cake, 245

Manhattan, Red Delicious, 254, *255*

Manischewitz Company, the, 124, *124*, *125*

Margarita, Boardwalk Bar and Grill, 256, *257*

Marinade, Meat, 171

marinara sauce

    Drunken Clams on Fire, 41

    Fat Darrell, The, 162

    Grandma Rosa's Tomato Pie, 202

Marinated Eggplant Sandwich with Soppressata and Mozzarella, 158

Mary Gibbons-Holl's Irish Soda Bread, 204, *205*

mascarpone cheese

    Stuffed French Toast, 10

Masi, Kimmee, 15, *15*

matzo, 124, *124*, *125*

meatballs

    Poached Chicken Meatballs in Pesto Cream, 142

    Unapologetic Carnivore's Slow-Cooker Sunday Sauce (North Jersey–Style), 200–201

Meat Marinade, 171

Mignogna, Steve, 83, *83*

Mompou [Tapas Wine Bar & Lounge], 248

mozzarella cheese

    Fat Darrell, The, 162

    Marinated Eggplant Sandwich with Soppressata and Mozzarella, 158

    Short Rib Poutine, 40

    Tomato and Mozzarella Salad, 78, *79*

MTQ BBQ Rub, 171

Muirhead [Foods], 57

mushrooms

    Baked Cauliflower Casserole, 74

    Sautéed Ricotta Gnocchi with

    Portobello Mushrooms, Tomato Confit, and Mushroom Butter Sauce, 134–35

mussels

    Backyard Clambake, 109

mustard

    Grilled Swordfish Panzanella with Cherry Tomatoes, Cucumbers, and Baby Kale, 106–8, *107*

    Whey-Fed Pork Chops with Berry-Mustard Sauce, 140, *141*

N

Nancy Friedman's Amazing Chopped Liver, 210–11

New Jersey Iced Tea, 27

New Jersey Sloppy Joe, 156

North Jersey Venison Chili with Cilantro Pesto, 121

nuts. *See specific type*

O

Octopus with Romesco Sauce, Frisée, and Marcona Almonds, Grilled, 98–99

onions

    French Onion Sliders, 160, *161*

    Grilled Swordfish Panzanella with Cherry Tomatoes, Cucumbers, and Baby Kale, 106, *107*

    Nancy Friedman's Amazing Chopped Liver, 210–11

    Tomato and Onion Salad, 56

onion soup mix

    Firehouse Chicken, 144

orange peel, candied

    Grand Marnier Truffles, 232-234, *233*

oranges/orange juice/orange zest

    Red Sangria, 248

    Rosemary-Citrus Soda Syrup, 86, *87*

Outslider, The, 160

oysters

    Cape May Salt Oyster and IPA Chowder, 94

    Oysters Braten, 90, 91

P

Paleo Salad, The Heal-Your-Liver, 62

Pancakes with Coconut Flakes, Almond-Cherry, 16, 17

Pan-Seared Lobster Tail over Corn and

Asparagus Risotto, 104–5, *105*

Papaya Salad with Pomegranate-Lime Vinaigrette, Arugula and, 59

Parmesan cheese

    Oysters Braten, 90, *91*

pasta

    Classic Lawrenceville Mac and Cheese, 132

    Fontanarosa's Eggless Pasta, 198

    Sautéed Ricotta Gnocchi with Portobello Mushrooms, Tomato Confit, and Mushroom Butter Sauce, 134–35

    Teresa Darcy's Weeknight Tomato Sauce and Pasta, 196, *197*

peaches

    Peach-Habanero Pocket Pies, 220–21, *221*

Pecorino Romano cheese

    Grandma Rosa's Tomato Pie, 202

    North Jersey Venison Chili with Cilantro Pesto, 121

    Stuffed Zucchini Blossoms with Heirloom Cherry Tomato Salad, 58

pepper. *See* black pepper

peppers. *See also* bell peppers

    Marinated Eggplant Sandwich with Soppressata and Mozzarella, 158

    North Jersey Venison Chili with Cilantro Pesto, 121

    Pork Roll Surprise, 7

pie

    Blueberry-Apple Crumb Pie, 218–19

    Cranberry Pie, 224

    Grandma Rosa's Tomato Pie, 202

    Peach-Habanero Pocket Pies, 220–21, *221*

Pignolia-Crusted Sea Scallops with Honey-Lemon Beurre Blanc, 100, *101*

Pilaf, Black Bean and Quinoa, 153

pine nuts

    Pignolia-Crusted Sea Scallops with Honey-Lemon Beurre Blanc, 100, *101*

Pint, 254

Poached Chicken Meatballs in Pesto Cream, 142

pomegranate seeds

    Arugula and Papaya Salad with Pomegranate-Lime Vinaigrette, 59

    Roasted Lamb with Pomegranate and Wine, 138

pork, 140, 151. *See also* bacon; ham; prosciutto

    Cantaloupe and Prosciutto, 33

    Cheese Curd Poutine with Pork Shank Gravy, 136–37

    Classic Pork Roll, Egg, and Cheese Sandwich, 8, *9*

    Crown Roast of Pork, 150

    "Health Be Damned Tonight" Jersey Disco Fries, The, 115

    Meat Marinade, 171

    Pork Loin with Sausage Stuffing, 152

    Pork Roll Surprise, 7

    Unapologetic Carnivore's Slow-Cooker Sunday Sauce (North Jersey–Style), 200–201

    Whey-Fed Pork Chops with Berry-Mustard Sauce, 140, *141*

potato chips

    Fresh Doughnuts with Beer Glaze and Chocolate-Covered Potato Chip Crumbles, 12–14, *13*

potatoes. *See also* French fries

    Backyard Clambake, 109

    Bacon-Cheddar Boxty, 203

    Cape May Salt Oyster and IPA Chowder, 94

    Cheese Curd Poutine with Pork Shank Gravy, 136–37

    Corned Beef Hash, 23

    Dry Vegetarian Curry, 181

    Grilled Venison Sausage Hash with Cider Jus, 148

    Hash Browns, 11

poutine

    Cheese Curd Poutine with Pork Shank Gravy, 136–37

    Short Rib Poutine, 40

Pressure-Cooker Corned Beef, 139

produce. *See also specific type*

    harvest dates, **3**

    types, in season, 2

prosciutto

    Cantaloupe and Prosciutto, 33

pubs. *See* bars/pubs

Pudgy's Street Food, 39

Q

quinoa

    Black Bean and Quinoa Pilaf, 153

    Carrot, Quinoa, and Spinach Soup, 130

    Vegetarian Stuffed Peppers, 146, *147*

R

radishes

    7 Fishes Caesar Salad, 52

    Radish Bread, 50, *51*

raisins

    Cranberry Pie, 224

    Mary Gibbons-Holl's Irish Soda Bread, 204, *205*

Raspberry Tartar Sauce, 114

Rat's [Restaurant], 99

Red Delicious Manhattan, 254, *255*

Red Sangria, 248

restaurants/cafés

    Americana Diner, 209

    Anthony David's, 46

    Asbury Festhalle & Biergarten, 92, *92, 93*

    Bent Spoon, the, *215–17, 216*

    Bernards Inn, 103

    Confections of a Rock$tar, 15, *15*

    Hobby's, 26, *26*

    Jenkinson's Boardwalk Bar & Grill, 60

    Langosta Lounge, 173, *173*

    Mompou, 248

    Muirhead, 57

    Rat's, 99

    Saltwater Café, 97

    Sam a.m., 22, *22*

    Seabra's Marisqueira, 180

    Small World Coffee, 86

    Talula's Pizza, 83, *83*

    Tre Piani, 100

    Viet Bistro, 186

rice

    Autumnal Brown Rice Salad, 56

    Pan-Seared Lobster Tail over Corn and Asparagus Risotto, 104–5, *105*

    Tofu Tikka Masala, 182–83

    Ukrainian Holubtsi (Stuffed Cabbage Rolls), 178–79, *179*

    Vegetable Fried Rice, 207

ricotta

    Limoncello Cheesecake, 240

    Sautéed Ricotta Gnocchi with Portobello Mushrooms, Tomato Confit, and Mushroom Butter Sauce, 134–35

    Stuffed Zucchini Blossoms with Heirloom Cherry Tomato Salad, 58

Ripper Dog and Jersey Relish, 164, *165*

Roasted Garlic Ranch Dip, 34

Roasted Lamb with Pomegranate and Wine, 138

rolls

    Buttered Roll, 6

    Spent-Grain Bread Rolls, 167

Romano cheese. *See* Pecorino Romano cheese

Ropa Vieja, 189

rosemary

    Rosemary–Black Pepper Shortbreads, 244

    Rosemary-Citrus Soda Syrup, 86

Russian Dressing, 170

S

salads. *See also* coleslaw

    7 Fishes Caesar Salad, 52

    Arugula and Papaya Salad with Pomegranate-Lime Vinaigrette, 59

    Autumnal Brown Rice Salad, 56

    Cracked Black Pepper–Salmon Pinwheel Salad, 68–69

    Crunchy Broccoli Salad, 70, *71*

    Cucumber Dill Salad, 73, *73*

    Escarole and Sun-Dried Tomato Salad, 63

    Farm-Fresh Beet Salad, 54

    Heal-Your-Liver Paleo Salad, The, 62

    Honey-Balsamic Roasted Beet Salad, 53

    Stuffed Zucchini Blossoms with Heirloom Cherry Tomato Salad, 58

    Summer Strawberry-Avocado

salads (continued)

Salad with Broiled Scallops, 60, *61*

Tomato and Onion Salad, 56

salami

Deep-Fried Salami Chips, 44, *45*

Sweet and BBQ Salami, 42

Salmon Pinwheel Salad, Cracked Black Pepper–, 68–69

salsa

Fresh Jersey Corn Cakes with Avocado Crème and Tomato Salsa, 64, *65*

Jersey Tomato and Corn Salsa, 66, *67*

Saltwater Café, 97

Sam a.m., 22, *22*

Samu, Francis, *22*

sandwiches

Fat Darrell, The, 162

French Onion Sliders, 160, 161

Happy Waitress, The, 163

Marinated Eggplant Sandwich with Soppressata and Mozzarella, 158

New Jersey Sloppy Joe, 156, *157*

Ripper Dog and Jersey Relish, 164, *165*

Tomato Sandwich, 158

Sangria, Red, 248

sauces. *See also* salsa

Bang Bang Sauce, 32

Kung Foo Sauce, "a Bruce Lee Favorite," 32

Raspberry Tartar Sauce, 114

Steak Sauce, 174, *175*

Sweet and Sour Cucumber Dipping Sauce, 172

Teresa Darcy's Weeknight Tomato Sauce and Pasta, 196, *197*

Tzatziki, 206

Unapologetic Carnivore's Slow-Cooker Sunday Sauce (North Jersey–Style), 200–201

sauerkraut

Kielbasa and Sauerkraut, 195

Oysters Braten, 90, *90*

sausage. *See also* salami

Backyard Clambake, 109

Beer-Braised Sausage and Peppers, 145

Crown Roast of Pork, 150

Grilled Shrimp and Sausage Skewers, 36, *37*

Grilled Venison Sausage Hash with Cider Jus, 148

Jersey Green Clam Chowder, 95

Kielbasa and Sauerkraut, 195

Pork Loin with Sausage Stuffing, 152

Sautéed Ricotta Gnocchi with Portobello Mushrooms, Tomato Confit, and Mushroom Butter Sauce, 134–35

scallions

Radish Bread, 50, 51

scallops

Barnegat Inlet Scallops with Charred Corn, Jalapeño, Cherry Tomatoes, Cilantro, and Lime, 102–3

Pignolia-Crusted Sea Scallops with Honey-Lemon Beurre Blanc, 100, *101*

Summer Strawberry-Avocado Salad with Broiled Scallops, 60, 61

Schlossbach, Marilyn, 173

Seabra's Marisqueira, 180

seafood. *See specific type*

Serrano, Carlos, 185

7 Fishes Caesar Salad, 52

Shallots, Caramelized, 85

Shannon Rose Irish pub, 203

shellfish. *See specific type*

Shortbreads, Rosemary–Black Pepper, 244

Short Rib Poutine, 40

shrimp

Backyard Clambake, 109

Grilled Shrimp and Sausage Skewers, 36, *37*

Shrimp with Garlic Sauce, 180

Simpson family, 57

Skewers, Grilled Shrimp and Sausage, 36, *37*

Sliders, French Onion, 160, *161*

Sloppy Joe, New Jersey, 156

Small World Coffee, 86

Soda Syrup, Rosemary-Citrus, 86, *87*

soppressata

Marinated Eggplant Sandwich with Soppressata and Mozzarella, 158

Sorbet, Strawberry-Basil, 214, *215*

soups, 128. *See also* chowder

Acorn and Butternut Squash Soup, 55

Carrot, Quinoa, and Spinach Soup, 130

Cucumber Gazpacho with Crabmeat, 84

TEC (Taylor Ham, Egg, and Cheese) Soup, 122

Tom Kha Ghai (Thai Chicken Coconut Soup), 191, *191*

sour cream

Tofu Tikka Masala, 182–83

Spent-Grain Bread Rolls, 167

spinach

Carrot, Quinoa, and Spinach Soup, 130

Cracked Black Pepper–Salmon Pinwheel Salad, 68–69

Dry Vegetarian Curry, 181

Jersey Green Clam Chowder, 95

Spoon Me Soups, 128

squash. *See also* summer squash

Acorn and Butternut Squash Soup, 55

Fall Vegetable Stew, 126, *127*

Steak Sauce, 174, *175*

stew

Fall Vegetable Stew, 126, *127*

Ropa Vieja, 189

Stewart, Josh, 83

stout. *See* beer

strawberries

Strawberry-Basil Sorbet, 214, *215*

Summer Strawberry-Avocado Salad with Broiled Scallops, 60, *61*

Stuffed Cabbage Rolls (Ukrainian Holubtsi), 178–79, *179*

Stuffed French Toast, 10

Stuffed Peppers, Vegetarian, 146, *147*

Stuffed Zucchini Blossoms with Heirloom Cherry Tomato Salad, 58

Summer Berries and Biscuits, 226–27, *227*

summer squash

    Ripper Dog and Jersey Relish, 164, *165*

Summer Strawberry-Avocado Salad with Broiled Scallops, 60, *61*

Sweet and BBQ Salami, 42

Sweet and Sour Cucumber Dipping Sauce, 172

Swiss chard, Swiss Chard and Poached Egg Toast, 80, *81*

Swordfish Panzanella with Cherry Tomatoes, Cucumbers, and Baby Kale, Grilled, 106, *107*

T

Talula's Pizza, 83, *83*

tarragon

    Apple, Fennel, and Tarragon Slaw, 75

Tartare, Lamb, 46

Tartar Sauce, Raspberry, 114

TEC (Taylor Ham, Egg, and Cheese) Soup, 122

Teresa Darcy's Weeknight Tomato Sauce and Pasta, 196, *197*

Thai Fish Cakes, 192, *193*

thyme, fresh

    Honey-Thyme Caramels, 236–37

Tofu Tikka Masala, 182–83

tomatoes, canned. *See also* marinara sauce

    Dry Vegetarian Curry, 181

    Lamb-Stuffed Eggplant, 208

    North Jersey Venison Chili with Cilantro Pesto, 121

    Teresa Darcy's Weeknight Tomato Sauce and Pasta, 196, *197*

    Tofu Tikka Masala, 182–83

    Ukrainian Holubtsi (Stuffed Cabbage Rolls), 178–79, *179*

    Unapologetic Carnivore's Slow-Cooker Sunday Sauce (North Jersey–Style), 200–201

    Vegetarian Stuffed Peppers, 146, *147*

    Vegetarian Three-Bean Chili, 120

tomatoes, fresh

    Barnegat Inlet Scallops with Charred Corn, Jalapeño, Cherry Tomatoes, Cilantro, and Lime, 102–3

    Fresh Jersey Corn Cakes with

    Avocado Crème and Tomato Salsa, 64, *65*

    Grilled Octopus with Romesco Sauce, Frisée, and Marcona Almonds, 98–99

    Grilled Swordfish Panzanella with Cherry Tomatoes, Cucumbers, and Baby Kale, 106, *107*

    Jersey Tomato and Corn Salsa, 66, *67*

    Ropa Vieja, 189

    Sautéed Ricotta Gnocchi with Portobello Mushrooms, Tomato Confit, and Mushroom Butter Sauce, 134–35

    Stuffed Zucchini Blossoms with Heirloom Cherry Tomato Salad, 58

    Tomato and Mozzarella Salad, 78, *79*

    Tomato and Onion Salad, 56

    Tomato Sandwich, 158

tomatoes, sun-dried

    Escarole and Sun-Dried Tomato Salad, 63

tomato juice

    Amish-Style Beef Chili, 194

    Steak Sauce, 174, *175*

Tom Kha Ghai (Thai Chicken Coconut Soup), 191, *191*

Tre Piani, 100

Truffles, Grand Marnier, 232, *233*, 234

Truong, Thuynhan, 186

Tuna Tataki with Edamame Succotash, Marinated Cabbage, and Grapefruit Ponzu, Black Pepper, 110–11, *111*

turkey

    New Jersey Sloppy Joe, 156, *157*

Tzatziki, 206

U

Ukrainian Holubtsi (Stuffed Cabbage Rolls), 178–79, *179*

Unapologetic Carnivore's Slow-Cooker Sunday Sauce (North Jersey–Style), 200–201

V

vegetables, **3**. *See also specific type*

    Fall Vegetable Stew, 126, *127*

    Vegetable Fried Rice, 207

Vegetarian Curry, Dry, 181

Vegetarian Stuffed Peppers, 146, *147*

Vegetarian Three-Bean Chili, 120

venison

    Grilled Venison Sausage Hash with Cider Jus, 148

    North Jersey Venison Chili with Cilantro Pesto, 121

Viet Bistro, 186

W

Waffles, Chicken and, 20–21, *21*

walnuts

    Boardwalk Fudge, 228, *228*

Warm Black and Blue Cobbler, 235

Weaver, Jim, 100

Wells, Vicki, *242*

Whey-Fed Pork Chops with Berry-Mustard Sauce, 140, *141*

wine

    Red Sangria, 248

    Roasted Lamb with Pomegranate and Wine, 138

Wraps with Avocado, Chicken Lettuce, 186, 187

Y

yogurt

    Tofu Tikka Masala, 182–83

    Tzatziki, 206

Z

zucchini

    Vegetarian Stuffed Peppers, 146, *147*

    Vegetarian Three-Bean Chili, 120

zucchini blossoms

    Stuffed Zucchini Blossoms with Heirloom Cherry Tomato Salad, 58

Also by John Holl

After visits to more than 900 brewpubs and taverns, the best beer-friendly recipes bubbled up to make this collection. From chopped Reuben salad to chocolate-covered strawberries, each recipe suggests perfect pairings.

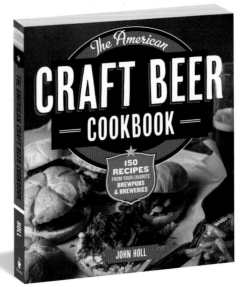

More Mouthwatering Mid-Atlantic Meals from Storey

Patrick Evans-Hylton

Colonial traditions mingle with contemporary flavors in this gastro celebration of Virginia. These 145 recipes serve up the best of the Old Dominion's farms, shores, and restaurants, with lip-smacking photos and decadent historical morsels.

Lucie L. Snodgrass

This culinary tour of the Old Line State includes 150 recipes highlighting Maryland's best — like soft-shelled crab, fried chicken, and the multilayered Smith Island Cake — plus tasty food lore and fascinating profiles of local chefs, farmers, and fishermen.